CONTEMPORARY
ECONOMIC SYSTEMS

CONTEMPORARY ECONOMIC SYSTEMS

A Regional and Country Approach

Nicholas V. Gianaris

PRAEGER

Westport, Connecticut
London

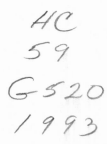

HC
59
G520
1993

Library of Congress Cataloging-in-Publication Data

Gianaris, Nicholas V.
  Contemporary economic systems : a regional and country approach /
Nicholas V. Gianaris.
      p.   cm.
  Includes bibliographical references and index.
  ISBN 0–275–94478–6 (alk. paper)
  1. Economic history—1945– 2. Comparative economics.   I. Title.
HC59.G520   1993
330.9—dc20   92–23063

British Library Cataloguing in Publication Data is available.

Library of Congress Catalog Card Number: 92–23063
ISBN: 0–275–94478–6

First published in 1993

Praeger Publishers, 88 Post Road West, Westport, Connecticut 06881
An imprint of Greenwood Publishing Group, Inc.

Printed in the United States of America

The paper used in this book complies with the Permanent
Paper Standard issued by the National Information Standards
Organization (Z39.48—1984).

10 9 8 7 6 5 4 3 2 1

It is clearly better that property should be private, but the use of it common; and the special business of the legislator is to create in men this benevolent disposition.

—Aristotle, *Politics*, 2.5, 1263a38

Contents

Tables and Figures

TABLES

FIGURES

Preface

The current interplay of economics and politics in the world arena presents new problems of production and distribution, as well as new rules and institutions of global dimensions. Historical and cultural geopolitical factors play a leading role in the performance of different economic systems. In order to facilitate the understanding of existing economic systems, a study of the most important countries with varying ideological conditions is needed. Such countries include the United States, the member nations of the European Community, and Japan with the main characteristics of capitalist or free-market economies; Sweden, as a welfare state; the Commonwealth of Independent States (the former Soviet Union); the eastern European countries; and China with their varying Communist or centrally planned economies and their recent reforms; and the developing or poor nations, which search for an economic system that would help them overcome their poverty conditions.

This book reviews traditional theories of economic systems and searches for solutions to contemporary problems by relating theory to practice. It examines up-to-date revolutionary changes and contemporary reforms toward privatization, decentralization, and democratization, primarily in the former planned economies. These reforms tend to support the theory of economic integration toward an "optimum regime."

Among the innovative features of the book is the study of the growing new system of employee and worker ownership plans or the sharing economic system as an alternative to "exploitative" capitalism and "oppressive" communism. Moreover, the book examines current movements of joint ventures and acquisitions, particularly in economies that are undergoing significant reforms as they try to successfully navigate through radically changing economic and political environments.

The book deals with the new trend of microeconomic convergence or synthesis of management–labor relations, through employee ownership and participation, and the macrointernational integration, through economic cooperation and joint ventures. It can be used as a textbook in a course on "comparative economic systems" and as a supplement in courses on "comparative politics" and "international economic relations," for students at the junior–senior level and partially at the graduate level. Also, it is useful in related research.

The purpose of this book is to examine the main characteristics of countries with different economic systems, as well as the structural changes and the main problems they face regarding economic policies, joint ventures, and developmental trends. After a brief introduction in Chapter 1, a review of the theoretical and historical developments of capitalism, socialism, and the share economy is presented in Chapters 2 to 4. The main features of the market economies of the United States, the European Community, and Japan are surveyed in Chapters 5, 6, and 7, respectively, as are those of Sweden in Chapter 8. Chapter 9 and 10 examine the economic and sociopolitical changes in the Commonwealth of Independent States (the former Soviet Union) and eastern European countries, and Chapter 11 examines the main features of the Chinese economy. Finally, the peculiar problems of the developing nations and the trends toward convergence or integration are presented in Chapter 12. Summaries are presented at the end of each chapter.

I wish to acknowledge my indebtedness to Professors Janis Barry-Figueroa, Ernest Block, Clive Daniel, George Kourvetaris, Victoria Litson, Gus Papoulia, John Roche, Shapoor Vali, and Paul Voura, as well as to tax and exchange rates experts George Alikakos and Christos Tzelios, for their stimulating comments during the preparation of this book. Maria Asedillo, John Fujiwara, Amy Hirsh, Marianne Nash, and Rosa Zak provided valuable services in reviewing, typing, copying, and other technical services.

1 Introduction

MAIN CHARACTERISTICS AND TRENDS

In the quest to find which economic system is more efficient, providing the best possible results with the least possible costs, many theories have been advanced regarding capitalism, communism, socialism, fascism, and other "isms." Such arguments present advantages and disadvantages of different economic systems concerning allocation of resources, stability, productivity, and distribution. The main goals are how to satisfy human wants and improve social welfare with limited sacrifice, preserving at the same time efficiency, justice, and freedom in production or enterprising and consumption or choice.

A significant difference between the two major systems, capitalism and communism, is the consumers' sovereignty versus the planners' preference. In the first case, production takes place in order to satisfy the consumers, who know best about their interest and ophelimity or utility. The sovereignty of consumers is the basis of economic and political freedom, whereas the leader's or planner's preference is related to dictatorship and oppression. Although consumers are influenced by advertisement and may not save enough for the next generations, the alternative may be misallocation of resources, lack of freedom, bureaucracy, and inefficiency in production and distribution.

Any economic system is comprised not solely of economic relationships. Social, political, and cultural, in addition to economic, components are embedded in every economic system. Individuals pursue not only material possession, but also their political freedom and their social standing, that is, their status in society.

Historical Trends

The process of change in economic systems has been given a number of interpretations throughout history. Ancient theologians, Greek philosophers, and

Roman and medieval writers stressed the moral aspects of economic behavior for further economic and social improvement. The physiocratic natural law (laissez-faire) and the mercantilistic emphasis on trade were the two main bases of capitalistic development, whereas communism was based on common ownership.

Regarding the efficient allocation of resources, which economic system can achieve higher economic growth and at what sacrifice? Is it the market-oriented capitalistic system more efficient than the plan-directed communistic system, or vice versa? What are the advantages and disadvantages of each system? Such questions are not new. For centuries, philosophers and economists have presented theories supporting or criticizing both systems. Their arguments are not purely economic. They are usually mixed with sociopolitical philosophies. Some twenty-four centuries ago, Plato had similar arguments with Aristotle, concerning the system of private versus common ownership.

Plato argued, primarily in his *Republic*, that private property causes selfishness, disunity, and conflicts in society, because each man wants to acquire more and tries to seize other men's property.[1]

Aristotle, a student of Plato, criticized the communism of the *Republic*. He said it is human nature, not property, that is to blame for selfishness and that property may serve, on the contrary, to elicit the finest moral qualities. Economically, Aristotle thought, "Common ownership means common neglect." Property is a necessary stimulus to maximum production. He doubted that common ownership would secure common-mindedness and higher overall productivity due to a lack of incentives—a problem from which the planned economies suffer today. Aristotle advocated private possession with common use so that the benefits of both individualism and communism would be secured. He wanted a better distribution, but he was not clear how this common use would be practiced in life. The principles of laissez-faire and natural law of the French Physiocrats of the eighteenth century, which were further developed by Adam Smith, had their roots in Aristotelian teachings.

The development of the Neo-Platonic Florentine Academy, during the years of the Renaissance, led to the new birth of the *Republic*. Thomas More, in his *Utopia*, advocated common ownership of all property by members of the state rather than only by the upper classes (guardians) as Plato had imagined. Later economists, such as Robert Owen and Karl Marx, drew upon Plato's ideal state for their own theories. Also, the Chinese communes of 1958–60 had great similarities with the principles Plato put forward in his *Republic*.

Adam Smith thought that the laissez-faire system along with the division of labor and the expansion of the market would increase the wealth of nations,[2] whereas the classical economists, primarily Malthus and Ricardo, expressed pessimism about the human race because of the rapid growth in population and the limitations imposed by land. John Stuart Mill started by questioning the advantages of the capitalistic development from the viewpoint of harmonious social advancement, and Marx strongly criticized it as based on exploitations, capital accumulation, and ever-increasing periodic crises.

Modern Arguments

Modern economists such as Frederick Hayek, Milton Friedman, and Harry Johnson of the Chicago School identify the rule of law and laissez-faire and market economy, where the voluntary contract and the forces of demand and supply dominate transactions.[3] According to them, any economic planning or control by government is in violation of the rule of law and inherently immoral. Strongly supporting the market mechanism in contrast to detailed planning, they complain that in the theory and policy of economic development, normally very little scope is permitted to the operation of market forces. In recent times, they argue, there has been a retreat both in economic theory and economic policy from the ideal principles of the free market and greater emphasis has been placed in favor of intervention. Factors antithetical to the market, according to them, are (1) the intellectual arrogance and impatience of idealists and reformers to organize, improve, and direct things themselves; (2) the antipathy toward entrepreneurship, by the established and bureaucratic-minded civil service, combined with associated changes and disturbances of an orderly economy; and (3) criticisms of the market by theories of monopolistic competition and welfare economics, along with shifts to aggregative and quantitative thinking after the 1930s. They think that the greater the controls, through wartime or peacetime planning, the greater spread of black markets. In contrast, the freer the market, the more efficient the allocation of resources, the greater the satisfaction enjoyed by consumers, and the higher the incentive for further accumulation and growth. The price system encourages productive enterprises through profit and discourages unproductive ones through losses, forcing them to bankruptcy. In central planning, unproductive enterprises may be kept in inefficient operation by government for a long period of time. This leads to misallocation of resources and low productivity.

PUBLIC SECTOR VERSUS PRIVATE SECTOR

One of the most important questions of economic policy regarding different systems is: What is the optimum size of the public versus the private sector, if any? Despite criticism of the bureaucratic public sector in many countries, it has been proved that, as income increases, demand for government services increases still more. The demand for public services includes, among other social necessities, Social Security and medical services, education, defense, administration of justice, domestic security, support for those who are unemployed and unable to work, environmental protection, and subsidization of certain sectors in the economy. All these elements loom significantly in government disbursement and lead to the growth of the public sector proportionally more than total production.

Fiscal operations in general and government spending in particular weigh heavily in the aggregate demand and the economic fluctuations. Moreover, de-

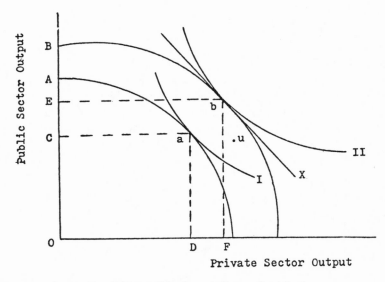

Figure 1.1 Production Possibility and Preference Curves for a Society

fense expenditures are relatively large in many countries, depending on political and territorial disturbances. Technological changes in weaponry, rapidity of obsolescence, and the nature of the equipment-intensive military establishment increase government outlays and impose a heavy burden on the budgets of countries. In addition, subsidies allocated to a number of economic sectors and production units are responsible for large portions of government spending.

A common characteristic of public enterprises is budget deficits. The main reasons for such deficits are high labor costs, low productivity, and bureaucratic inertia. Laying off tenured employees is difficult or impossible in these enterprises. What remains to be explored is the introduction of new technology for higher productivity and the adjustment of labor costs to related price and revenues.[4]

Although there is no way to escape the interaction between the public and private sectors, it is difficult to determine what policies or what blends should be adopted by each country. For the public sector to be more of a benefit than a burden to the economy, good public management, sound industrial and agricultural policies, and an effective financial system are all important.

Figure 1.1 shows the production possibility curves (A and B) and the social indifference curves (I and II) regarding public- and private-sector outputs. At full employment of factors of production, if public-sector output OC is produced, the largest output of private-sector output would be OD, and so on. With economic growth, the new output mix demanded would shift from point a to point b, which is the best point of production and consumption; that is, the point of optimal intersector allocation, where the production possibility curve *B* is tangent to social indifference curve II, providing *OE* in public-sector output and *OF* in private-sector output. Line *X* (tangent to both curves *B* and II) shows the marginal rate of substitution in consumption and the marginal rate of transformation in production. If there is unemployment, then the country is not utilizing its maximum productive potential and the economy will be operating inside the curve, such as point *u*, for example.

SOCIOECONOMIC INEQUALITY

The problem of inequalities in the distribution of income and wealth is of major importance not only from an ethical and economic point of view but, more important, from a social and political point of view. Distribution of income means who gets what; wealth means who has what. Extensive inequality in income and wealth is a source of social unrest and instability. It creates feelings of inferiority and generates self-hate, anger, and violence. People hardly starve quietly. Even pollution is more concentrated in poor neighborhoods, whereas the wealthy can always get away and enjoy fresh air and other amenities.

Critics of income equality, on the other hand, argue that inequality provides work and creative incentives as well as greater amounts of saving and investment. According to them, under a completely egalitarian system, society would be dull and stagnant. However, great disparities in living standards and wealth distribution, through inheritance and other socioeconomic measures, breed tensions between the political principles of democracy and the economic principles of capitalism.

From the standpoint of income and wealth distribution, there is a trend toward a private utopia, away from community and social togetherness. Isolation occurs not only through television and other media, but also through residential clusters in the suburban sections or housing projects. These social clusters tend to have about the same income and similar education and consumer habits. It can be said that the trend is toward creating economic enclosures, according to the economic conditions of the communities involved. The result is greater inequality in community services and living standards. For example, in the United States, the income of the top fifth of the working people is more than that of the remaining four-fifths together. In addition, more responsibilities are currently shifted to local communities.[5]

Figure 1.2 shows income inequalities, which can be measured by the Gini ratio, that is, the distance of the Lorenz curve of inequality over the total distance below the equality (45°) line (*EB/EP*), or 20/80 = 0.25. Also, *EA/EP* = 40/80 = 0.50. Such a Gini ratio is estimated to be about 0.40 for the United States. Mostly, it is expected that inequality (the Gini ratio) is higher for developing nations and lower for planned economies.

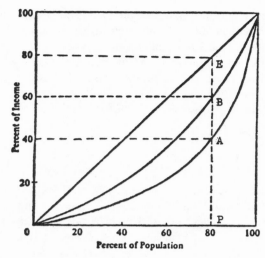

Figure 1.2 Lorenz Curve of Inequality

Cost–Benefit Analysis

Cost–benefit analysis is the process of weighting costs and benefits of government programs in order to rank them according to their merits. Because of their intangible and largely nonmonetary nature, evaluation of public projects or programs is difficult in practice. Thus, social benefits from reduction in pollution, betterment in literacy, avoidance of accidents, and improvement in health from investment in hospitals, sewage, and other facilities are difficult to assess.

As far as collective choices are concerned, the rational citizen would favor government expenditures in a public project when the expected cost or the tax share is lower than the expected personal benefit. If the marginal or additional cost is higher than the marginal or additional benefit, the individual voter would not support such a project. If the marginal cost or the tax share is equal to the marginal benefit, the voter would be indifferent and might not bother to vote. From that point of view, politicians are expected to approve public activities that offer net benefits to their constituency and thereby gain votes.

In the real world, decision makers face problems different than those of Pareto's optimality, that is, of improving the position of an individual without harming that of somebody else.[6] The principle of nonexclusivity or the sharing of benefits by all people in public goods, regardless if they pay for them or not, prevents the market mechanism from determining individual preferences. Consequently, all rationally behaving citizens are expected to be free riders, in the sense that they enjoy external benefits produced by others with no cost to themselves. If all citizens choose such a free-rider strategy, though, there would be no production of a public good and benefits would be forgone.

In cost–benefit analysis, used in the fiscal decision process, projects can be ranked according to the difference of the present value of the stream of benefits, B, minus the present value of the stream of costs, C, that is, $B - C$.

The present value of a benefit stream $B_1, B_2, \ldots, B_n$ for n years, discounted at the rate of discount, or the time preference rate r, is

$$B = \frac{B_1}{1 + r} + \frac{B_2}{(1 + r)^2} + \frac{B_3}{(1 + r)^3} + \cdots + \frac{B_n}{(1 + r)^n}$$

The same thing holds for the stream of costs.

The present value of a project is equal to the stream of benefits minus the stream of costs, as follows:

$$V = \sum_{t=1}^{n} \frac{B_t - C_t}{(1 + r)^t}$$

A project that gives a positive present value V can be expected to be approved. If it gives a negative value, it should be rejected.

GROWTH PERFORMANCE

As Table 1.1 shows, the performance of the United States and the European Community (EC), regarding rates of economic growth, is, more or less, cyclical and not much different for the last two decades. Comparatively speaking, Germany performed better in recent years than the other large EC countries, whereas Japan had higher rates of growth for all years considered than the other market economies.

From the planned economies, China performed much better than the former USSR and the eastern European countries, which followed a declining path of real economic growth during the last two decades. This may be the main reason of economic reforms introduced recently by these countries.

It would seem that, in the near future, the United States, the EC and other western countries would have low growth rates, mainly because of heavy capital accumulation and economic maturity. But the eastern European ex-Communist countries and the former Soviet republics would probably have even lower or negative growth rates, primarily because of the ongoing drastic changes in their economic systems toward the market economy. According to the Department of Commerce, the rates of growth of 1991 were −0.7 for the United States, 1.4 for the EC, −13.0 for the former USSR, −10.0 for eastern Europe, 4.5 for Japan, and 6.5 for China.

Table 1.1
Growth Rates in Real GNP, 1971–90 (percentage change)

Area and Country	1971–75	1976–83	1984–88	1989	1990
	(annual average)				
United States	2.2	2.5	4.2	2.5	.9
Japan	4.3	4.4	4.6	4.9	6.1
European Community	2.9	2.3	2.8	3.5	2.9
Britain	2.1	1.7	3.8	2.2	1.6
France	4.0	2.5	2.3	3.6	2.5
Germany (W)	2.1	2.4	2.6	3.9	4.2
Italy	2.4	3.3	3.1	3.2	2.6
U.S.S.R.	3.0	2.0	1.9	1.6	-3.0
Eastern Europe	4.9	1.2	1.9	- .3	-4.0
China	7.4	6.7	11.5	3.9	4.4

Source: Derived from U.S. Government, *Economic Report of the President*, Washington, D.C.:
U.S. Government Printing Office, various issues.

DRASTIC CHANGES TOWARD THE MARKET SYSTEM

Reforms in Europe

The old continent of Europe is undergoing drastic economic and geopolitical changes that present problems of worldwide dimensions. From the dawn of history to the present day, Europe played a vital role in the formation and development of economic and sociocultural world events. Although centuries have passed and a unified Europe remains largely a dream, the near future may prove that the dream of yesterday will become a reality of tomorrow and "all nations of the Continent will merge . . . and form a European fraternity," as Victor Hugo envisioned.

The potential effects of the integration of western Europe on the rapid opening of eastern Europe and the German reunification are expected to dramatically change mutual trade and investment, as well as global political and cultural relations. The new trend toward privatization and democratization in the previously planned economies of Europe makes joint ventures and acquisitions attractive and profitable, particularly in Hungary, Czechoslovakia, and Poland, as well as the Commonwealth of Independent States (CIS). The removal of technical, monetary, and trade barriers within the European Community creates challenges and opportunities from the standpoint of trade, investment, and economic growth. However, as the EC moves toward closer economic and political integration, the question is whether the bloc will eliminate internal barriers only to create a larger barrier around the community.

The three centers of economic power, that is, the United States, the EC, and Japan, should combine economic resources to rebuild the new democracies of eastern Europe, Latin America, and other developing countries. New capital investment, accompanied by modern technology and efficient management, and a reduction of the barriers to trade and investment would help elevate these economies from the vicious circle of low performance and poverty and lead to stability and global economic growth. It is in the interest of all countries, particularly those of Europe, to help avoid a collapse of the economies of the former Soviet republics and those of eastern Europe that may affect negatively the world economy. It would seem that free-market democratic systems, such as those of Japan, the United States, and the EC, offer a path to success for other countries to emulate. On the other hand, the failure of the ex-Soviet and eastern European economies proved that communism is the long, hard path from capitalism to capitalism.

The Balkan Triangle

The countries of the Balkan peninsula are located at the crossroads of Europe, Africa, and Asia and constitute a natural bridge between Europe and the Middle East. Although their economic systems are different, they tend to accept similar institutions and models of development. This causes a need for closer economic and cultural cooperation among them. However, it should be recognized that there are so many other social, political, and ethnic elements involved that it would be improper to concentrate only on economic issues and disregard non-economic factors.

Reforms in former Yugoslavia emphasized the novel concept of worker self-management as an evolutionary process that would transform capitalism to socialism and "wither away the state," as the supporters of the system argued.

Greece, on the other hand, like Odysseus in Homer's epic, returned to her European home after a long period of uncertainty and historical disturbances. As a full member of the European Community, it is included in the related chapter, whereas Albania, Bulgaria, Romania, and the former Yugoslav republics are dealt with other eastern European countries.

SCOPE

In addition to the important changes in countries or country groups with alternative economic systems, a related historical background is presented for a better conceptualization and understanding of the reader.

With the collapse of communism in eastern Europe and the former USSR, it seems that capitalism proved to be superior of socialism from the standpoint of production incentives, technological innovations, and economicopolitical liberties. Not only market economies used privatization programs and deregulations for higher efficiency, but centrally planned economies abandoned government ownership and central controls in favor of private ownership and the free market. Similar trends can be observed in the developing or poor nations as they try to overcome their poverty conditions due to overpopulation and heavy debts.

An important contribution of this study is the review and analysis of the current dramatic changes in former socialist countries concerning organization, structure, and economic policies, as well as the trends toward economic integration or formation of common markets among countries. The lack of production incentives in planned or centrally controlled economies forced them to introduce drastic reforms toward privatization, decentralization, and democratization. Moreover, national interests, in the context of rapidly changing economic systems, are gradually subordinated to regional groups and eventually to a global economy. The growing interdependence of trading nations requires a shift from isolated and hierarchical decision making to negotiations and common domestic and foreign economic policies.

There seems to be a trend toward a system of workers' capitalism and a progression from management ownership to employee ownership. Expectations are that more and more firms will come under the Employee Stock Ownership Plans (ESOPs). Indeed, the survival of one form or another of the employee participation system for a relatively long period of time, in spite of all its difficulties, suggests that workers' alienation can be reduced and cooperation and work incentives for high productivity can be stimulated through a system of share economy. Such a system is expected to reduce differences among nations and accelerate the process of economic and political integration.

The economies of the United States, the European Community, and Japan are used as the models of the free market or capitalist system with decision making via the price mechanism. Sweden, with its welfare system, is treated separately as a peculiar case of economic organization. The former Soviet Union, the eastern European countries, and China, where the Marxian or Communist system was, or is still, practiced, are reviewed as case studies of different models of command or planned economies with their recent dramatic economic and political changes and reforms toward a democratic and free-market system.

SUMMARY

Out of a number of different economic systems (capitalism, communism, socialism, fascism, feudalism), capitalism and socialism were and still are the most important systems in the world.

The main characteristics of capitalism are private ownership, free enterprise, low level of government expenditures, and the sovereignty of the consumer; whereas in communism, state or cooperative ownership, economic and political controls, high government expenditures, and the planners' preference prevail.

As income increases, the size of the public sector in capitalist or market economies tends to increase, but in Communist or centrally planned economies, it tends to decrease. The new trends toward privatization and democratic free markets in the previously Communist countries of Europe proved the triumph of marker economies vis-à-vis the command or planned economies.

Developing or poor nations, with problems of overpopulation, limited industrialization, and high inequality, search for an economic and political system that can bring rapid economic growth without restrictions on political and economic freedoms. Perhaps, a system that combines the advantages of both capitalism and socialism, or a form of "people's capitalism," may be the answer for their future development. No matter how we classify countries around the world, the fact is that more than half of the total population lives in poverty and the gap in per capita income between poor and rich countries is widening in absolute if not in relative terms.

2 The Economics of Capitalism: History and Theory

INTRODUCTION

Even though the field of "economic systems" gained attention in the twentieth century, previous writers on social and economic matters throughout history did not neglect to stress the importance of different economic organizations. Early writers of Greece, Rome, and Medieval Europe contributed ideas that proved to be helpful in understanding and further promoting economic evolution along with social, cultural, and political changes.

The mercantilists and the classical economists of the eighteenth and nineteenth centuries centered attention on matters of capital accumulation or acquisition through economic growth or the wealth of nations, as Adam Smith called it. Malthus, Say, Ricardo, and Mill, all belonging to the classical school, however, were concerned with the limits of economic growth and capital accumulation because of expected rapid growth of population.

Marx and Schumpeter provided new insights into the problems of economic organization and business fluctuations, whereas Keynes, Hansen, and Galbraith see progress from the point of view of stagnation, economic concentration, and state intervention.

All those pioneer economists contributed valuable ideas that deserve far more discussion than the brief review offered in the following sections of this chapter. It is important, therefore, to find out which elements those economists considered responsible for economic organizational changes of their periods and what the similarities are with the problems of current developments regarding different economic systems.

THE GRECO-ROMAN PERIOD

From the dawn of human history, the survival of humankind and the improvement of life have been associated with the struggle to gain economic benefits from nature's endowment. Humankind's increased knowledge of the environment and the application of energies to the process of production speeded up economic changes and progress.

One should not ignore, however, the misdirection of resources and the human suffering in the process of development. Kings imposed heavy taxes or contributions upon their subjects to support large armies and servants.[1]

After the decline of the Egyptian civilization, the Greeks extended from Crete to Athens, Asia Minor, and Macedonia, creating the city–states (polis) as independent political and economic units. The expansion of city–states brought about the development of trade and commerce during the seventh and sixth centuries B.C. It was during this time that the first coins appeared in Lydia and Aegina. Banking services, ship building, and agricultural production flourished along with the expansion of the market. Regulations, similar to our present antitrust laws, were enacted by the city government to prevent price fixing and the development of market monopolies. Monopolies were permitted only when they supported state policy and when they offered free meals to the poor.

Philosophers, primarily Plato and Aristotle, wrote on matters of government and economics. Plato in his *Republic* said that the city arises because of the division of labor, which is the result of natural inequalities in human skills and the multiplicity of wants. He stressed the economic advantages of the division of labor from the viewpoint of production. Happiness or the good life, according to Plato, must include all the people and can be achieved not only through material growth, but also by elimination of desires. Thus, "poverty results from increase of man's desires, not from diminution of his property."[2] Slavery was condemned also by Euripides, who strongly advocated equality of men and women in his *Medea*. For him, the noble and the slave were both unnatural. Aristotle, in his analytical writings (*Politics* and *Ethics*), distinguished between advantages and disadvantages of private and common ownership, between value in use and value in exchange, and between real wealth and money accumulation— ideas that Adam Smith and other writers used extensively more than 2,000 years later. He thought that private ownership provides incentives for individual and social development.

During the period of the Roman Empire (31 B.C. to A.D. 476), writers such as Pliny, Cato, and Palladius were interested in reforming land ownership and improving methods of production. Small landholders and free laborers left the countryside and crowded into the towns to increase the number of plebeians (low class). The possession of large estates (latifundia) by the wealthy upper class (patricians) and the nobles, together with the inefficiency of slave labor and the introduction of heavy taxation, accelerated the decline of the Roman Empire. The creation of a new commercial class, the patricians, and the new landowners necessitated a body of laws that later had a profound influence on legal and economic institutions. The recognition of juristic or artificial persons by the Roman laws was, perhaps, the most important development from the viewpoint of invention and expansion of modern states and enterprises.

THE MIDDLE AGES

With regard to its effect on economic organization, the period following the fall of the Roman Empire, which is known as the Middle Ages (A.D. 476 to about 1500), is characterized by scientific and economic stagnation. Thomas Aquinas (1225–74) and Nicholas Oresme (1329–82) were the main writers on matters of economics during that period. They justified trade if prices in the exchanges were just, that is, equal to the cost of production and morally ensuring equal advantages to both parties.

During the Middle Ages, including the period of the Byzantine Empire with Constantinople its capital, ever greater administrative powers were placed into the hands of the owners of large estates (the largest owner being the Church), which became new political and economic units. This is known as the manorial or feudalistic system with a class distinction between the landlords, acting as independent rulers, forming their own laws and courts, and the peasants who tilled the land (serfs). In the towns, merchants formed themselves into craft guilds for protection, economic organizations that later became monopolies with considerable power from which the capitalistic system emerged. The pressure of the landlords upon the serfs brought about the migration of young serfs to the cities, where they could enjoy greater economic and social freedom. This movement of young workers from rural to urban areas, together with the creation of new markets and new methods of production further stimulated by trade as a result of the Crusades, led to a new economic climate favorable to trade and handicrafts.

CAPITALISM AND THE PROTESTANT ETHIC

Some writers, such as R. H. Tawney and Max Weber, tried to explain the rise of capitalism and the entrepreneurial class in religious terms. According to them, the development of the capitalistic system in the sixteenth and seventeenth centuries was the result of a new religious doctrine, Protestantism.[3] During the medieval period, the Catholic Church opposed usury and emphasized the sin of avarice, thus setting a barrier to capitalistic development. It discouraged the pursuit of profit and the accumulation of capital and stressed the importance of just prices and just wages. The Protestant Reformation (1517 and later), mainly Calvinism, justified the pursuit of wealth, the payment of interest, and profit making as acts deserving religious blessing. The process of capitalistic enterprising had a divine connotation for the supporters of this doctrine.

Individual responsibility and freedom of enterprise gave rise to extreme individualism and to the laissez-faire ideology, which were considered to be the two main poles of capitalistic development. Also, the principle of the joint stock company, which was first considered by Roman writers, was further developed by the Protestant ethic.

A great deal of criticism has been made of these, basically Calvinist, economic teachings by later writers. Thus, on the one hand, there is the lagging growth of Scotland and the southern section of the United States with their Calvinist and other Protestant religions; but, on the other hand, there is the rapid progress of Japan with its different religious denominations.

THE MERCANTILISTS AND THE APPEARANCE
OF CAPITALISM

The main characteristics of mercantilism (1550–1776) were (1) the emphasis on foreign trade as a means of accumulating precious metals, as the most desirable form of national wealth; and (2) the supremacy of the state over the individual. The state, being the locus of power, should support exports, create state monopolies, and establish colonies to increase national wealth. Commercial expansion by monopolies, such as the Merchant Adventurers, the Eastland Company, the Muscovy Company, and the East India Company, was associated with colonialism.

State and Church authorities used credit and facilitated wealthy families, such as the Bardi, Fuggers, and Medici (mainly by Machiavelli, 1469–1527, in Florence), to undertake commercial and financial adventures and thus displace the medieval feudal lords. This new system of commercial capitalism was characterized by economic freedom, technical progress, and profit seeking, regardless of the social consequences and communal relationships.

The quest for material wealth, self-interest, and liberalism by the rising merchant and industrial classes, during the mercantilist period, broke up the medieval controls and replaced religious noneconomic values with worldly material ones. The gradual development of maritime commerce and the capitalist reforms introduced by the Renaissance (around the fourteenth through sixteenth centuries), and the Protestant Reformation, provided the necessary incentives for material success, technical advancement, and scientific progress.

Toward the end of the mercantilist period, the physiocratic economic school appeared (1756–78). This school was based on the natural order that prevailed over all the activities of man.[4] According to the Physiocrats, there is a circular process of production and expenditures in any economy. Production generates purchasing power or income so that the commodities produced are sold in a natural manner.

The Physiocrats were against the mercantilistic system, especially governmental controls, and advocated economic freedom and competition between producers and consumers. Competition, profit incentives, and free enterprise, which the Physiocrats and Adam Smith supported, constituted the cornerstone of the then emerging capitalistic system.

CLASSICAL SCHOOL

Adam Smith's Arguments

Adam Smith, in his famous work known briefly as the *Wealth of Nations* (1776), was primarily concerned with the problem of increasing national wealth. He stressed that division of labor leads to specialization and increases in productivity. Humans increase productivity through division of labor, but they also cease to be independent of others.[5]

Smith was influenced by Bernard de Mandeville's poem "Fable of the Bees" (1714) that private vices lead to public benefits, whereas cooperation from other members of society comes automatically. As they try to achieve their own ends, their own interests and advantages are led as if by an invisible hand to promote the interests of society as a whole. However, external and internal security and certain public works (roads, bridges, coinage, post office) belong to the state.

Contrary to the mercantilistic support of strong states, Smith thought that government interference and monopoly were harmful to the economy because of bureaucracy, corruption, and inefficiency, with which they were usually associated. The economy should also regulate itself, through competition between buyers and sellers, instead of being regulated by the state.

John Stuart Mill's Prospects

Mill emphasized that the laws of production of wealth are physically determined, whereas the laws of the distribution of wealth are man-made. The institutions and customs of a society determine the distribution of product among the factors of production and affect the process of development. To obtain progress and economic development, there should be an improvement in material prosperity, an increase in production and population, and growth of humankind's power over nature. Continuous progress, according to Mill, requires security of persons against violence and arbitrary power of government, cooperation in business such as the joint-stock companies, and the association of producers or consumers in the form of cooperatives. Throughout his writings, he stressed the interdependence of many social forces and condemned luxurious living because it reduces capital formation.

Even though he followed Ricardo's dynamic analysis in his treatment, Mill added a chapter, "Of the Stationary State," in his *Principles*, where he argued that the increase in wealth must come to an end because the law of diminishing returns, the accumulation of capital, and the working of competition in market economies combine to produce declining profits and rising rents. He stated that "the richest and most prosperous countries would very soon attain the stationary state, if no further improvement were made in the productive arts."[6] He felt though that the stationary state might be more desirable because industrial progress is associated with symptoms of individual struggle and social uneasiness. He thought that "the best state for human nature is that in which while no one is poor, no one desires to be richer, nor has any reason to fear being thrust back by the efforts of others to push themselves forward."[7] He believed that there would be much room for cultural, moral, and social progress in the stationary state, because human minds would cease to be engrossed in the art of struggling to get ahead.

According to Mill, free competition, where capital and labor move freely from one employment to another, brings about the best allocation and efficiency in the production process. But, as John Cairnes pointed out later, "noncompeting" labor groups in the economy act as obstacles to competition,[8] and that not a whole population is competing indiscriminately for all occupations, but a series of industrial layers, that is, several isolated strata from unskilled laborers and artisans to producers and learned professionals.

Competition might have some effect within the same group, but is very difficult between groups. Thus, textile workers or shoemakers cannot compete with pilots or electricians and lawyers with physicians or engineers. Such stratification and specialization between different professions make the smooth working of the free competitive market impossible and modern antiinflationary development policies difficult.

CLASSICAL CAPITALISM AND THE PRICE MECHANISM

Perfect and Monopolistic Competition

Under conditions of perfect competition, average revenue and marginal revenue are the same and are represented by a horizontal demand curve, as Figure 2.1 indicates. In such a pure competitive system, the producer is a price taker not a price maker, and the consumer's sovereignty prevails. In this model, the market is the best planner of resource allocation and the principle of profit maximization, under which marginal cost of the firm equals marginal revenue, coincides with the optimum resource allocation.

Mixed economies, such as that of the United States, the European Community, and Japan, are more and more departing from the model of perfect competition and moving toward a monopolistic market structure, primarily under the model of monopolistic competition. In that model, in which a relatively large number of firms is producing or selling differential products (cloth, shoes, food products, entertainment), average cost equals average revenue at point a, as Figure 2.2 indicates. However, the government can subsidize the firm to expand production to the optimum social point b with quantity Q_2, or even to Q_3 (point c), so that idle capacity be reduced.

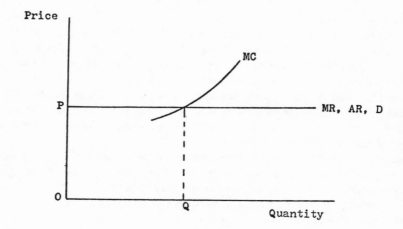

Figure 2.1 Price and Output Under Perfect Competition

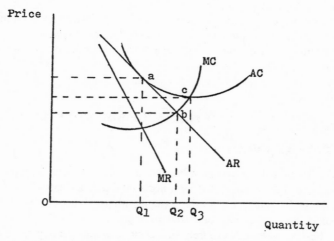

Figure 2.2 Price and Output Under Monopolistic Competition

Imperfect Markets and Monopoly

Figure 2.3 shows that at point c, a firm is producing quantity Q_2 at a price P_2, which is equal to average cost, leaving no losses. At this break-even point, imposed probably by a public utility regulation, the firm may realize a small "normal" economic profit, which is included into average cost, perhaps as an insurance premium against losses. This is the proper size of an enterprise, public or private, to achieve the highest possible output at the lowest possible price without any losses. However, profit maximization is achieved at point a, where

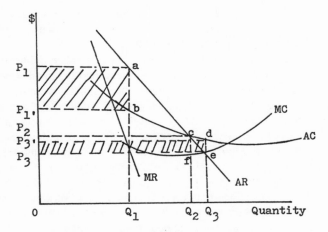

Figure 2.3 Optimal Social Allocation in an Imperfect Market

marginal cost is equal to marginal revenue, with price P_1 and output limited to Q_1. At this point, total profit is shown by the area abP_1P_1' (or $ab \times aP_1$). This profit-maximization model is normally used by private enterprises.

In contrast, for public enterprises or public policy aiming at the highest possible output and employment, point e, where marginal cost is equal to average revenue, is the point of optimal social allocation with price P_3 and output expanded to Q_3. At this optimal social output Q_3, there is a loss edP_3P_3' (or $ed \times OQ_3$). For the production of this good to continue at Q_3, the government should subsidize the losses of the producing enterprise. On the contrary, a public enterprise producing at point a and charging a price OP_1 is like the government imposing an excise tax on the product, a tax collected by that public enterprise.

The loss in total benefits to consumers from consuming Q_1 rather than Q_3 is the area under the demand curve Q_1aeQ_3. However, the saving in resource costs from reduction in output from Q_3 to Q_1 is the area under the marginal cost curve. The net cost to society is the difference between these two areas. In other terms, the net loss to society is the consumers' loss less the producer's gain. On the other hand, the net loss to society from average cost pricing at point c (in a regulated firm) and a pricing at marginal cost at point e (in a public-owned enterprise) would be the area cfe.

REFORMS TO TRADITIONAL CAPITALIST THEORY

Contrary to the classical model, which calls for reduction in consumption to increase saving, the Keynesian model calls for increase in consumption to avoid unemployment and preserve the capitalist system. As the average income increases, the propensity to consume would decline,[9] that is, consumption would not increase in the same proportion as income. The continuation of this phenomenon would lead to a gradual decrease in the rate of growth and finally to a situation of economic stagnation, except when proper fiscal and monetary policy measures are taken to stimulate spending.

In cases of unemployment, the government or any other public institution should increase its spending, primarily in investment, in order to increase demand and thereby generate more income and employment. Such governmental spending, which would be covered by deficit financing, would have a "multiplier effect," generating additional income several times the amount originally spent.

Public works would be necessary in case of severe unemployment, even if they are of doubtful utility (such as digging holes in the ground and filling them again). Such public works or any other form of spending would stimulate demand, employment, and growth. The Keynesian theory, in brief, is a short-run theory of income and employment and to a limited extent a theory of long-term growth.

Many fiscal and monetary measures Keynes suggested in this system of reformed or planned capitalism were applied in several countries, but it is questionable whether these measures and tools are responsible for the inflationary bias many countries practiced during the postwar years.

Keynes was fearful that fascism and communism would appeal to nations with high unemployment and poverty in the 1920s and early 1930s. The Bolshevik revolution in Russia and the reparations imposed on Germany and Italy by the Treaty of Versailles, as a result of World War I, led to doubts in the free market and liberalism and the adoption of authoritarian systems, to wit, fascism in Germany and Italy and communism in Russia as alternatives to the laissez-faire system and the capitalist individualism. This was a deviation from the Say's Law that supply creates its own demand and that a self-regulating market would lead to full employment and economic stability.

The Use of Fiscal Policies in Market Economies

Figure 2.4 shows that a $5 trillion spending for consumption, C, leads to an equal amount of national income, Y, as the consumption function (line C) indicates. An additional spending for investment, I, of $0.4 trillion creates a new equilibrium of spending and income ($Y = C + I$) and pushes national income or output to $6 trillion. That is, each dollar invested adds $2.5 more income to the economy, which means that the multiplier k is equal to 2.5 (or $k = \Delta Y/\Delta I = 1.0/0.4 = 2.5$).

Here, full employment, F, in the economy can be achieved at an income or production of $7 trillion. The difference between actual income and potential or full-employment income ($7 - 6 = 1$) is lost income or output due to unemployment. If there is no additional spending, the economy faces what Keynes called chronic unemployment, which is equal to this difference. The resultant gap, ab, is called the deflationary gap. An additional spending by government, G, to point a will push total spending to $7 trillion and lead the economy to a full-employment equilibrium of aggregate demand and supply, where total spend-

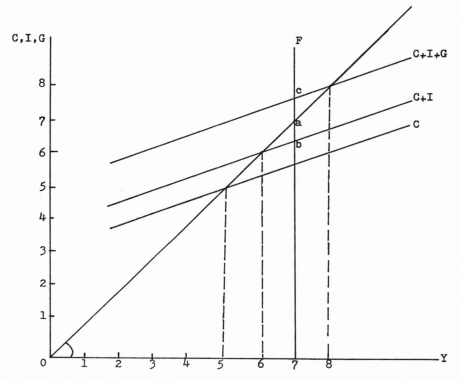

Figure 2.4 National Income (*Y*) Determination with Government Expenditures (*G*)

ing is equal to total earning ($C + I + G = Y$). This will be the ideal position of the economy, with full employment and stability.

However, if governmental spending is more than that required for the full-employment level, an inflationary gap *ac* would be created and the increase in national income from \$7 to \$8 trillion is an increase in prices or inflation; that is, it is an increase in nominal, not real, income and production.

The relationship between interest rates and national output or product, when planned spending equals income, that is, when aggregate supply equals aggregate demand, can be shown with the *IS* curve in Figure 2.5, which explains the goods market equilibrium schedule. The *IS* curve shows the equilibrium points of investment (*I*), at different rates of interest, and savings (*S*), at different levels of income. Thus, the lower the interest rate, the more the investment and the higher the income. The higher the income, the more the saving for investment financing. The steepness of the negatively sloped *IS* curve depends on how sensitive investment spending is to changes in the interest rate or return to investment.

The money market equilibrium, or the upsloping *LM* schedule (liquidity pref-

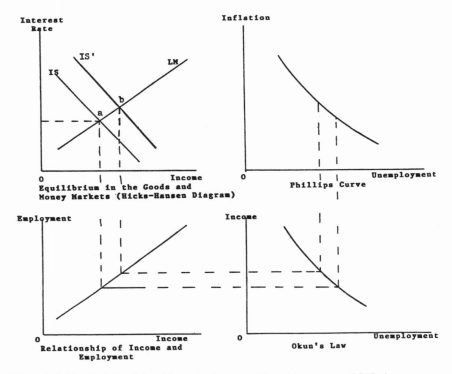

Figure 2.5 The Relationship of Interest, Income, Unemployment, and Inflation

erence function), is derived by the demand for money (L) curve, at different levels of the interest rate, and the money available at various levels of income and a given money supply fixed by the monetary authorities. With the level of income rising, the need for transactions money rises and the amount left over (supply of money, M) declines.

At the equilibrium level of income, saving (S) is equal to investment (I), whereas at the money market equilibrium supply of money (M) and demand for money or loans (L) are equal. The investment-saving (IS) curve shows the level of national income when intended (ex ante) saving and intended investment are adjusted to be equal. The lower the interest rate, the less people want to save and the more corporations and entrepreneurs want to borrow and invest. The demand for loans and supply of money (LM) curve shows the equilibria of the money market at different interest rates and income levels.

Different interest rates are associated with different income levels. At equilibrium point b, the shift in the IS curve to a new position IS', mainly because of government spending, leads to a higher interest rate and higher income, compared to equilibrium at point a. Depending on the labor-intensive method of production introduced, this leads to more employment and, *ceteris paribus*, to less unemployment but higher inflation. This is shown in the Okun's Law curve, which relates income or production and unemployment, on the one hand, and the Phillips curve, which relates unemployment with inflation, on the other hand.

The points where the *IS* and *LM* curves meet indicate the interest rates and the levels of income at which both the investment-saving market and the money market are at equilibrium. Expansionary fiscal policies, through an increase in public expenditures or a decrease in taxes, would shift the *IS* curve outward, increasing income but also raising interest rates. However, an expansionary monetary policy would shift the *LM* curve outward, but then interest rates would be lower and national income higher. Therefore, all things being equal, a monetary easing would keep interest rates down, stimulate investment, and increase income and employment toward the full-employment level of the economy.

When people are trying to save much but investors want to invest little, a downturn in the economy and an increase in unemployment is expected. In such a case, the government can fill the gap by stepping up spending, that is, by increasing the budget deficit. However, easy money may be preferable because it reduces interest rates and stimulates investment, whereas large budget deficits will increase interest rates and discourage new investment.

INNOVATIONS AND DISHARMONIOUS DEVELOPMENT IN CAPITALISM

Joseph Schumpeter, an Austrian economist who taught for many years (1927–50) at Harvard, noted that there is a circular flow in economic life, which demonstrates the mutual interdependence among the elements of which the economic cosmos consists and in which commodities, money, and factors of production all fit into a constant stream that circulates within the economic whole, similar to the way blood circulates within a living organism.

Considering business cycle trends, Schumpeter predicted that successive economic fluctuations, which depend on technological changes and innovations, would eventually destroy the capitalistic system. Personally, though, he admired capitalism more than socialism, but he felt that the system would fail not because of its failures *per se*, but because of its very successes. In making this pessimistic forecast, he compared himself to a doctor who predicts that his patient will die even though he does not desire it. The role of entrepreneurs would gradually decline, just as that of the military commander, because of an unfavorable social climate and changes in technology that produce conditions inimical to their function in society and mechanization of the process of decision making. Social welfare programs, strong labor unions, progressive taxation, governmental operations of public utilities, and similar measures that tend to squeeze out the earning of profits would discourage business investment and further entrepreneurial ventures. New firms and new men with business leadership to exploit innovations would cease to appear and capitalist economies would face chronic depressions.

The gradual reduction of competition and the growing role of research departments of large firms prevent the emergence of new entrepreneurs and pave the way for a new system characterized by huge oligopolistic corporations that use their own profits or securities for financing, controlling the market, and dictating to consumers. Schumpeter contended that concentration and bigness contribute to economic progress but weaken, at the same time, the basic capitalistic institutions of private property and freedom of contract. Moreover, the hostility of the oversupplied intellectuals tends to influence movements toward anticapitalist reforms and lead society down the road to socialism.[10] He believed that the capitalistic system is engaged in the process of "creative destruction" and predicted its euthanasia. Not many economists, however, accepted his conclusion that capitalism was gradually destroying itself because of its achievements.

STAGNATION AND INDUSTRIAL CONCENTRATION

A number of economists, including Keynes and Alvin Hansen, maintained that countries at a high level of development are subject to rising underemployment and chronic stagnation unless proper fiscal and monetary measures are taken by the government to correct the situation.

Many countries are developing increasingly into dual economies, that is, joint partnership of private enterprises with government. The private sector would concentrate on the production of material goods, and the government would provide a wide range of services (welfare state services), such as Social Security, health, education, and community projects. It is argued[11] that this private–public partnership will enable low-income people to reach high levels of development.

Recently, a new form of organization has appeared in market economies. This is the world of large corporations, which is served by people and markets, instead of serving them. The consumer, the public sector, and the market accommodate themselves to the needs of the producer's organization.[12] National or international corporations may dominate the state, and the state, in turn, will secure the ends and goals of the corporations, providing training for research scientists, engineers, and skilled personnel, as well as protective legislation, to make the system continue to work.

In present societies, economic and even political power are primarily exercised by small inner groups and an impersonal bureaucracy. In market economies, the assets of a corporation may be represented by stocks owned by thousands of people, many of whom might be ignorant about the economic standing and the performance of the corporation. Sophisticated speculators, innocent orphans, greedy widows, and a host of other persons may put their money in stocks and trust their investment to the decisions of a management group of a company about which they know little, if anything. Similarly, a small managerial group and impersonal industrial bureaucracy prevail in socialist economies. Developing countries, including China and Cuba, are expected to become equally bureaucratic when they achieve higher industrialization because advanced industrial technology goes together with organization or bureaucracy.

Depending on the level of economic development, market economies may face difficult problems when it comes to concentration of economic power. Wealth and political power may be concentrated in the hands of a small minority of the population, excluding the masses from many incentives for improvement. Owners of companies and corporations may be, at the same time, parliamentary representatives, ministers, or military generals of the country controlling or influencing governmental decisions on matters of economic development and social justice. If the largest amounts of economic gains accrue to a few individuals who influence national policy, incentives of the employees and workers may be very low.

In a number of countries, there are not elected governments to care about the development of the masses. Military men or political zealots have become great exploiters and predatory individuals. They care about their own best interests and the interests of their collaborating foreign and political oligarchies, ignoring social benefits.

SUMMARY

The capitalist system, which increased the material well-being for most of the people most of the time, gained importance in the eighteenth century and later. However, ancient theologians, Greek philosophers, and Roman and medieval writers stressed the moral aspects of economic behavior. Aristotle criticized the ideal Communist state of Plato and supported the system of private property against common ownership, which leads to common neglect.

The economic reforms introduced by the Renaissance and the Protestant ethic of hard work and profit making contributed to the development of capitalism, and the physiocratic natural law (laissez-faire) and the mercantilistic emphasis on trade were the two main bases of the capitalist system. Adam Smith thought that the free-market system along with the division of labor and the expansion of the market would increase the wealth of nations. Other classical economists, primarily Thomas Malthus, David Ricardo, and John Stuart Mill supported laissez-faire but expressed pessimism, regarding population crises, stagnation and injustice, and started questioning the advantages of the capitalist system, the very success of which would lead to its "creative destruction," according to Joseph Schumpeter.

Government fiscal and monetary policies to stimulate aggregate demand and avoid crises or stagnation of the capitalist or free-market system were suggested by John Maynard Keynes and Alvin Hansen. To mitigate income inequalities, market economies have introduced various social measures and "welfare" schemes that stabilize demand and stimulate economic growth.

3 Socialism and Economic Planning

SOCIALISM BEFORE MARX

Many people believe that socialism, that is, the economic system in which a large part of the means of production is owned socially, started with Karl Marx and the Russian Revolution. Nevertheless, socialism has a long history, both in theory and practice.

Practically, primitive societies used some form of common ownership of means of production and the distribution of food among the members of the tribe. Adam Smith, the father of the laissez-faire system, mentioned that in primitive cultures, there was no appropriation of land and no accumulation of stock.[1] There was no conceptualization of ownership as tribes moved from place to place in search for food and other means of subsistence.

In ancient Egypt and Mesopotamia, almost all the land and other resources were owned by the state. Economic activities were mainly controlled and co-ordinated by strong central authorities that had great power over the individuals and mobilized resources to build public projects in a similar fashion as in modern planned economies. For arguments of Plato and Aristotle, regarding private versus common ownership, as well as other related contentions, see Chapters 1 and 2.

Early Christians practiced a life with common ownership in land and houses and equal distribution of income on a voluntary basis. Such a collectivist experiment could be observed in Jerusalem, primarily to take care of the needy persons.

The Industrial Revolution in England, with its urban blight, child labor, and other unsocial side effects, resulted in wealth accumulation by the capitalists and an increase in poverty. The unrestrained laissez-faire doctrine caused misery on workers and created a fertile ground for socialism toward the end of the eighteenth century. Moreover, the American and the French revolutions for political equality and economic betterment inspired a new social movement around the world.

Saint Simon, who is considered an inspiration for the French indicative planning, had not opposed private ownership, but condemned idleness and supported collectivism and universal association.

In 1800, Owen, an industrialist, used profits from his New Lamark factory in Scotland to raise wages, shorten working hours, and provide education to children, housing, and other workers' benefits, keeping a 5 percent return on capital invested. In 1826, and after the British government did not approve his project of "villages cooperatives," he came to America and created a cooperative society in New Harmony, Indiana. He advocated the use of labor notes based on work time instead of money. But he failed after 2 years and return to Britain, where he continued to support unions and the abolishment of private property.

John Stuart Mill, although familiar with the dark side of the naked capitalism during the Industrial Revolution, supported the laissez-faire of the classical school. He was in favor of competition and against monopoly, which he considered as the taxation of the industrious for the support of indolence. He rejected the idea of directing the economy by a single center and administering the capital of a country on the public account. However, he favored public-sector involvement in education, health, and social reforms.

Although Mill was a firm believer in capitalism, he thought that, regarding labor remuneration and social justice, the system has serious loopholes. He said, "If, therefore, the choice were to be made between communism with all its chances, and the present state of society with all its sufferings and injustices; ... if this or communism were the alternative, all the difficulties, great or small, of communism would be but as dust in the balance."[2] He accepted that labor produces more than is required for its support and, like David Ricardo, arrived at the conclusion that profits depend on the cost of labor.

MARXIAN APPROACH

According to Karl Marx, socioeconomic changes occur because of conflict or clash of opposites. Every existing condition (thesis) develops its counteraction (antithesis), and the interaction between the two brings about a new situation (synthesis). The new condition, synthesis, then becomes the thesis and begets its negation, which causes a new synthesis, and the struggle continues. The history of all hitherto existing society is the history of class struggle between freeman and slave, patrician and plebeian, lord and serf, in a word, oppressor and oppressed. On the basis of these struggles, he distinguished the following main socioeconomic stages: primitive communism, slavery, feudalism, capitalism, and what he expected in the future, socialism and, finally, ideal communism.

Primitive communism was a stage where there was a classless society without private property. In the slavery stage, the master, possessing some form of patriarchal authority, could buy, sell, or even kill his slaves. These brutal treatments of slaves brought about revolts against the master class and the emancipation of slaves who became serfs. This process introduced a new economic stage, that of feudalism. The serf was tied to the estate (manor), but he had more personal dignity than the slave.

Capitalism, based upon the private ownership, initiated the world of free competition, freedom of movement, and a new bourgeoisie social order with a capitalist class (the owners of the means of production) and the propertyless proletariat class.

The core of the Marxian theory of capitalist development consists of the "surplus value," which in turn leads to capital accumulation, wealth concentration, and profit decline. By surplus value or profit, Marx meant the difference between what workers produce and what they receive from their labor. Surplus value does not originate from raw materials and capital equipment, which themselves have been prepared by previous labor and gifts of nature, but from the exploitation of labor.

In order to survive the competitive race and maintain or increase profit or surplus value, capitalists introduce labor-saving technological progress. They are engaged in a dog-eat-dog struggle with other competitors, squeezing the workers more and more for their survival. They invest in new machines that save labor. Unemployed workers, on the other hand, compete for jobs against their brethren, forcing wages down. Workers' income, which is the only source of their subsistence, declines, first, because of unemployment and, second, because of reduction in wages to below even subsistence levels.

Accumulation of capital is transformation of surplus value, s, derived from variable capital, v, which is spent on the purchase of labor, into constant capital, c, which includes raw materials and means of production. Dividing both parts of the equation $Q = c + v + s$ by $v + c$, we have

$$\frac{Q}{v+c} = 1 + \frac{s}{v+c} = 1 + r$$

where Q is total income or output, and r the rate of profit, which Marx defined as the rate of returns on advanced capital, that is,

$$r = \frac{s}{v+c} = \frac{s/v}{1+c/v}$$

or the rate of profit rises as the rate of exploitation (s/v) rises and falls as the organic composition of capital (c/v) rises. The main goal of capitalist activity is "Accumulate, accumulate! That is Moses and the Prophets."[3]

The capitalistic system follows an unbalanced expansion process in favor of the capital goods sector. As such, it is expected to lead to rapid development in its early stages because of capital accumulation and technological improvement. Eventually, extensive unemployment, created by automation and the squeezing out of small firms, would lead to overproduction and ever-increasing economic crises. Periodic crises would progressively intensify the struggle of the proletariats (the industrial reserve army) against the capitalists until common ownership of the means of production finally replaces private ownership.

Marx predicted that the capitalistic stage would be replaced by a period of socialism and then a final stage of communism. Then what was left of the capitalist state would gradually be allowed to "wither away," and bad economic and noneconomic institutions, which were created in the planlessness of economic society, would disappear. In its place would evolve a classless society representing the acme of perfection that would last forever.

COLONIALISM AND IMPERIALISM

According to Marx and his followers, advanced capitalist countries encountering resistance at home become desperate for new markets, new sources of cheap labor, and needed raw materials. By establishing colonies and conquering foreign markets, national crises and the consequent destruction of capitalism could be postponed, but only temporarily.

During the years of colonialism, metropolitan countries discouraged manufacturing activities in colonies, thus creating markets for their manufactures. Colonies, in turn, provided cheap labor and needed natural resources while their traditional habits were destroyed, handicraft industries were wiped out, and the masses were stripped of their means of production. In short, poorer countries were exploited instead of getting benefits from capitalist development.

The capitalist, thirsting for exploitation, constantly throws capital into the colonies, where a growing labor supply and cheap raw materials give higher returns. Colonial expansion cannot prevent the contradictions of capitalism even in the less-developed areas, where class conflict will eventually grow sharper. The vicious nature of capitalist development will continue on an international scale and capitalism will reach its highest stage.

Vladimir Lenin, a theoretician and practictioner of the Marxian system, called this stage imperialism. At this stage, the gap between poor and rich nations will be wider because "finance capital and the trusts are increasing instead of diminishing the differences in the rate of development of the various parts of the world."[4] The antagonism between capitalist countries to secure new and cheap resources leads to imperialistic wars. Although this new imperialistic phase may postpone the collapse of capitalism, the final destruction of the system is inevitable, Lenin argued, because of the gradual depletion of cheap resources, the deterioration in the living standards of poor people, and the heavy burdens of military expenditures.

Paul Baran tries to give a Marxist twist to the problem of barriers to economic advancement. He argues that in many countries, the ruling, owning elites do

not invest productivily and markets are monopolistic. Moreover, large corporations, feudal landlords, and industrial royalists, in alliance with the rising
bourgeois middle classes, impose governments that cannot move low-income
societies forward.[5]

ECONOMIC PLANNING

Although the planning system is criticized as bureaucratic and the market
system as anarchic, there is not mutual exclusivity between the two. Experience
shows that many capitalist countries use planning, whereas in all the socialist
countries, there exist some market relations. Efforts to eradicate the market
mechanism in the Soviet Union in 1918–21 (War communism) and in China in
1958–60 (Communes) had adverse effects. Presently, many market economies
in third world countries do not use imperative planning, but developing planning,
whereas France and Yugoslavia use "indicative" or democratic planning.

Central Planning

The main characteristic of central planning is that a central authority, a government agency, formulates the projects and supervises their implementation.
This central agency, be it a planning commission, a ministry, or the national
government itself, controls all economic organizations and processes and directs
all vital forces of the national economy. Short- and long-term goals are set for
attainment, in specified times, usually in 5-year periods, and a vast administrative
and managerial machinery, with vertical and horizontal interconnections, at-
tempts to fulfill those goals.

The allocation of resources and the coordination of individual decisions between consumers and producers are a matter of central planning, not market
economy. A state bank (Gosbank in Russia or People's Bank in China) exercises
financial control over the state enterprises. The managers deposit their receipts
in the bank, which, in turn, provides them with enough money to pay for labor
and all required materials. Thus, an automatic control is provided by the central
bank for fulfilling plans from a financial or value point of view parallel to basic
physical input–output plans. Other national and regional commissions deal with
the supply of materials and equipment and provide statistical data on available
resources and commodities.

Regarding the distribution of national product, the prevailing principle in
planned economies is that remuneration will take place "from each according
to his ability, to each according to his labor." The application of this principle
is regarded as a necessary precondition toward the Marxian final or ideal stage
of communism, in which distribution would take place "from each according
to his ability, to each according to his needs." At this stage, society will reach
abundance because of the mechanization of production and high productivity.
Scarcity and the need for individual incentive will disappear; work will be

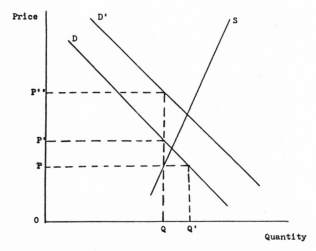

Figure 3.1 Turnover Tax in Planned Economies

humankind's second nature, because work will be done cheerfully and efficiently; there will be no need for money and prices or wages, no classes or state. Ideologically, countries with centrally planned and controlled economies claim that they are in the stage of socialism and are still building the base for the final stage of full communism. Many western writers, however, claim that such economies have created elite classes (the class of the communist party and that of managers) and deviate from the principle of classless socialism with social justice and no oppression.

Shortages, Subsidies, and Controls

The planned economies follow largely economic policies that rely heavily on turnover taxes to provide revenue and to balance supply and demand. If the authorities establish a low price *OP* for a commodity whose market supply (*S*) and demand (*D*) curves meet at a higher point, as shown in Figure 3.1, the difference *QQ'* is shortage. In this case, rationing would take place. When the planners want to avoid shortages and rationing, they impose a turnover tax, *PP'*, thereby moving prices close to the equilibrium of supply and demand and collecting budgetary revenue equal to *PP'* per unit of the commodity considered. If there is a shift in demand to *D'* and planners prefer to have the same quantity, they simply further raise turnover taxes *P'P''*, thus determining a final price *OP''* and collecting *PP''* unit taxes.

The turnover taxes, therefore, play an adjustment role of supply and demand similar to profits in capitalist economies and a distribution role by discriminating between necessary goods (housing, medical care, transportation, education,

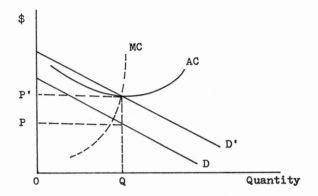

Figure 3.2 Subsidization of a Nationalized Firm

books) for which there is a small or no turnover tax and luxurious goods (cars, videos, vodka) with high taxes. Prices incorporating taxes then play a limited allocative role in socialist economies and are used for demand-and-supply manipulation, for income distribution, and partially for tax revenue.

Figure 3.2 shows government subsidization PP' per unit of a commodity to keep the low price P and the same quantity produced Q by a nationalized firm. In this case, the firm can produce and sell a quantity Q, where the marginal social benefit, indicated by D', equals the marginal cost. It can sell at price P and receive a subsidy by the government (PP') per unit to cover its costs.

Shortages in houses and rent controls exist not only in planned economies, but in market economies as well, where there is a strange phenomenon, particularly in large cities with large numbers of homeless families, although many buildings have been abandoned and remain vacant.

Figure 3.3 shows that under a free housing market, with no rent or other controls, supply and demand would determine the point of equilibrium E at a price (rent) OP and quantity OQ of apartment units. The rent control price brings about an increase in the apartments demanded and a decrease in supply, creating a shortage AB. In restricting the amount of housing available, the new price would be OP_1, which is higher than that at equilibrium (OP). By eliminating rent control, the equilibrium price would be restored and the amount of housing offered would rise.

Input–Output Tables

One of the main functions of the planner is the allocation of resources among many sectors and subsectors in such a way as to achieve the optimum volume of output from each sector. This can be achieved by equating the marginal value product of resources in each sector. However, one or more sectors may not be able to produce without input from other sectors or industries. The planner then

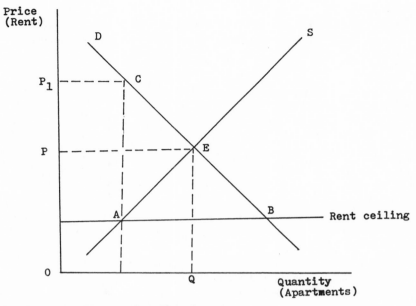

Figure 3.3 Housing Shortages from Rent Controls

must coordinate the flow of inputs claimed and the output produced by each sector. His main task, therefore, is how to measure required inputs and expected outputs in such major sectors as agriculture, mining, manufacturing, electricity, transportation, housing, public administration, and other services. In such a process of resource allocation, which can be facilitated by high-speed computers, considerations of balanced versus unbalanced growth must be taken into account by the planner.

Estimations of required inputs of factors and material for the projected output can be facilitated by the preparation of an input–output table, that is, a matrix showing the interrelationship among sectors or industries of the economy.[6] Specifically, the rows of such a table indicate where the outputs of each industry go, and the columns show the sources of inputs of each industry. Thus, policy makers have a picture of sources, the amounts, and the destinations of materials. They can see, for example, how much of the agricultural output goes to agriculture (for seed, feed, breeding livestock, and so on), industry, and other services, as shown in Table 3.1.

As the table shows, agriculture purchased or used its own products for a value of 45, and its sales to industry amounted to 40 and to services 15. Similarly, industry used its productions for a value of 30 and its sales to agriculture were 14, and so on. By comparing these figures with total outputs of agriculture, industry, and services, the input coefficients are obtained. Thus, for the agricultural use of its own productions, the coefficient is 0.45 (= 45/100); for the

Table 3.1
Input-Output Relations (Hypothetical Figures)

PURCHASING SECTOR

		Agriculture		Industry		Services		Total
		Units	Coef.	Units	Coef.	Units	Coef.	Units
PRODUCING SECTOR	Agriculture	45	.45	40	.80	15	.25	100
	Industry	14	.14	30	.60	6	.10	50
	Services	22	.22	20	.40	18	.30	60
	Total	81		90		39		210

industrial use of agricultural products, the coefficient is 0.80 (= 40/50); for the industrial use of services, the coefficient is 0.40 (= 20/50); and so forth.

If X_1 is total agricultural product, X_2 total industrial product, and X_3 total services product, we have the following equations:

$$X_1 = 0.45X_1 + 0.80X_2 + 0.25X_3$$
$$X_2 = 0.14X_1 + 0.60X_2 + 0.10X_3$$
$$X_3 = 0.22X_1 + 0.40X_2 + 0.30X_3$$

COLLECTIVE FARMS AND LAND REFORMS

The planned economic system is based on the following main principles, which are different from the free-market system: (1) state ownership and (2) central economic planning. Private ownership is largely abolished and socialist ownership is established in the form of state property, cooperatives, and collective farms. Collectivization of farms, that is, common ownership and use of land by a number of families or whole villages, was first introduced in Russia (*kolkhoz*) by the First Five-Year Plan in 1928 and it is now used, with varying degrees of control, in all planned economies, including China, North Korea, Vietnam, and Cuba.

The different reforms, varying from small-scale peasant farming to large plantations and the Russian *kolkhozes*, the Mexican *ejido*, and the Israeli *kibbutz*, constitute special types of the cooperative use of land. In the *kibbutz*, a large farm is owned and operated by a group of families that shares the income and manages the farm through an elected board that assigns jobs and supervises the cultivation of land. In the Mexican *ejido*, land is assigned to a village that in turn assigns it collectively or to individuals. The individuals cannot sell or mortgage their land, but they can keep it as long as they cultivate it. The Israeli *kibbutzes* seem to be successful. But the Mexican *ejidos* were oriented toward dividing the land into small plots that did not preserve the technological benefits from large-scale farming. Also, the *Gizera* plan for Sudan, a joint venture by the government, a commercial firm, and the tenants (receiving 40, 20, and 40 percent of the profits, respectively) achieved good results.

MARKET SOCIALISM

From a theoretical point of view, Enrico Barone, an Italian economist, pointed out in 1908, as did Vilfredo Pareto (an Italian–French economist) in 1896, that a large number of equations can be used to express the interactions of consumers and producers. Regardless of the economic system, market capitalism or centralized socialism, the demand-and-supply equations would look the same. However, Barone recognized that it is difficult in practice to have a centralized mathematical solution even if armies of employees are used to gather and evaluate the huge amounts of data required.

On the other hand, Ludwig von Mises, an Austrian economist, pointed out in 1920 that, as long as capital and natural resources are owned collectively, efficient allocation of resources is impossible. In socialism, there are no markets to determine prices of resource–services, making it difficult to compare cost with benefits and to maximize social welfare by achieving the best possible results with the least possible cost. According to von Mises, therefore, a socialist economy is bound to be less successful than a capitalist one.[7] However, some practitioners of central planning argue that the valuation problem could be solved by mathematical techniques, linear programming, and, currently, by computers. Nevertheless, socialists should be grateful to von Mises, the *advocatus diaboli* of their cause, because his challenge forced them to recognize the importance of economic accounting in resource allocation in socialist planning.

The Theory of Oskar Lange

According to Oskar Lange, a Polish economist who developed his theory of market socialism in 1936, cost minimization or output maximization could be achieved when marginal cost is equal to average revenue or price of a product. This would be so for consumer goods and labor services. However, ownership of capital and natural resources, or the means of production, would reside with society (public property). In the case of consumer goods and labor services, prices would be determined by supply and demand in a free market, whereas the prices of producer goods would be determined by a Central Planning Board (CPB), by trial and error until supply and demand are equated. The planning board would appoint the enterprise managers, determine investment (as percentage of GNP), set an interest rate to equate the supply and demand of capital, and distribute a social dividend to households to reduce inequality. However, the board would not set physical input requirements and output targets, that is, no physical input–output tables would be used.[8] In a later publication, Lange argued that centralized calculations are feasible, particularly for long-term planning, because of the development of computers.

Severe criticism to Lange's model of market socialism was based mainly on the difficult task of price determination for so many products. Consumer tastes, production costs, and future expectations change continuously, and it is impossible for the CPB to adjust prices to maintain equilibrium of supply and demand. Moreover, a huge bureaucracy is needed for central planners to obtain information for so many goods and services.

In his model of "market socialism," which was largely supported by Abba Lerner, Lange argued that if prices were set above the intersection between marginal cost and demand or average revenue (MC = AR), then managers would produce less (at the point where the new price equals MC), demand would exceed supply and depletion of inventories would lead to price increase, which would make things worse.

In the event of declining marginal and average costs, that is, continuing economies of scale, as the majority of empirical cases have proven to be, the market seems to fail in its allocative mechanism, producing limited output at MC = MR. This is so because of the higher production concentration and monopolization, which is justified in this case on the grounds of declining per unit costs in larger firms.

Figure 3.4 shows that an enterprise, private or public, would produce quantity Q_2 at price P_2 equal to cost per unit (AR = AC). At this break-even production point, there would be no profits—and no losses either. At Q_3, however, there is a loss equal to the difference of AC and MC per unit, that is, equal to the average fixed cost (AFC). This loss can be covered by subsidy from the public sector if it is desirable to produce large quantities of output at Q_3. On the other hand, implementation of the profit-maximization principle would mean production of output OQ_1, which is far less than OQ_2, and at price P_1, which is far higher than P_2 at the break-even point.

Confusion of Socialism and Communism

Socialism is a political and economic ideology somewhere between oppressive communism, a centralized economic system as practiced in the recent past, and unfettered capitalism. However, because the Communists used the term "socialism" for their totalitarian regimes in the Soviet Union and elsewhere, many people confuse Socialists with Communists, although they are opposing each other since their split more than 70 years ago. It seems that the model of market socialism resembles a mixed economy of democratic socialism.

As the Socialists argued during the Socialist International in New York in October 1990, true socialism or social democracy advocates a democratic society,

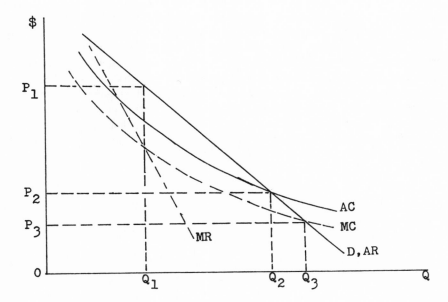

Figure 3.4 Social Allocation with Declining Costs

a parliamentary style of government, and a mixed economy. Prominent Socialists or Democratic Socialists, such as Willy Brandt, former German Chancellor, and Jean-Pierre Cott, the leader of 180 Socialists in the Europarliament of 518 members, said that as communism defuncts, socialism became a troublesome and even dirty word. It has been discredited by the bureaucrats of the abhorrent previous economic systems of central and eastern Europe. Nevertheless, according to modern Socialists, after some years of adherence to the laissez-faire or unregulated market system, people will wake up with a hangover and turn to democratic socialism, in which private interests are attuned to public interests and social justice. In the meantime, they advise the supporters of economic reforms "not to go faster than the music," as the French are saying.

SUMMARY

Socialism or communism is different from capitalism on property rights, economic organization, and state controls. Socialism is primarily based on state ownership of the productive factors, collectivism, and government controls on market operations, regarding production, distribution, and the determination of wages and prices.

Although socialism has a long history, Karl Marx set out to explain its tenets and to give a sociohistorical interpretation of economic changes. He strongly criticized capitalism as based on labor exploitation, capital accumulation, through the "surplus value,'' and ever-increasing periodic crises. Vladimir Lenin argued that the collapse of capitalism would be postponed through imperialistic expansion.

A central government authority formulates 5-year plans, using input–output tables for project coordination, and supervises their implementation. However, bureaucracy and lack of incentives are mainly responsible for low performance, which leads to severe shortages and poor quality in centrally planned economies.

Market socialism, as an alternative system was suggested, primarily by Oskar Lange, with capital and natural resources owned by society and consumer goods and labor service prices determined in a free market at the point of intersection between marginal cost and demand.

4 Employee Ownership and Share Economy as Alternatives

INTRODUCTION

In the previous review of the two major systems, capitalism and communism, their main advantages and disadvantages were examined. Economic fluctuations or business cycles, associated with unemployemnt and inflation, constitute the main dilemmas of capitalism and the free-market economy. Bureaucracy, inefficiency, and lack of economic and political freedom are the main disadvantages of communism or the centrally planned economy. The question then is whether there is an alternative viable system that reduces or eliminates some of the disadvantages of both extreme economic systems.

In recent decades, a remarkable development in industrial organization has been introduced in a number of countries, signifying a deviation from both the private and public sectors. Gradually and quietly, workplace committees of workers and employees have come to play a significant role in enterprise decision making concerning wages, working conditions, investment, and similar matters. Such work groups have been developing in the EC countries and recently in the United States. In cooperation with capital, or under a system of employee ownership, they aim at stimulating incentives and improving productivity and welfare. Although they grow at the expense of the traditional labor unions, which behave like tamed dogs presently, they do not seem to raise questions of replacing the authority of owners of property and state. From the standpoint of the public sector, such a trend unloads the government subsidy expenditures to moribund enterprises and undesirable controls to a new form of decentralized social activity.

In a number of instances, management encourages labor representation in enterprise decision making, especially in the EC and the United States, so that strikes and other union disturbances may be avoided as workers become responsible for decisions affecting them. Moreover, when enterprises, public or private, are not profitable or approach bankruptcy, employees are asked, and frequently accept, to take over management to keep the firm in operation and preserve their jobs. In such cases, the government, or any other responsible authority, is not required to finance and rescue weak or bankrupt enterprises.

In prosperous times, a competitive labor market permits improvement in wages because of the increase in demand for labor relative to supply. But increases in wages and improvements in working conditions may equally or better be achieved under the system of industrial democracy than through the countervailing power of labor unions versus management. However, in times of severe recessions and automation, unemployment increases and workers and unions (with dwindling power) are unable to protect their jobs, let alone keep constant or improve real wages, as was evidenced during recent recessions.

DEMOCRATIC PARTICIPATION

Incentives of participation in a democratized workplace may be able to replace conventional incentives (pay, promotion, discharge) in the market economies of all the nations. Industrial democracy may strengthen and stimulate production. This is important in modern societies because of growing specialization, which makes the person stupid and ignorant, according to Adam Smith, and which increases nervousness and rivalry among workmates.[1] Inventiveness and accomplishment, affection, relief, and happiness in the workplace may require replacement of heirarchical and authoritarian structures in enterprises, whether private or public.

Along these lines, John Stuart Mill and Jean Jacques Rousseau believed that collective decisions and participatory democracies advance human intellect, reduce bureaucracy, and increase efficiency.[2] However, care should be taken through employees' training to make participation workable and practical, otherwise there is the danger of frustration and inefficiency, which may drive, or keep, communities and nations into stagnation. A frantic participation or apathy and too great a public preoccupation with politics may make the systems unworkable and inefficient, or may lead to the creation of a professional elite in place of an old bureaucracy.

Moreover, John Stuart Mill believed that society would improve if laborers became owners of the capital with which they work and elected their own managers. That is, he advocated a system of democratic market socialism, with labor-managed cooperatives or workers self-management. According to Mill, for the betterment of mankind, production should be dominated by laborers "collectively owning the capital with which they carry on their operations, and working under managers elected and removable by themselves."[3]

Years ago, Joseph Schumpeter suggested that a new economic system, known as "people's capitalism," may combine the advantages of both capitalism and socialism. Recently, some success lessons in that direction can be observed in the United States, the EC, Japan, and other economies through the spread of ownership.[4]

The decline of the competitiveness of some companies usually leads to unemployment and loss of income. The question posed, therefore, is: Can employee ownership save such companies? Recent trends show a positive response, as more and more important companies approaching bankruptcy come under the Employee Stock Ownership Plans (ESOPs). They manage to cut costs and, as a result, to line up financial backing from banks and other institutions.[5]

CAPITAL WORKERS AND PRODUCTIVITY OF LABOR

Employee ownership, as practiced in many western countries, is democratizing access to capital and transforms labor workers into capital workers by using corporations' credit to allow employees to buy their shares. Modern capital formation and new technology require commercial financing and insurance and not so much old-fashion saving and self-financing. Not only wealthy persons with accumulated savings or inheritances can buy companies, but employees and workers as well through the availability of credit by financial institutions. This is the way to split ownership, instead of having wealth concentration. (For example, all nonresidential productive assets are owned by only about 5 percent of American families.) Moreover, productivity and competitiveness would increase by a motivated work force of employee-owners. Automation and demand stabilization require that the economy supplements labor employment with capital ownership and labor workers with capital workers—a transition and a combination essential to private property and a free market.

In addition to commercial financing, employee owners may finance capital formation and introduce new technology by contributing part of their remuneration for the expansion of their firms. Through the accumulation of capital, as well as work incentives, worker-owners can contribute also to the overall economic development and growth of the economy.

The neoclassists, who disagreed with the classical argument that the economy would reach a stationary position, were optimistic about the growth of the market economies, through factor competition and technological improvement. Using the Cobb–Douglas production function as their base, they found that the relative share of labor to output, over many years, was fairly constant and equal to 0.75. In this case of constant returns to scale, and assuming labor L and capital K as the only factors of production, the share of capital was 0.25. That is, $Q = L^{0.75}K^{0.25}$. In an incremental sense, $\Delta Q/Q = 0.75\ \Delta L/L + 0.25\ \Delta K/K$.

Capital investment and technological progress help labor to increase efficiency and thereby its remuneration. In other words, as capital per worker K/L increases, output Q per worker (Q/L) increases, as Figure 4.1 shows. Line K/Q indicates a constant capital output ratio, and production function F_t (which shows the technical position in period t) indicates a declining contribution of capital to output as capital per worker (capital labor ratio) increases proportionately more

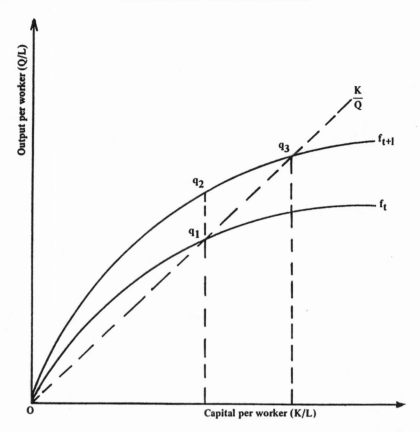

Figure 4.1 The Relationship of Output per Worker (Labor Productivity) and Capital per Worker

than output per worker (output labor ratio). However, new investment and high-production incentives by worker owners are expected to move the function from f_t to $f_t + 1$, thereby increasing the productivity and the wages of workers.

The rate of growth of labor productivity in Japan was 5 percent in 1964–84 compared to less than 1 percent in the United States. This was so mainly because of the high growth rate of gross capital per worker in Japan (8 percent) compared to that in the United States (2 percent).

ARGUMENTS IN FAVOR AND AGAINST EMPLOYEE OWNERSHIP

Employee ownership is a new paradigm of economic organization in which managers or bosses become employees of their workers and unions negotiate with union members acting as employers. From that standpoint, neither the state nor the market can fully explain this mythical phenomenon. Neither the laissez-faire doctrine of Adam Smith nor the Marxian theory of socialist development, not even the Keynesian antidepression prescription, can answer fully the workings and the results of this system. It is a *nova terra* that needs further exploration and research.

Such employee ownership and flexible performance-based wages lead to a broader distribution of wealth, which helps the stability and dynamism of the economy, because it is based on many. This also helps the spread of political freedom that stems from economic freedom, and reduces concentrated power, which is the enemy of liberty, as the American founding fathers proclaimed. Moreover, the problem with capitalism is that there are not enough capitalists, as Senator Russell Long, a strong supporter of ESOPs in Congress, mentioned. In relation to that, it should be mentioned that 80 percent of the privately owned wealth in the United States belongs to 2 percent of the population.

Many companies are turning their employees into shareholders, not so much to make them work smarter and harder, but to support management against hostile takeovers by making it difficult for raiders to finance such bids. The use of poison pills, sophisticated forms of employee ownership, shark repelling, golden parachutes, and other antitakeover ploys aim at reducing the risk of takeovers.

Although the law encourages employee ownership, the ESOP movement may not always boost productivity. For example, encouragement was given to owner-farmers by the Homestead Act by U.S. Congress passed in 1862, but not too many farmers remained with the agricultural sector. A similar "industrial homestead" act, through ESOPs, enacted by Congress in 1974 may not always assure high productivity. As economies move to more advanced stages, productivity might decline in the industrial sector and more emphasis should be given to ESOPs in the service sector. From that standpoint, the term "worker ownership" is gradually replaced by "employee ownership."

For some executives, employee ownership may be an anathema. They may not be willing to involve the new owner-employees in decision making. Furthermore, they may abuse tax-advantage ESOPs, covering their actions with the mantle of employees' capitalism in order to keep power. Managers may support theoretically employee ownership and compensation according to productivity, but they may hesitate to implement such measures in practice. Therefore, employee ownership may not be an elixir that always works on better performance, especially if employees do not have a voice in the conduct of company business. ESOPs make capitalists out of people with voting rights for work incentives and antitakeover defense, but there may be cases in which employee owners may vote in favor of a corporate raider as well.

LABOR-UNION REACTIONS

Labor unions are largely confused regarding the principle of employee ownership and participation in management. Sometimes, they are supportive of this new trend because of the benefits provided to workers; sometimes, they are critical and even cynical; and at other times, they feel threatened from the rapidly growing employee ownership plans. On the other hand, labor laws are not facilitating unionized workers to participate in such plans.

Previously, labor unions were mostly against ESOPs because they feared that they would radically lose control and worker-owners would be eventually transformed into capitalists who would oppose unionization. The union chiefs or union "fathers" were against such plans mainly because of the decline of their authority and influence regarding negotiations on wages and benefits, working conditions, strikes, and other labor disturbances in exercising contravening power against management. Moreover, some labor unions, and mainly the international unions, feared that ESOPs were established to save moribund companies, jeopardizing workers savings, or were used as substitutes for pension funds. However, in recent years, a number of unions, including Steelworkers, Teamsters, Communication Workers, and Autoworkers, as well as the AFL–CIO, started supporting their locals in ESOPs initiatives. This was due mainly to the decline of the power of unions, which began behaving like tamed dogs. Perhaps, with union involvement and support, employee ownership would acquire more importance. Otherwise, the way to strengthen the interest of their member is through ESOPs, which do not take away workers rights to unions.

FINANCIAL CONDITIONS

The components of ownership include the right to possess, use, or destroy, exchange, and transmit something. Involving workers in ownership and management in the companies they work makes the use of machinery and equipment more effective and safer. However, governmental intervention modifies these rights by taxation and other controls. On the other hand, banks and other financial institutions, extending loans to ESOPs with full ownership and voting rights to workers, initially were reluctant to provide financing, but gradually they accepted the challenge and even preferred such financing to firms totally or partially owned by employees.

A number of companies add large amounts of money to their employee stock ownership plans to enjoy tax benefits and avoid hostile takeovers. In many cases, their ESOPs borrow money from banks and other financial institutions with the companies guaranteeing the debt. The interest rates for such borrowing are low because not only the interest but also the payments for principal can be deducted from the companies' taxable income. Also, the lenders pay taxes only on half of the interest they receive.

From that point of view, leveraged ESOPs became popular, because, normally, the money is used to buy shares from the public and give them to friendly owners, that is, the employees, who thus would have voting rights. Until the companies use the money to buy stocks, they will have the cash available for other purposes.

Allocation of ESOP shares usually is based on the salary level and the number of employees in the company. Such shares in the hands of the employees can serve as a blocking group against hostile takeovers. Moreover, annual dividend payments and grants to the ESOPs by the companies may be used for interest and principal payments on the related loans.

Retiring small entrepreneurs and business people are selling their firms to all their employees in a number of cases, making them whole employee-owned firms.

Many companies in the United States, and to a lesser extent in the EC, offer ESOPs for pension funds and profit sharing and others use leverage ESOPs to avoid unwanted takeovers. Employees and workers agree to buy the firms in which they work and offer concessions to avoid buyouts by other firms.

Because pension funds of some thirty million employees were used to finance hostile takeovers, legislation was introduced in the U.S. Congress to give the employees control over $1 trillion of their pension funds. It requires the participation of an equal number of employee and employer representatives on a joint board of trustees when issues regarding corporation pension funds are discussed. This means that employees would have a voice in how these funds are invested, but not in a company's contributions or benefit payments. Although corporate executives argue that employees lack the sophistication necessary to make modern financial decisions affecting the investment of pension funds, employees think that the pension funds are a form of deferred compensation for which they should have a say, instead of letting management invest these funds in "junk bonds" and other risky ventures.

REVENUE-SHARING SYSTEM

Different schemes of employee participation in decision making, revenue, and ownership have been developed in a number of countries, including the EC and the United States. In the system of revenue sharing, employees would receive a certain percentage of revenue instead of fixed wages. Paying part or all of workers' compensation in the form of periodic bonuses has the financial advantage of providing the enterprise with working capital for several months. Part of these bonuses may remain with a special fund for additional pension or for extra payment after a number of years of work. This system is used effectively in Japan.

The revenue-sharing system, in one form or another, gradually acquires worldwide importance. One can argue that the relaxation of the rules of wage determination through union–management negotiations in the United States and the EC countries is due to the abandonment, in many cases, of the fixed-wage system. Even the nonadjustment of the U.S. minimum wage ($4.25 per hour for years) to inflation may be considered as an indirect way of accepting the principle of revenue sharing.

There seems to be a built-in mechanism in the revenue-sharing system, which tends to lead the economy to equilibrium at full employment of labor. On the other hand, the existing wage system may require long periods to slowly move the economy, through an invisible hand, toward full employment. Because of the inflexibility in wages and other sticky variables, only by accident may there be full employment in the economy. In a share economy, with wages determined as percentages of revenue, employers will not tend to lay off workers in recessionary periods. Rather, they will tend to employ more workers because of absolute lower wages. Likewise, during the upswings of the economy, aggregate demand increases, the economy expands, and more workers and employees are expected to be employed.[6]

Nevertheless, in a stationary or unchanging economy, there is not much difference between the share system and the wage system. In the real world, however, sociopolitical and economic changes are customary and unpredictable disturbances and disequilibria are expected, especially in the market economies of the EC and the United States. Therefore, a balancing or equilibrating mechanism, notably that of a share economy, may be of great importance in leading the economy to stability and full employment. The revenue-sharing system may achieve full employment without inflation. Thus, the United States, the EC, and other market and even planned economies may solve the sticky dilemma between inflation and recession with share economy. Perhaps the problem of the inflationary pressures, that the Keynesian system introduced through deficit spending, may be solved forever. The synchronization of wages with revenue may mitigate the problem of cost-push inflation without increasing unemployment. At the same time, there may be no need for raising budgetary expenditures for countercyclical purposes and the bureaucratic and inefficient public sector may be reduced or at least not increased.

The system of the share economy, practiced successfully in Japan, may provide a solution to the problem of recession or stagnation and inflation (stagflation), which have troubled the market economies of the EC and the United States for more than two decades. The dilemma of simultaneous unemployment and inflation or their alternating path in economic fluctuations may be tackled effectively with a system of labor compensation related to the motivation of the employees and the performance of the enterprises in which they work.

A system of labor remuneration, in which employees are paid a significant part or the total amount of their wages in the form of bonuses according to the revenue of their companies, instead of fixed wages, could increase incentives of production and reduce unemployment. The difference between the revenue-sharing and the profit-sharing systems is that even in the case of no profits or losses workers would receive payments based on the amount of revenue of the company.

A new method of workers' participation that attracts attention in the United States and the EC is the team production system introduced at NUMMI (New United Motor Manufacturing Inc.), a joint venture of General Motors Corporation and the Toyota Corporation in Fremont, California, and Gencorp Automobile in Indiana. The team system is shifting control from the management hierarchy down to the workers who know better how to speed production and correct defects. Also, it eliminates middle management.

EMPLOYEE OWNERSHIP AND PARTICIPATION IN MARKET ECONOMIES

Employee ownership is rapidly growing in both market economies and planned economies. For example, in the United States, employee stock ownership plans (ESOPs) increased rapidly during the last two decades and include about 10,000 plants with some 10 million employees. Likewise, in the European Community (EC) countries and the seven EFTA (European Free Trade Association) countries, labor participation in the form of ESOPs (Britain), workers consultation (France and Sweden), labor capital comanagement or codetermination (Germany), and self-management (Yugoslavia) are also growing. Specific cases of such participation in individual countries are presented in subsequent chapters.

Many large and small companies around the world realized that employees are the key to better performance. Creative human resource management, with increasing employee involvement, is vital in promoting quality performance in the present highly competitive world. Economic performance is improved through greater employee responsibility, continuous on-the-job training, teamwork production, and work motivation. This investment in human capital and organization has been implemented by Germany and Japan with very good results.

In order to increase the employees' involvement, some companies offer a certain number of stocks to them at a lower than market price, with the option to keep or sell the stocks after 5 years.

Such an offer of 100 shares to each of 37,000 employees was made by Merck and Company of the United States in September 1991. This and similar partial ownership of stocks increase the motivation and the productivity of the employees, as they feel that good company performance eventually will increase their money return.

WORKERS' CAPITALISM IN PLANNED ECONOMIES

A serious dilemma concerning the economic reforms in planned economies is the ownership and management of enterprises. In labor management, where ownership rights belong to a work collective or to employees of enterprises, wage discipline is the Achilles' heel of economic stabilization. In state-owned enterprises, wage discipline is enforced by mandatory directives. In privately owned firms, wages are determined according to the principle of profit maximization and cannot be higher than the marginal productivity of the workers. In labor management, though, the management, elected by the workers, does not like to enforce unpopular measures of curbing wages and this leads to cost-push inflation. Moreover, multiparty elections for labor management often turn into party struggles as factory doors open to political rivalry. From that standpoint, the system of self-management may be an ineffective substitute. Therefore, vain hopes and illusions about introducing a genuine democratic system of labor management in place of state suppression or private exploitation in the production process are difficult to entertain.

Nevertheless, in the planned economies under reforms, public sector is gradually declining in favor of private entrepreneurship and, to some extent, labor management.[7] However, until a proper proportion, a symbiosis, of the private–public sectors, similar to that of the western market economies, is achieved, more bureaucratic constraints need to be dismantled. *Mutatis mutandis*, certain enterprises of monopolistic nature that serve large segments of society, such as sewage and water works, garbage collection, fire protection and the like could belong to the public sector, mainly to the city or village governments democratically elected.

Moreover, various forms of pseudo-cooperatives, with all the characteristics of bureaucratic state enterprises, exist in almost all planned economies. Nonetheless, the gradual transformation of such cooperatives takes place toward some kind of private partnership. In this case, the cooperatives are run by freely elected managers and not appointed by the party or the central government. Also, free entry and exit are possible, and the share of the accumulated capital can be taken by withdrawing members.

In the process of ownership transformation, individuals should be free to buy state-owned realties at a real market price, mainly through auction. Credit institutions should facilitate the purchase of state property by residents of the country or foreigners. Also, state-owned enterprises can be converted into joint stock companies with their shares sold to various owners, including their employees.[8] On the other hand, state assets can be leased to the private sector at competitive or reasonable rents. Such privatizations and leases of state assets provide revenue for the public sector, reduce budget deficits, and suppress inflationary pressures, as part of the money of individual buyers will be directed from consumer spending to asset ownership.

In the efforts of planned economies to change from state-controlled to market economies, serious questions appear as to the transformation and the new organization these economies will take. Are small and large enterprises to be transferred from the public to the private sector and in what form? How would the transfer of ownership be achieved? Through state sales to individuals and foreign investors or by making workers and employees total or partial owners of the firms in which they work?

Although we do not have much experience in applying such economic reforms, some form of workers' capitalism or Employee Stock Ownership Plans (ESOPs) could be used in the process of privatization. This economic system avoids extreme wealth accumulation and monopolization by individuals or the state and combines advantages from both the capitalist and the socialist systems and it is in accordance with Joseph Schumpeter's theory of "people's capitalism."

Under this system, which has been implemented to some extent by the United States, Japan, and the European Community, work incentives and labor productivity improve, strikes and other disputes are less likely because employee-owners share in decision making, and income distribution is more equitable. Thus, low-production incentives, bureaucracy, and controls prevailing under communism may not be relevant to a workers' capitalism implemented in the former planned economies under reforms.

WORKER–MANAGEMENT SYSTEM

Incentives and Problems

In worker-managed firms there are problems of ownership rights to capital, the right to a market rate of economic rent, and the right of liquidation. An individual worker, for example, should be compensated for the capital contributed to a firm through underpaid labor, especially when he or she leaves the firm. Also, differences in income-leisure preferences of workers, as well as inflexibility in short-run adjustment of labor input, can pose problems in the process of decision making, because workers may be suspicious of changes affecting their share in income and decision making. When they deal with leased capital goods, they may show little interest in preserving the equipment. Workers may prefer short-run activities with quick payoff, neglecting long-run capital formation. These difficulties may lead the system away from optimality and toward something less than the best social utility, in which the winners gain more than the losers lose.

The incentives to worker-entrepreneurs for the formation of a new enterprise or the introduction of innovations into an established enterprise seem to be weak, because they do not have unique claims to the residuals generated by these enterprises, which they must share with the other workers. Although certain nonpecuniary rewards may be offered in place of income renumeration, there may be dissatisfaction with private benefits for entrepreneurial activities; this could result in fewer innovations, fewer new firms, and inefficient factor allocation. Moreover, in the voting procedures a well-organized and energetic minority may dominate an apathetic majority of workers who may be ignorant of policy making. This can take place through manipulating voters, using demagoguery, shifting positions, and forming coalitions.

The sharing by workers in enterprises also means participation in losses, that is, acceptance of lower wages in recessions and business slumps. Such sharing in the profits and losses of enterprises makes the workers feel that they are the owners and they belong for life to the enterprises in which they work. Therefore, strikes, boycotts, or other labor disturbances are avoided and incentives for high-productivity increase, in a way similar to that of the Japanese system.

Nevertheless, fusing managerial and labor-supply functions in a self-management system is another problem. Thus, workers acting as managers may face conflicts of interest as they wear two hats at the same time. As suppliers of labor, they are interested in maximizing short-term wages and benefits. As managers, they are under pressure by banks and local and central authorities to maximize returns on equity and achieve a good long-run standing for the enterprise they manage. Also, there are questions whether workers' interests are better served through bargaining, forcing management to accept their demands, or through participation in decision making, in which case they become their own supervisors. However, in cases of recessions and widespread layoffs, workers' demands through bargaining may be ineffective, as it has been proved in market or capitalist economies, whereas under self-management workers largely hold on to their jobs. Such a system, seeds of which can be found in the Commune of Paris (1870s), is used in former Yugoslav republics.

Wage Determination

If a labor-managed firm follows the principle of profit maximization per worker, not total profit, then the new worker will receive a share in profits, not a fixed wage. In this case, income per worker, y, is equal to total value of production, V, minus total nonlabor cost, C, over the number of workers employed, L. That is,

$$y = \frac{V - C}{L}$$

Thus, if $V = \$1,000,000$, $C = \$800,000$, and $L = 200$ workers, then

$$y = \frac{\$1,000,000 - \$800,000}{200} = \frac{\$200,000}{200} = \$1,000$$

Figure 4.2 shows that the maximization of income per worker will be achieved by a firm at L, where marginal cost, MC, is equal to marginal revenue, MR. In this case, the slopes, or the tangents to the average nonlabor cost (C/L) and the average revenue (V/L), are parallel.

Depending on the availability of resources and the related cost and technology, self-managed or any other firms can determine the stage of production in which they will operate.

Figure 4.3(a) shows the relations among total product, TP; average product, AP; and marginal product, MP. Regarding the relationship of labor to output, Q, production stage II is preferable. To use more and more labor, the firm should

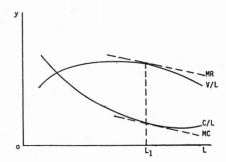

Figure 4.2 Income Maximization per Worker

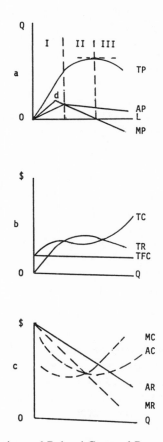

Figure 4.3 Stages of Production and Related Cost and Revenue

move toward the end of the second stage, where the marginal product of labor is zero. It is assumed that labor L is the varying factor, while other factors remain fixed. If the supply of labor is limited, then stage I, with growing average product, will be used. At point d, the law of diminishing returns is applicable. The uneconomical stage III, where total product is declining and marginal product is negative, can be used if the government subsidizes the firm to keep extra (unproductive) labor employed. This is a familiar phenomenon in overmanned public enterprises, whereas in self-managed firms, workers would oppose the employment of additional unproductive labor because this would reduce their remuneration.

Figure 4.3(b) shows the relations of total cost, TC, which is composed of total fixed cost, TFC, plus total variable cost, TVC, and total revenue, TR. Figure 4.3(c) shows the familiar relations of marginal cost, MC, marginal revenue, MR, average cost, AC, that is, total cost divided by output, and average revenue, AR, for varying quantities of production, Q. The best point of production, from the standpoint of profit (return) maximization, is where marginal cost equals marginal revenue (MC = MR). In this example, this coincides with the lowest average cost, which corresponds to the highest average product (in Figure 4.3(a)).

SUMMARY

Employee ownership and share economy may be considered as an alternative system that reduces or eliminates some of the disadvantages of both extreme systems, "exploitative" capitalism and "oppressive" communism. This system, which is rather encouraged by management and is not opposed by unions, reduces labor disturbances and increases work incentives. The spread of ownership to employees and individuals, mainly in the United States, Japan, the European Community (EC), and recently to eastern Europe and the Commonwealth of Indepent States (CIS) (former Soviet Union), may lead to a new economic system known as "people's" capitalism.

About 10,000 companies with more than 10 million workers or more than half of the labor unions are under Employee Stock Ownership Plans (ESOPs) in the United States. Tax reductions and other benefits are offered by the government to encourage such plans and to avoid bankruptcies and monopolization through takeovers. Similar measures have been introduced in Britain and other EC countries to facilitate employee ownership. Moreover, the revenue-sharing system, which is used effectively in Japan, the worker-management and the comanagement or codetermination systems, used in Yugoslavia and in Germany and Sweden, respectively, give workers and employees a voice in enterprise decision making regarding wages, profit sharing, layoffs, and other important business matters. Workers capitalism is also rapidly spread to ex-Communist countries of Europe and, to some extent, to developing countries.

5 The United States

A SYSTEM OF CAPITALIST EXPANSION

Early Expansion

Since America was discovered (1492), sectionalism and cleavage could be observed not only between individual colonies, but also between the coastline and the interior, as well as between the north and the south, primarily up to the American Revolution (1776). There were the mainly British colonial aristocrats (landlords, merchants, and slave owners) with economic and political power, and the small farmers and poor people in the back country who paid relatively more taxes and other fees. They were the debtors compared to the creditor eastern seaboard commercial establishment. Taxation was levied primarily on persons, not on property.

With the termination of the Anglo–American war in 1783, the estates of the loyalists were confiscated and land was redistributed. More important were the vast lands the new nation obtained from the peace treaty of 1783. This national domain played a major role in American (United States) economic and political developments (notably in the Homestead Act of 1862) regarding religious freedom, the separation of Church and State, and commercial expansion. Wages were determined primarily by the supply and demand for labor, and the constant flow of immigration delayed the growth of labor movements for many decades. From the time of its discovery to the present day, the New World (America) has been populated mainly by immigration from Europe.

American workers, under pressure of cheap labor from the flood of immigrants, opposed unrestricted immigration. As a result, Congress enacted legislation prohibiting advertising by employers that stimulated immigration and made it selective on grounds of nationality with other restrictions against undesirable aliens, including criminals, prostitutes, and polygamists. The main reasons for such restrictions were nativism, labor pressure, and the decline in the railroad industry due to shipping competition and particularly to rapidly growing motor vehicle transportation of freight and passengers.

The influx of European capital, together with European workers and investors, helped the development of a large railroad industry and the corporation form of business, which increased economic growth in the United States.

Because competition from Europe was strong and American industries were at an experimental stage, protection was needed until the infant industries matured enough and were able to compete with their European counterparts. Alexander Hamilton, using the infant industry argument, proposed tariffs and Congress approved them in 1789.

For governmental revenue and, to some extent, for industry and labor protection, 8.5 percent tariffs were imposed on imports in 1789. In 1792, the average rate of tariffs increased to 13.5 percent. Tariffs were increased on a number of occasions, and the average level was over 47 percent in 1864 and 49.5 percent in 1890 (McKinley Tariff). The highest tariffs in American history were established in 1922.

In 1863, under the presidency of Abraham Lincoln, gold certificates with 100 percent gold backing, and in 1878, silver certificates backed 100 percent by silver were placed in circulation. Also, in 1890, treasury notes (a temporary currency also backed by silver) were introduced. To charter and supervise national banks, the post of Comptroller of the Currency in the Treasury Department was established by the National Bank Act of 1863. National banks could also be established by transfer from state charters. The inelasticity or arteriosclerosis of currency and credit to meet seasonal and cyclical changes ignited the crisis of 1907, the "rich man's panic." This led to the creation of the Federal Reserve Bank (Fed) in 1913, which controls the economy's supply of money and credit and supervises the commercial banks.

The outbreak of World War I in Europe in 1914 helped the U.S. economy to grow mainly because of the heavy demand for American raw materials and war supplies for the belligerent European nations. As a result, the United States was transformed from a debtor to a creditor nation, whereas the European nations became debtors.

Public Policy Measures

During the economic depression of the 1930s, President Franklin D. Roosevelt introduced the New Deal, a program of spending in public works through the Public Works Administration and other agencies and industrial self-regulation. Also, a number of regulations was introduced to stimulate demand and to improve the economy through deficit spending, according to the Keynesian prescription. The United States came off the gold standard in April 1933, but gold could be used for international transactions, and the dollar was devalued by 50 to 60 percent. Federal Reserve member banks were not permitted to engage in stock market speculation, and insurance on deposits was provided. Also, a personal Social Security System was introduced in 1935, much later than similar programs in Germany (1880s), England, and other European nations. Furthermore, the Congress of Industrial Organizations (CIO, 1938) helped improve the position of labor unions.

After the defeat of Germany and Japan in 1945 and the end of World War II, U.S. industry managed to switch to peacetime production without a severe recession or inflation. It continued to provide Europe and the rest of the world with vital materials and industrial products. As a result, the United States emerged as the richest and most powerful nation on earth.

Although in the United States, direct productive operations belong primarily to the private sector, there are certain activities of a mainly public utility nature that are regulated or owned by the public sector. They include the Tennessee Valley Authority, the Bonneville Dam in the northwest, the Hoover Dam in the southwest, rural electrification, the space program, and some direct or indirect projects on atomic power. Also, a number of activities and operation on the local level belong to the public sector, for example, airports, subways, and buses. As a result, some people talk about creeping public-sector trends in the United States. Yet in western countries, such as Canada, Britain, Sweden, and France, a number of other enterprises belong to the public sector. They include coal mines, railroads, steel mills, airlines, radio and TV broadcasting, and even car industries that are totally or partially owned by the state.

A new economic tendency or necessity, which appeared recently with great force in the United States and other market economies, is that of bailing out or rescuing troubled enterprises by providing rescheduling state loans and other subsidies. Such firms include Lockheed, Chrysler, Continental Illinois, Amtrak, Eastern Railroads and Conrail, Home Savings Bank in Ohio, Old Court Savings and Loan Association in Maryland, savings banks in Texas and elsewhere, and probably other auto, steel, and airline companies, as well as banks with problem loans to developing debtor nations. This bailing-out phenomenon took place in Italy during the Mussolini era and is presently taking place in Britain, France, Germany, Spain, Greece, Turkey, and even Japan, where the governments struggle to keep moribund enterprises alive to avoid extensive unemployment.

ANTIMONOPOLY CONTROLS, MERGERS, AND ACQUISITIONS

To discourage monopolization of the market, special laws and regulations have already been introduced by the United States and the EC. They aim at the protection of the consumers from adulteration, pollution, resource depletion, and misrepresentation of quality and prices. In the United States, such laws include the Sherman Act (1890), prohibiting activities that restrain trade and monopolize the market; the Clayton Act (1914), forbidding price discrimination and elimination of competition between corporations through interlocking directorates and other devices; the Trade Commission Act (1914), prohibiting unfair methods of competition; the Robinson–Patman Act (1936), making it illegal to try to eliminate smaller rivals by charging unreasonably low prices and using other supply discrimination techniques; the Celler–Kefauver Antimerger Act (1950), prohibiting acquisition of real assets if it substantially lessens competition; and other laws and regulations that were enacted to achieve these goals, that is, to restrict monopoly and maintain competition. Similar antitrust laws prevail in the EC countries and aim at the protection of the consumers from unfair trade practices.

However, in spite of all these pieces of legislation and the accompanying judges and lawyers to implement them toward discouraging monopolies, monopolization and oligopolization of the American and the EC markets continue to grow. This may be due to economies of scale that large firms can achieve through concentration of capital and modern technology. As long as large monopolistic or oligopolistic firms can utilize mass production methods and reduce cost per unit, it is difficult to discourage their formation and operation through controls and regulations in the economy. The dilemma, therefore, is how to encourage competition and entrepreneurial intuition without hurting efficiency and economic progress.

Antitrust legislation may be considered as being, to a large extent, not much realistic just as are the models of competition it aims to protect. Breaking down large enterprises or prohibiting mergers and other monopolistic formations does not seem to accomplish much from the viewpoint of optimal resource allocation and entrepreneurial innovations. The problems that antitrust laws face today resemble the heads of the mythological Lernaean Hydra, for in the place of every problem solved, two others appear.

Consolidations and mergers may lead to better organizations and research and lower unit costs. To break or discourage such efficient formations is to punish efficiency and success. Antitrust laws and related restrictions should probably discourage price fixing and employment malpractices rather than obstruct mergers that can improve quality and reduce the cost of production. One could argue in favor of replacing all antitrust laws with modern and simplified pieces of legislation that would recognize the present real conditions of the oligopolistic and monopolistic structure of the domestic and international markets. This is what can be observed in the EC and to some extent in the United States, particularly for firms dealing with foreign trade and investment in the face of severe competition.

Public regulations and public enterprises appeared as an alternative to the shortcomings of the antitrust legislation. The responsibility of public utility regulations in the United States is mostly entrusted to state and local agencies. However, federal government commissions have also been introduced to reinforce local and state controls, mainly during and after the Great Depression.[1] They include the Federal Power Commission (FPC), regulating gas and electricity; the Securities and Exchange Commission (SEC), regulating stock and security markets; the Federal Communications Commission (FCC), controlling telephone and telegraph as well as radio and TV services; the Interstate Commerce Commission (ICC), regulating interstate and foreign trade movements; the Federal Aviation Agency (FAA) and the Civil Aeronautics Board (CAB), responsible for enforcing airlines safety rules and economic aviation regulations, respectively. However, the CAB was abolished at the end of 1984, after 46 years in operation, and the Department of Transportation assumed some of its remaining functions.

Government regulation of airlines, for example, was responsible for high labor costs and low efficiency.[2] Since 1978, however, when the U.S. government's sheltering regulations of airlines ended, increased competition suppressed operating costs, including wages, which were reduced in a number of cases. Similar deregulation trends can be observed also in EC countries. However, there is the danger that smaller companies are swallowed up by large ones, which eventually may control the market and charge higher prices.[3] Also, problems of proper maintenance and dangers of air accidents may appear.

LABOR UNIONS AND ESOP

Collective Bargaining

The importance of labor unions and the collective bargaining process in solving labor–management disputes has flourished after the Great Depression of the 1930s. The Wagner Act, along with other related pieces of legislation, played a significant role in upgrading collective bargaining. Specifically, Section 8(a)(5) of the Act does not permit the refusal of collective bargaining.

A number of academicians, including Archibald Cox of Harvard University, asserted the importance of the Wagner Act in encouraging workers to join unions and discouraging managerial interference. In relation to that, corporations resorted to the courts to decide whether management has the prerogative to determine workers' merit payments, vacations, pensions, and other labor-related issues. On the other hand, labor leaders thought that these problems should be solved jointly by management and labor and that this is the way to avoid strikes and other disturbances. However, it is questionable if the legal system and the courts, including the Supreme Court, were able to accommodate collective bargaining and if the judges had knowledge of the many important cases of industrial relations. In any case, historians, politicians, economists, and other scholars seemed to agree that workers and unions cannot be deprived of their rights to judicial consideration of their disputes with employers. And this is true in spite of the fact that the importance of the Wagner Act and the vitality of labor unions have declined lately.

The Wagner Act aimed at prohibiting employer actions that cause economic warfare by encouraging collective bargaining. It was designed to promote industrial democracy that had different meanings in American history. Workers were expected to behave rationally regarding workplace disputes, thereby avoiding actions that might cause harm to the company involved and the national economy. For that reason, the Taft–Hartly Act amendments of 1947 were introduced to prohibit certain kinds of union conduct, preserving though the protection of the right to collective action.

From the period of the New Deal to recent years, the unchallenged U.S. economic superiority in the world and the growing prosperity reinforced the bargaining power and the demands of labor unions. However, with competition from Japan and other countries, peace was needed between labor and capital, and strikes and other labor conflicts were to diminish so that American corporations could be able to compete effectively in the domestic and international markets.[4] In other words, the jobs of the workers and the survival of unions were and still are at stake. This became obvious particularly since the mid–1970s as price inflation, a weaker dollar abroad, and severe competition from foreign corporations increased. As a result, historians of law such as Christopher Tomlins and other legal theorists such as James Atleson and Katherine Stone shared the argument of the degeneration of the Wagner Act and the downgrading of the system of industrial relations of the New Deal. On the other hand, the U.S. government encouraged the establishment of the employee representation plans and provided certain benefits for such plans.

As long as business grew, the Wagner Act and the National Labor Relations Board (NLRB) were supported by labor unions, although not much by local activists, during the post–World War II years. However, with the recession of the early 1980s and later, the conditions of the unionized sectors of America became dismal. Even the AFL–CIO president Lane Kirkland and members of the NLRB, as well as the federal courts, called for the repeal of the Wagner Act.

Nevertheless, the Wagner Act and the NLRB have contributed to the humane revolution in the workplace. Unions and corporations that used to solve their problems with violence gradually learned to respect each other and negotiate their differences at the bargaining table. Although violations continued by employers and unions, workers have found rational and peaceful ways to solve their problems.[5] Such collective bargaining covered not only industrial workers, but public employees as well.

ESOPs

Employee Stock Ownership Plans (ESOPs) have spread rapidly all over the United States. Some 9,800 plants with about 10 million workers, compared to about half a million in 1976, are under such plans, according to the National Center for Employee Ownership. They include such companies as Phillips Petroleum, Weirton Steel (the largest completely employee-owned company), LTV Steel Company, ARCO, Dan River, U.S. Sugar Corporation, Cone Mills Corporation, Time Warner Corporation, Houston Industries, O and O (Owned and Operated), Rochester Products, Fastener Industries, American Standard Company, Stone Construction Equipment, Procter and Gamble, Polaroid, Bera of Ohio, Gore and Associates (makers of Goretex), Avis, Oregon Steel Mills, Quad/ Graphics, Texaco, Ralston Purina, J. C. Penney, TWA, Seymour Speciality Wire, National Can Corporation, Publix Supermarkets (Florida's largest chain totally owned by employees), Todd Products, Thermo Electron, Bell Atlantic, McClouth Steel Company, Conrail, Kerr–McGee Corporation, PPG Industries, and the Bureau of National Affairs (a business–law publishing firm).

Although labor unions have in many cases opposed employee ownership, especially in the United States, they recently started to support the establishment of employee-owned firms, as happened in the case of the United Automobile Workers (UAW) and the United Press International (UPI). Today, the employee-owned companies represent as much as 8 percent of the U.S. workforce and in some 15 years are expected to increase to 18 percent, equal to the present members of labor unions.

Tax deductions, up to 25 percent of the annual payroll of the company's contributions to ESOPs, and other incentives are offered by the federal government to encourage employee ownership. Also, lenders to ESOPs in the United States do not have to pay income taxes on half of the interest they collect. Such tax breaks are estimated to be $2 to $3 billion each year.

The U.S. House Ways and Means Committee, however, is considering restrictions on current tax breaks for ESOPs, unless the participants own at least 30 percent of a company's stock. Such restrictions refer to the repeal of the tax preference that allows financial institutions to avoid taxes on up to 50 percent of the interest they receive from loans to ESOPs. Also, the committee might repeal the deduction for dividends paid on employers' securities obtained by ESOPs and require taxpayers who sell securities to ESOPs to have held them for 3 years before the sale in order to be eligible for tax benefits. The legislation aims at closing an "abusive loophole" and collecting revenue for the governmental budget.

SECTORAL MOVEMENT OF LABOR

Regardless of the economic system, there is a trend of labor to move out of agriculture, first into industry and then into services. Such a movement is faster in capitalist or free-market economies than in centrally planned or controlled economies.

In the United States, workers have moved in large numbers from the agricultural into the manufacturing and, finally, services sectors. As Figure 5.1 shows, the size of the labor force engaged in agriculture declined from more than 60 percent in 1840 to about 30 percent in 1910, 12 percent in 1950, and only 3 percent in 1989. In western Europe, where industrialization started earlier, this structural change occurred years back and continued thereafter but at a slower pace.

After the introduction of the steam railway in 1828, industrial growth was

Percent

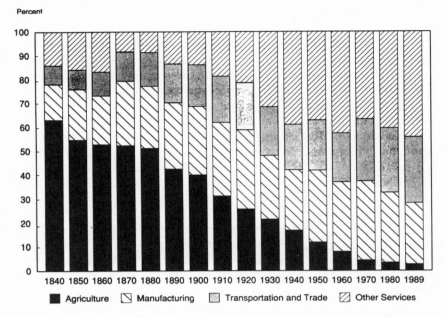

Figure 5.1 Labor Force Shares by Industry
Source: U.S. Government, *Economic Report of the President* (Washington, D.C.: U.S. Government
Printing Office, 1991), 114.

enhanced. Gradually, and mainly from the early 1900s, workers moved rapidly
in services such as trade, communications, transportation, education, health,
finance, accounting, and, lately, computers and other business services. Because
more and more women have entered the labor force during the postwar years,
primarily in the service sector, and more and more manufacturing jobs have been
lost to foreign competition, the labor movement to services has intensified.

It seems that the pressure of foreign competition will continue because American companies and institutions do not pay as much attention to research and
development as foreign firms. They are interested in short-term results at the
neglect of long-term improvement. Because of this policy, they are pushed aside
in quality competition. Thus, the Japanese companies employ more than five
times the number of robots used by American firms and competition is severe
mainly in consumer electronics, steel, and particularly in automobiles. Toyota,
for example, is using only 10 percent of the labor General Motors is using to
produce the same number of cars. Furthermore, American firms are interested
in diversification instead of paying more attention in eliminating waste, driving
costs down, and improving quality. On the other hand, there is not a comprehensive industrial policy with connections between business and government in
the United States as there is in Japan. This leads to Japanese dominance (Pax

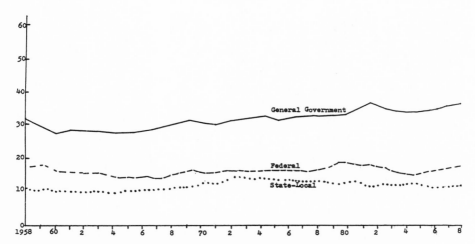

Figure 5.2 Total Receipts of General, Federal, and State–Local Government as
Percentages of National Income (current prices)
Source: Organization for Economic Cooperation and Development, *National Accounts*, various
    issues.

Nipponica) in technology, trade, and investment. Already, a good part of American manufacturing and bank assets is owned by Japan.

FISCAL AND MONETARY POLICY

Government Expenditures and Revenue

The ratio of public-sector spending to national income remains high, as do
budget and trade deficits, despite the tough talk on fiscal discipline and reduction
in government expenditures. During the postwar years, the percentage of national
income absorbed by the public sector increased from 23 percent in 1950 to close
to 40 percent in recent years. About 25 percent of national income is absorbed
by the federal government and the rest, 15 percent, by state–local governments.[6]
The same trend can be observed in federal and state–local tax revenues as
percentages of national income, as Figure 5.2 shows. Table 5.1 shows government deficits and debt, unemployment, and other economic indicators.

Government spending for subsidies and a lobby-driven tax code leads to
decisions according to what is tax-efficient rather than economically efficient.
This overloads the private sector, stifles the genius of capitalism, and makes the
blessings of the invisible hand less attractive.

Historically, the federal debt was changed from $75.5 million in 1791 to $24.3
billion in 1920, $260.1 billion in 1945, $906.4 billion in 1980, and close to $4
trillion in 1992.[7] Corporation debt amounted to about $2 trillion in 1990, mort-

Table 5.1
GNP, Per Capita GNP, Unemployment, Inflation, Federal Government Deficit, and Debt for the United States

Year	GNP (billion$)	Per Capita GNP ($)	Unemployment %	Inflation %	Federal Deficit (billion$)	Federal Debt (billion $)
1970	1,115.5	4,922	4.9	5.7	0.7	369.0
1975	1,598.4	7,334	8.5	9.1	45.3	532.1
1980	2,732.0	11,804	7.1	13.5	50.4	906.4
1981	3,052.6	13,077	7.6	10.3	58.5	996.5
1982	3,166.0	13,424	9.7	6.2	112.6	1,140.9
1983	3,405.7	14,282	9.6	3.2	186.7	1,375.8
1984	3,772.2	15,705	7.5	4.3	161.0	1,559.6
1985	4,014.9	16,581	7.2	3.6	185.5	1,821.0
1986	4,231.6	17,307	7.0	1.9	212.8	2,122.7
1987	4,515.6	18,297	6.2	3.6	160.7	2,347.7
1988	4,873.7	19,558	5.5	4.1	144.1	2,599.9
1989	5,200.8	20,904	5.3	4.8	130.3	2,836.3
1990	5,463.0	21,730	5.5	5.4	158.2	3,210.9

Sources: U.S. Government, *Economic Report of the President*, Washington, D.C.: U.S. Government Printing Office, various issues; Organization for Economic Cooperation and Development, *National Accounts*, various issues; and International Monetary Fund, various issues.

gage debt and consumer loans climbed nearly twentyfold during the last three decades to about $1.5 trillion, and state and local government debt to about $1 trillion.

The Banking Sector

In the United States, the power to coin money rests with Congress. With the establishment of the Federal Reserve Bank (Fed) in 1913, the amount of money supply is determined by the Fed, which is an independent institution. The seven members of the board of governors of the Fed are appointed for 14 years by the president with the consent of the Senate. All these seven members, and the director of the New York Fed and four other directors from the twelve regional Feds in rotation, form the powerful Federal Reserve Open Market Committee

(FOMC). The FOMC is responsible for buying and selling U.S. government securities and setting money supply targets, thereby affecting prices, employment, growth, and other economic goals of the country. When the Fed buys a government security, it pays with Federal Reserve notes or draws checks upon itself, thus creating money and directly monetizing the debt. However, the U.S. Treasury may borrow, primarily from the public at large, and thereby avoid such monetization.

In addition to the open market operation (buying and selling government securities to influence the economy), the Fed can use the discount rate and the reserve requirement to combat unemployment and inflation. The discount rate is the interest rate commercial member banks pay when they borrow money from the Fed. Reserve requirement is the percentage of demand deposits (checking accounts) the banks must keep in cash or deposit with the Fed. Changes in the reserve requirement, which now is 10 percent of demand deposits, substantially affect the amount of money in circulation because of the effect of the banking multiplier (which is equal to one over the reserve requirement).

Unlike the banking organizations of other countries, which are based primarily on the branch system, the U.S. banking organization is based on the unit system with a large number of banks (about 14,000). Directly or indirectly, the commercial banks are under the supervision of the Fed, which determines the money supply (currency, that is, paper money and coins, and demand deposits) and controls credit.

Government authorities frequently spend more than they collect from tax revenue and finance the difference by borrowing from the public or through money creation. In the United States, the supply of money is regulated by the Fed, which has control over bank reserves. In most other countries, the control over money rests with the central banks, which are under the control of the government.

Recently, there was a significant increase in the money supply in many countries, which is related to the increase in the nominal gross national product (GNP), that is, the real GNP plus inflation. For the United States, the velocity of money, the speed by which the average dollar is changing hands in a year, was declining or relatively constant and around 6 in the 1980s. However, there was a gradual increase in velocity during the 1960s and 1970s.

As Figure 5.3 shows, the velocity of money, that is, the ratio of GNP over the money supply, increased gradually from 3.5 in 1960 to 6.8 in 1981, that is, by 94 percent. This supports the argument that the velocity of money is not constant over time as the monetarists argue. From that standpoint, inflation during that time and particularly in the 1970s was largely due to the increase in velocity of money, which is mainly the result of fast spending promoted by advertisement and the United States' advanced monetary system. Therefore, velocity (V) of money (M_1), or $V = \text{GNP}/M_1$, is primarily responsible for the inflation of 1960–80.

To isolate the effects of inflation from wages, Social Security payments, and

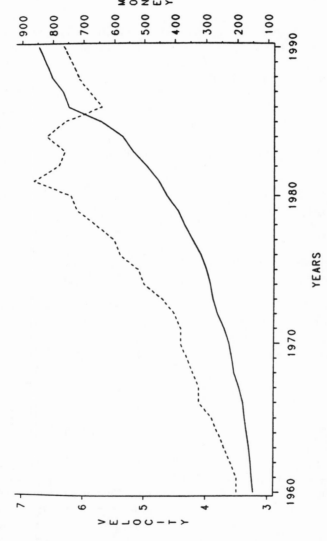

Figure 5.3 Money Supply (M_1) and Velocity of Money (GNP/M_1)
Source: International Monetary Fund, *International Financial Statistics*, various issues.

progressive taxation, a price-level index is needed to make the standard of living and the tax rate structure inflationproof, which, at the same time, removes the bias toward a growing public sector.

The present U.S. consumer price index, CPI, which can be used for tax indexing, is based on a survey of 23,000 businesses, instead of the former 18,000 retailers, and in 85 cities, instead of the former 56 cities. The spending patterns include workers, clerks, the self-employed, retirees, and the unemployed in the new all-urban consumer index, and the number of commodities includes several thousands in the base year and the current year.

ECONOMIC POLICY AND FOREIGN INVESTMENT

Effects of the Twin Deficits

A serious problem of the U.S. economy is the deficit in the budget as well as in foreign trade. The main cause of the twin deficits is the governmental policy of reducing tax revenue, mainly through the Economic Recovery Tax Act of 1981 and the Tax Reform Act of 1986, without reducing as much spending. The idea was that tax cuts would encourage people to work more, save and invest more, and the growth in the economy would yield more tax revenue. However, these tax cuts did not produce the surge of working effort and the proportionate tax revenue. The result is a continuation of internal and external deficits and growing interest payments. In essence, this is an illusion of well-being based on borrowed money and borrowed time that leads to a gradual decay of influence and reduced standards of living, making Americans renters of the property they once owned. This is what happened, for example, with the recent Japanese purchase of MCA Inc. (which deals with movies, books, and records, for $6.1 billion), 51 percent of the Rockefeller Group (owner of Rockefeller Center for $864 million), CBS Records (for $2 billion), Columbia Pictures (for $5 billion) and many buildings in Los Angeles, as well as a number of other companies.

For the anxious European and the patient Japanese investor, ownership of American land, which is cheaper than in other countries (mainly because of the drastic depreciation of the dollar since 1985), and other assets is important from an economic and social point of view, while Americans gradually lose their economic independence.[8]

Because Americans are living well by running up huge domestic and external foreign debts, foreign creditors, mainly Japanese and Europeans, use their surplus and buy American assets. It is like an individual enjoying life by spending borrowed money, running up debt, and selling off property.

A multiple regression analysis of trade deficits (TDs) on budget deficits (BDs), gross domestic product (GDP), and interest rates (IRs), 1960–88, indicates that, for the United States, "budget deficits" and "interest rates" are more significant variables in explaining changes in "trade deficits." That is,

$$TD = -23.37 + 0.41BD + 0.12GDP + 0.75IR$$
$$(3.72) \qquad (1.47) \qquad (4.55)$$

(Figures in parentheses are t values.)

The fit of regression was very good ($\bar{R}^2 = 0.937$) and no serial correlation existed ($D - W = 1.63$). Thus, reductions in budget deficits are expected to reduce trade deficits, percentage wise, by more than 40 percent. A similar regression analysis for the European Community (EC) shows a weak or no correlation for these variables ($\bar{R}^2 = 0.263$), particularly between trade deficits and budget deficits, mainly because of nonuniform budgetary and monetary policies in EC countries.

A North American Common Market?

In order to improve mutual trade and investment, the United States and Canada formed a free-trade agreement that was approved by Congress and the House of Commons and went into operation at the beginning of 1989. This is expected to increase the Canadian GNP by 5 percent and that of the United States by more than 1 percent annually in about a decade when all tariffs would be eliminated. There is no doubt that the timing of the agreement was influenced by the movement in the EC to eliminate all remaining economic and other barriers. The hope in both countries is to match the new expected competitiveness of the large unified market in western Europe.

Already, the United States and Canada decided to speed up tariff cuts in chemicals, electrical motors, printed-circuit boards, and other items. Moreover, entrepreneurs and multinational companies of both sides accelerated their efforts to trim costs on imported components and other products.

Furthermore, expected closer cooperation between the EC and the other countries in Europe may bring the United States, Canada, and Mexico closer together in the face of growing competition.[9] On August 8, 1992, the three nations signed an agreement to gradually eliminate tariffs in 15 years.

If foreign products are sold in the United States at less than their fair value, the U.S. Department of Commerce can impose antidumping duties to eliminate price differentiation. If such imported products harm or threaten to harm American firms producing similar products, then duties could be collected by the Customs Service to eliminate the difference between cost of foreign products and the lower prices at which they are sold in the United States.

Perhaps together with Canada, Mexico, and other neighboring countries, an eventual American Economic Community (AEC) would be able to compete with the EC and probably with another group in east Asia in which Japan, Korea, Taiwan, and other neighboring countries might participate.[10] Therefore, it is expected that these three economic groups or common markets would be the future competitors in the western world. However, after a period of negotiations and adjustments, and under the aegis of the 107 nations' General Agreement on

Tariffs and Trade (GATT) and other international institutions, these groups are expected to move toward more economic coordination through barrier reductions joint ventures, mutual trade, and foreign exchange policies.

SUMMARY

The influx of immigrant workers and capital, mainly from Europe, helped the development of the U.S. market economy. During the economic depression of the 1930s, a number of macroeconomic measures were introduced to stabilize demand and avoid high unemployment. Such measures constituted a deviation from the laissez-faire system.

Although productive operations belong primarily to the private sector, there are certain activities that are regulated by the public sector. Despite the extensive antitrust legislation, there is a trend toward market monopolization or oligopolization through mergers and acquisitions, mainly because of economies of large scale and pressures from foreign competition. Growing oligopolies and monopolies, as well as unyielding labor unions, restrict competition and invite government regulations.

To avoid severe recessions and high rates of inflation and unemployment, fiscal and monetary policy measures are used by the government and the Federal Reserve Bank, respectively. However, high budgets and foreign trade deficits persist, federal and foreign debts pile up, the future burden of the American economy from debt services increases, and the laissez-faire system is under pressure from the growing public sector.

6 The European Community

EVOLUTION OF THE EUROPEAN COMMUNITY

From the ancient times of the Greco-Roman period on to the Middle Ages, the Industrial Revolution, and later, efforts for a united Europe were promulgated on many occasions. Writers and rulers in ancient Greece and Rome supported or enforced, from time to time, unions of city–states for parts or the whole of Europe. For centuries, emperors, kings, feudal lords, theologians, artists, and many common people vainly yearned for unity among the divided and, in many cases, belligerent nations of Europe.

From 1815 to 1854, five European powers (Britain, France, Prussia, Austria, and Russia) formed some kind of alliance (Concert) after the Napoleonic wars that reduced conflicts and kept peace for 40 years. Also, they established buffer zones, held regular conferences, and undertook joint actions, including military operations so that costly military buildups could be reduced and domestic economies strengthened.

After World War I and particularly at the beginning of the Great Depression, new totalitarian fascist governments came into power all over Europe. The end of the depression of the 1930s came finally with World War II in 1940–45. Thereafter, mostly labor parties came to power in western Europe. They introduced reforms regarding distribution of income, extension of welfare services by the state, and nationalization, particularly in railroads, power, coal, and other heavy industries.

The European Economic Community (EEC) was established by the Treaty of Rome in 1957 with six members: Belgium, Luxembourg, the Netherlands, France, West Germany, and Italy, commonly known as the "Inner Six." It was formed to gradually reduce internal tariffs. Because the group was successful, the United Kingdom and Denmark, as well as Ireland, joined the EEC in 1973.

Greece became a member in 1981 and Spain and Portugal in 1986.[1] Because of political and other noneconomic integration movements, the EEC is currently named the European Community (EC).

There are four major institutions in the European Community for the formulation and implementation of economic and other related policies: the Commission, the Council, the European Parliament, and the Court of Justice.

The Commission formulates and proposes related legislation and provides for the implementation of the Community's policies. There are seventeen commission members (two each from Britain, France, Germany, Italy, and Spain and one from each of the other member–states) chosen for 4-year terms by the twelve EC member–state governments.

The Council approves the legislation of the Community and is its decision-making institution. In contrast to the Commission, its members act as representatives of the particular member–state governments.

The European Parliament, elected by the voters of the individual member–states, has 518 members seated in nine political party groupings. With the closer integration of 1992, the parliament acquired more power in decision making.

FISCAL AND MONETARY POLICIES

Public Finance

This section deals with similarities and differences in fiscal and monetary policies. It examines governmental expenditures and taxation and their changes over time, as well as the relationship of money supply and credit to inflation, interest rates, and other related variables.

With a growing public sector in the EC economies, fiscal policy acquires great importance not only on matters of financing governmental expenditures, but also on matters of countercyclical policy. General government expenditures include central or federal, state, and local government spending. The federalism of Germany establishes a division of powers between the national and the state governments, in contrast to other nonfederal countries such as Britain, France, Italy, Spain, Greece, and Portugal. Governmental spending involves payments for goods and services and other transfer and intergovernmental activities.

The EC public sectors have grown proportionately at a faster rate than the overall economy in the long run. For the EC countries (average of Britain, France, Germany, and Italy), general government expenditures increased from 36 percent of national income in 1950 to 50 percent in current years. Figure 6.1 shows the growing public sector in the EC and the United States, and Figure 6.2 shows the trend of indirect taxes.

The expansion of the public sector, or the growing average propensity to spend, is the result of ever-increasing demand for government services, including those of regional and local units of government.

Moreover, loans and other support measures are provided particularly by the

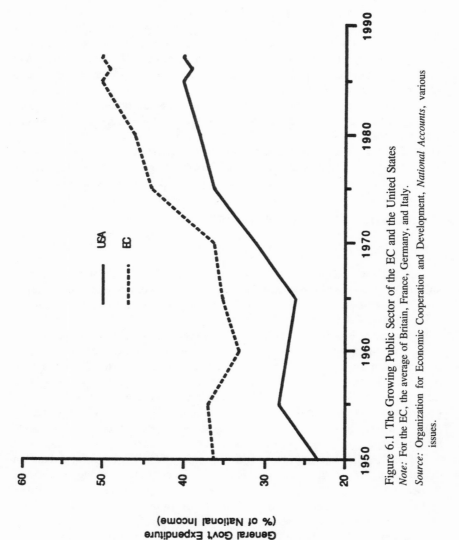

Figure 6.1 The Growing Public Sector of the EC and the United States
Note: For the EC, the average of Britain, France, Germany, and Italy.

Source: Organization for Economic Cooperation and Development, *National Accounts*, various issues.

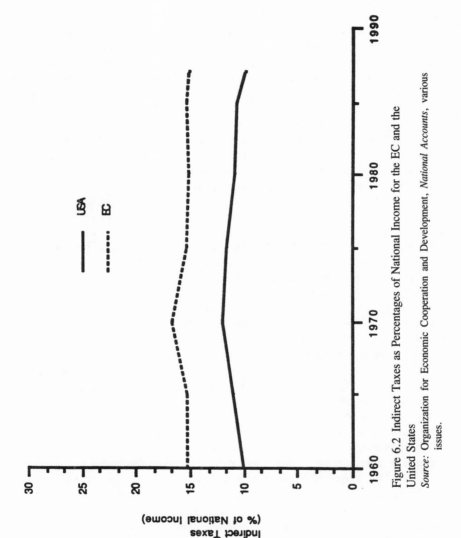

Figure 6.2 Indirect Taxes as Percentages of National Income for the EC and the
United States

Source: Organization for Economic Cooperation and Development, *National Accounts*, various
issues.

EC member states to problematic and moribund firms. As long as the states preserve complete or partial control of such firms, these rescue operations tend to be institutionalized and introduce a modern form of undesirable fiscal activity. However, with the introduction of a share economy and the employee ownership of enterprises, such government interventions and undesirable controls can be reduced or eliminated.

Direct (or income and profit) taxes that are imposed primarily on individuals absorb relatively higher proportions of income in the advanced economies of the European Community (except France and the Netherlands) than in the less-developed economies of Greece, Portugal, and Spain. Likewise, they account for higher proportions of the total tax revenue for these EC countries, as well as for the United States, Japan, and Sweden, compared to the indirect taxes (or taxes on goods and services). Tax revenue from Social Security is relatively higher in France, Germany, Italy, and Spain than in Japan, Sweden, United States, and Britain.

Indirect taxes, as percentages of total taxes, are higher in low-income EC countries such as Greece, Ireland, and Portugal than in the advanced EC countries. From that standpoint and as a result of the EC integration, a relative decrease in indirect taxes and structural changes in both direct and indirect taxes are expected to occur in the near future in the foregoing low-income countries. Table 6.1 shows public-sector expenditures and other variables of EC countries.

In the European Community, the value added taxes (VATs) have either replaced inefficient turnover or cascade taxes (e.g., in France, Germany, and the Netherlands), or have been required for EC membership in the Community. The VAT was introduced in France in 1954. Presently, it raises about 50 percent of tax revenue in that country. In Germany, the VAT was proposed in 1918 and introduced in 1967. There it provides 13 percent of government revenue. In Britain, it provides 15 percent.

The revenues of the EC countries as a group come primarily from value added taxes (1 percent of the VAT collected by the member nations), customs duties, and special levies on agricultural imports (including sugar duties). Revenue from VAT is about 50 percent of the total revenue of the EC as a unit separate from that of the individual member countries.

Most of the collected revenues are spent for the support of prices of agricultural products by a special EC fund known as FEOGA (Fond Européen d'Orientation et de Garantie Agricole) (about two-thirds); around 10 percent for the regional development of backward areas; and the rest for social policies, research, energy, and for aid to third world countries (about 6 percent). Greece, Italy, Portugal, Spain, and to some extent France, are the main recipients of subsidies for agricultural products and regional development.

The EC VAT rates vary from 6 percent for basic goods to 16 percent for most goods and services, and up to 38 percent for luxury goods. However, exports, agricultural and some other goods, and small firms are exempted.

Table 6.1
Population (in millions), Per Capita GDP (in dollars), Growth of GDP, Inflation (average annual rates 1980–89, %), Unemployment (%), and General Government Expenditures over National Income (GG/Y) for the EC, 1990

Country	Population	Per Capita GDP	Growth of GDP	Inflation	Unemployment	GG/Y
Belgium	9.9	16,220	1.8	4.5	8.5	50.2
Britain	57.2	14,610	2.6	6.1	7.0	46.9
Denmark	5.1	20,450	2.2	6.0	7.7	68.4
France	56.4	17,820	2.1	6.5	9.4	56.7
Germany	62.1	18,354	1.9	2.7	5.5	50.3
Greece	10.0	5,350	1.6	18.2	7.8	41.4
Ireland	3.5	8,700	1.8	7.8	17.0	54.4
Italy	57.7	15,120	2.4	10.3	10.8	44.5
Luxembourg	0.4	16,220	1.9	4.5	1.8	42.6
Netherlands	14.9	15,920	1.7	1.9	8.7	59.5
Portugal	10.5	4,250	2.5	19.1	5.0	40.7
Spain	39.0	9,330	3.1	9.4	17.0	39.9
EC	326.7	13,328	2.2	6.4	8.2	49.6

Note: In some cases, earlier years' data were available. The growth of GDP, inflation, unemployment, and GG/Y for the EC is the average of Britain, France, Germany, and Italy.

Source: International Monetary Fund, *International Financial Statistics*; Organization for Economic Cooperation and Development, *National Accounts*; World Bank, *World Development Report*; all various issues; and ELEFTHEROTYPIA (newspaper), Athens, July 8, 1991, 24–25.

Policies on Mergers and Acquisitions

Concerning the new trend of economic organization and market monopolization via mergers and acquisitions, there are questions of weakening national sovereignty and rising corporate colonialism in market economies. Although ideologies pass and nations remain, antitrust and takeover regulations in almost all nations become ineffective because of the growing capital concentration required by modern technology and international competition.

There are national differences in antimonopoly and takeover regulations that present more opportunities in certain countries, such as the United States, Britain, and the Netherlands, than in others, such as Germany, France, and Japan. For example, Germany has its traditional differences in takeovers through worker participation in management changes and Japan through its cultural and family-type relations of companies and their employees.

On the other hand, banks in Germany may hold up to 20 percent of a company's shares, and in Italy, the government controls some 26 percent of the entire stock market and the Agnelli, Benedetti, and Feruzzi families another 32 percent. Moreover, companies in the Netherlands can limit the voting power of shareholders or issue defense preference shares with a sizable discount in price, but in Belgium, with a more liberal legislation on takeovers and acquisitions, more than 50 percent of the market is owned by the French.

However, such limitations and differences in the EC and other European countries present problems for the integration of Europe and the formation of "Europeanized" companies, as well as for further economic cooperation with the United States, Japan, and other investor nations.

Nevertheless, the United States' merger mania does not prevail in Europe. Thus, according to Securities Data Company, there were only 852 mergers or acquisitions in Europe in 1990, compared with 3,894 in the United States, where, as someone once said, "Everything is for sale except your kids, and maybe your wife." Mostly, company stocks are held within families or related institutions and mergers and acquisitions are primarily friendly. In Europe, joint ventures are preferable to takeovers.

WORKERS' PARTICIPATION

In order to boost the single market's "social dimension," the European Commission considers certain ways of workers' participation in the process of decision making of the companies in which they work. One way is to follow the German model in which workers are represented on supervisory boards. Another way is that of France with separate workers' councils. Or a new system to be agreed upon by management and the work force via collective bargaining may give the workers the option to participate or not. It seems that the Commission would base its decision, regarding workers' participation, on Articles 54 and 100A of the Treaty of Rome, which allow majority voting on such matters. To smooth out disagreements, particularly from Britain, the commissioners prefer to use the term "involvement" instead of "participation." Moreover, proposals are advanced that workers would merely share information on plant closures, alliances, and other strategic decisions, but not consultation on day-to-day operations. Nevertheless, the European Parliament wants some form of workers' involvement in decision making.

A company under the European statute would be subject to EC rules not only regarding workers' involvement, but mergers, acquisitions, and joint ventures, as well as a single tax code. Companies incorporating under EC rules could be able to write off losses in one member nation against taxes in other member nations. However, a number of the EC governments object to this privilege because they fear that their tax revenue might be reduced.

In July 1991, the Council of Economic Ministers of the EC proposed and the related European Committee adopted the workers' participation in the annual results of enterprises in which they work, through their sharing in the capital stock. This measure covers both private and public enterprises.

Employee ownership and producer cooperatives with worker participation in management and different forms of profit sharing can be observed in a number of European countries, such as Britain, Germany, Italy, and Spain. Small producer cooperatives in Britain were found to have higher incentives and productivity than larger enterprises, and in Germany, high degree of participation of employees and workers in management and decision making proved to be very productive. Likewise in Spain, the Mondragon's worker cooperatives, with some 18,000 workers, proved to be more productive than the 500 biggest industries in the country. This was due primarily to flexible wages, high rates of investment, high incentives from worker ownership, and a high degree of cooperation in the region.

All over western Europe, the trend is toward denationalization, privatization, and employee participation in enterprise decision making. Many state enterprises are expected to be transferred to individuals, private companies, and the employees. Also, more and more private firms are expected to transfer partial ownership to their workers and employees. The main reason for such transformation is to encourage competition, reduce subsidies, and increase efficiency.

THE BRITISH ECONOMY

Great Britain, a great power in the nineteenth century, was formed in 1707 by the union of England, Wales, and Scotland. Its union with Ireland in 1801 formed the United Kingdom. In 1922, Ireland withdrew. Northern Ireland, though, was retained and continues to struggle for independence. By the beginning of the twentieth century, Britain, the largest colonial power, controlled about one-fourth of the world, on which "the sun never set." It was the birthplace of the Industrial Revolution, and in 1870, had the highest per capita income in the world ($2,031 valued in 1983 U.S. dollars). However, in 1913, the United States had the highest per capita GNP on earth ($3,119) and continues to do so up to now. Presently, the British GNP per capita is lower, not only than that of the United States, but that of Canada, Japan, Germany, France, Belgium, and a few other countries.[2]

After the Labor Party came to power in 1945, substantial economic changes were introduced. High rates of unemployment and widespread inequalities that prevailed in prewar British capitalism had to be corrected. Socialization of health, nationalization of a number of industries, and other reforms made Britain, one of the oldest capitalistic nations, a welfare state, similar to Sweden and other Scandinavian countries. On the other hand, the independence of a number of colonies from the British hegemony deprived it from vital resources and markets and resulted in an unfavorable balance of payments and low rates of economic growth.

Although the British economy is performing relatively well from the standpoint of stability and growth, it remains somewhat behind compared to other economies regarding the rates of economic growth.

The long decline of the British economic power is primarily due to growing foreign competition, a current problem for the United States as well, and the expansion of government controls of the economy through nationalization and social welfare programs. Also, the growing power of labor unions, which denounced the blind forces of the market, the encouragement of mergers at the detriment of competition, and the anticolonial trends contributed to the decline of the British empire, particularly during the post–World War II years.

A form of indicative planning, similar to that of France, was formulated in 1961, but it became ineffective in implementation. In practice, stop–go fiscal and monetary policies were used to stimulate the economy when unemployment was high or to reduce inflation and balance of payment deficits. After 1979, when the conservatives took power, emphasis was placed on monetary policy, reduction in progressive tax rates, and denationalization.

In addition to the Bank of England (the central bank of Britain established in 1694), there are also seven large commercial banks. The Bank of England was nationalized in 1946, whereas the commercial banks remained under private ownership. The government appoints the governors of the central bank, which is not as independent as the U.S. Federal Reserve Bank (established in 1913).

Privatization and Employee Participation

Immediately after World War II, a number of industries were nationalized in Britain by the Labor Party in power. Thus, the coal industry was nationalized in 1946 and put under the National Coal Board, which still operates a number of mines today. It is expected, though, that the industry would be transferred to the private sector if the Conservatives remain in power. More than 25 enterprises were sold to the private sector since 1979, when Margaret Thatcher took office, providing some $50 billion for the British Treasury. Also, garbage collection services were contracted to private firms. A number of firms were sold totally or partially to their workers and employees, including the National Freight Consortium.

The British privatization program is closely related to a wider share ownership policy. Recently, the proportion of adults owning shares increased from below 7 to 19 percent. About 52 percent of all individuals owning shares have shares in only one company. This is due primarily to the employee share ownership, which is present in a number of firms mainly in privatized enterprises. One of these firms is British Telecom with 98 percent of its employees being shareholders. However, the proportion of the total shares owned by employees is relatively small in many such enterprises, privatized or not, and the influence of employee-owners on decisions regarding wages and other matters is limited. From that point of view, the privatization program has impact on the width and not much on the depth of employee ownership in Britain.

In recent years, the British government moved toward further denationalization or privatization of state or semistate enterprises. Thus, British Telecom (the state-owned telephone monopoly), Ferranti (the industrial electronics firm), British Aerospace (the aircraft and missiles firm), Britoil, British Sugar, Jaguar (the luxury car maker), British Petroleum, Cable and Wireless, and British Airways, which were totally or partially owned by the state, have been or are in the process of total or partial denationalization (this is called Thatcherism) or have been taken to the market with employee participation. The main reason is to encourage competition and increase efficiency. Thus, the stocks of the denationalized British Telecom were divided between British institutions (47 percent), Telecom employees and the public (39 percent), and foreign investors (14 percent, United States, Canada, and Japan). Also, the National Freight Company (producing trucks) was sold to its employees in 1981, as was the John Lewis Partnership many years back.

Although there are not many ESOPs in Britain, compared to those in the United States, the tax relief and other advantages they enjoy would speed their spread to other companies as well. A conventional management buyout (MBO) would enjoy tax relief only if it includes an ESOP through distribution of shares to the workers. The split of ownership through ESOPs is supported by almost all political persuasions, including the right-wing Adam Smith Institute and the left-wing Fabian Society in Britain. ESOPs are neither a capitalistic tool, as wealth and power are split to many workers, nor a creeping collectivist tool, as employees and workers become capital or wealth owners. The tax relief applies to those British ESOPs that distribute all shares to workers within 7 years. However, the law discourages family-owned firms from establishing ESOPs as yet, because they must pay taxes on capital gains realized from sales of equity to an ESOP.

At times, labor unions buy and sell companies instead of letting others do that. Also, cross-Atlantic raiders are involved in ESOPs. Thus, Sir James Goldsmith, the British raider who acquired the parent Crown Zellerbach Corporation a few years ago, will keep 10 percent of the equity and the rest (about 30 percent) will go to union's financiers, employees, and debt holders.

Britain and the EC

Many British are uncomfortable with the novel idea of the EC single market. Moreover, with the completion of the Calae tunnel connecting Britain with France, they feel that there would be an economic invasion by other Europeans, especially from France. Furthermore, the British, along with other EC member nations, have been in two serious wars in the present century and many other conflicts before. However, from the point of view of exports, the British, as well as the Germans, the French, and the Italians, feel more comfortable with the EC integration.

The vision of the British government and the Tories is not a United States of Europe similar to the United States of America, where people went to avoid oppression and enjoy freedom and opportunity. They think that frontier controls should not be abolished for purposes of protecting Europeans from drug movement, crime, illegal immigrants, and terrorists. Moreover, Europe should not be allowed to come under a network of regulations that stifle initiative and enterprise. Such objections may bring fears of what Charles De Gaulle thought in the 1960s, when he objected to Britain's entrance in the EC, arguing that Britain will be "the Trojan horse of the United States" and may destroy the vision of a United Europe.

THE FRENCH ECONOMY

Economic Trends

France, which was always different from other market economies, is known as a country with new political and economic ideas. The French Revolution of 1789 has inspired the creation of democratic institutions for the past two centuries. The Physiocrats of the eighteenth century, with their teachings on a natural economic order and a laissez-faire ideology, influenced Adam Smith and other classical economists. Even the present democratic planning has some similarities with the national economic planning under an industrial parliament proposed by Saint-Simon in the 1820s. On the other hand, a tradition of government control over economy was established by such reigns as Louis XIV between 1661 and 1715 (with creation of colonies in Canada and Louisiana) and Napoleon Bonaparte between 1749 and 1816 (with stronger mercantilistic policies than those of the Physiocratic school and Jean Baptiste Colbert, the finance minister at that time).[3] The highly centralized system of Charles de Gaulle under the Fifth Republic of 1958 still remains influential in present French political and economic policies.

Under the competitive pressure from other EC countries, France's political ideology became less important as related to the economic issues of recent years. Thus, in 1981, when François Mitterand and the socialist candidates won the elections, the French stock market fell 20 percent in 2 days and the franc declined substantially. In 1988, however, after the second victory of Mitterand, both the stock market and the franc rose and the investment climate improved, because of less social spending promises.

Indicative Planning

After the destruction of World War II, Jean Monnet proposed the creation of a Planning Commissariat for which he was appointed director in 1946. The main principles of French planning were to coordinate the economy through the co-operation of trade unionists, industrialists, and civil servants toward the mod-ernization and growth of the economy. This form of decentralized democratic (*indicatif*) planning was to improve and not replace market operations. That is why the *Commissariat General au Plan* remained small with a staff of about 100 until it was merged into a new ministry in 1981.

The postwar 5-year plans, from the first one of 1947–51 and up to the tenth one of 1989–93, as well as some interim plans or miniplans for specific un-foreseeable reasons, aimed primarily at formulating economic targets and using fiscal and monetary policies to achieve these targets. They show the directions in which the economy ought to go rather than providing specific targets for individual firms. In recent years, entrepreneurs gradually orient their production and distribution activities toward the EC rather than within a national framework, and French planners have increased difficulties in projecting and communicating national economic targets. Overall, because of the peculiar characteristics of France's "indicative planning," it is argued that it is mostly talk or that it is more French than planning.[4]

The economic policy of France is based on macrostability, through de-mand management, decentralized or indicative planning, and microeconomic coordination, through the free-market mechanism. Individual firms form their investment production and distribution plans and try to correct inconsisten-cies between them and other related firms and sectors. To achieve a prede-fined rate of growth, a process of economic coordination is pursued through national planning. Usual and pragmatic fiscal and monetary policies, ad-justed to the EC relative directives, are used during the implementation stages of the plans. The process of planning is one of cooperation among producers, workers, consumers, and the government in a way that planning would supplement and inform the market to perform better, thereby preserv-ing the dynamism of competition.

In contrast to Dutch short-term stabilization plans, French medium-term or 5-year plans aim at guiding resource allocation based on forecasts regarding final demand, labor supply, and investment requirements, assuming a certain technological level and a relatively constant incremental capital output ratio (ICOR). Although French planning is not a command-type of China plan-ning, input–output tables are used, as they are in controlled or planned economies, but not with imperative force. The plans are self-fulfilling docu-ments based on consultations. They are supported by tax alleviations, subsi-dies, and credit policies.

Nevertheless, forecasts of individual firms and the aggregated sectoral pro-jections are largely unfulfilled in practice and, in many cases, they become wild guesses, mainly because of unforeseeable changes, such as the students' riots and the general strike of May 1968. However, this does not mean that planning does not have pedagogic and predictive values for business executives and public enterprises. Also, policy makers on fiscal and monetary matters may use plans' predictions, not only on domestic stabilization and growth policies, but also on issues of foreign trade and exchange rates, compatible with EC integration policies and long-term socioeconomic trends in the country.

France and the EC

In France, all political parties support European integration, and they expect their country to be the first among equals both economically and politically. The drive for economic unity leads the Socialist Government of François Mitterand to adjust its policies to those of the EC. Such policies include privatization of state-owned enterprises, reduction in public-sector expenditures, and other austerity measures to curb inflation and eliminate budget deficits. This is a deviation from previous policies France, Spain, Greece, and other EC countries followed in stimulating demand through generous wage increases, expansive monetary policy, and social spending policies that led to inflation, high trade deficits, and currency depreciation.

Many French politicians and executives of big business expect the European Community to be a single free market, similar to that of the United States. Then, German, Italian, Spanish, and other professional people would be able to open offices in Paris or Lyon, and French or other EC nation's lawyers and professionals in general would be able to operate in any other member nation.[5] However, a nationalist backlash might be created among farmers, workers, and small business people with chauvinistic tendencies who might react to this challenge of European unification.

Nevertheless, even Gaullists and others, who opposed unification in the past, gradually abandoned their objections and adjusted to the expansion of the EC operations. They think that eventually Paris will be capital of the EC, and after the construction of the Calae tunnel, France will be a vital transportation and commercial center of Europe. On the other hand, the antiimmigrant National Front, the extreme right-wing party of Jean-Marie Le Pen, with some 14.4 million voters, is against the EC market unification because its members are afraid of "labor invasion," and the Communist Party favors a larger European community from the Urals to the Atlantic.

Privatization and Workers' Consultation

In order to distribute the power of decision making, through workers' consultation (autogestion); reduce wealth concentration, through private ownership; and achieve a better distribution of income, the French government nationalized a number of public utilities and other private firms. The nationalization process, which started with railroads in the 1890s and was intensified after World War II, included such industries as armaments, telecommunications, coal and gas, electric power, insurance, some steel and auto companies, as well as banks and other chemical and textile firms. In the early 1980s, about one-third of the labor force worked for the government or for firms controlled by the government. A number of firms, close to bankruptcy, were nationalized to avoid unemployment, but were supported with subsidies by the public sector, a policy that is known as "lemon socialism." Currently, however, in order to improve efficiency, a privatization policy is implemented.

Along these lines, France embraces "popular capitalism" and it is in the process of selling off government-owned industry to employees and other private investors. The campaign of denationalizing some 65 public enterprises, a number of which had been nationalized by Charles de Gaulle, has been warmly received by employee-investors and other domestic and foreign financiers. They include such companies as Paribas, Saint-Gobain, Agency Havas, Compagnie Générale d'Électricité, and three major commercial banks.

THE GERMAN ECONOMY

The Nazi and the Social Market Systems

During the Middle Ages and until 1871, Germany was composed of a number of disunited states. The free-trade doctrine held until the formation of Customs Union (Zollverein) in 1834, when *ad valoren* tax rates were erected against external trade. Otto von Bismarck, the Prussian politician, united feuding states into a powerful state in which he served as a chancellor from 1871 to 1890. He raised tariffs and encouraged the establishment of cartels and monopolies and introduced the world's first Social Security system in the 1880s. With the defeat in World War I and the Treaty of Versailles, Germany lost its colonies and was punished with sizable reparation payments. These heavy obligations and the Great Depression helped to bring Adolf Hitler and the Nazi (National Socialist) Party in power.

The Nazi economic system, which started in 1933 under the fascist regime of Adolf Hitler, was based on private property and state controls on production and distribution. It was a regimentation of the economy in which economic and social groups and individuals were subordinated into sectorial groups (industry, trade, power, handicrafts, banking, insurance, and tourism) and regional or territorial groups. Decisions on management, prices, wages, and production quotas were determined by the government. There was a state representative (leader or führer) in each enterprise to direct operations in accordance with the desires of the Nazi Party.[6] Small firms were forced to join cartels and independent labor unions were replaced with appointed ones by the government. Supervisory agencies (Reichstellen), mainly under the control of the Ministry of the Economy, put production priorities for armaments and import substitution. It was a regimented or command capitalist economy for the purpose of achieving the political and military goals of the fascist or Nazi state. Wages were determined by decree, whereas during the Weimar Republic (a democratic regime established in 1919), compulsory government boards were used to conclude wage agreements between employers and employees.

The economy of today's Germany can be characterized as a social market economy (soziale Marktwirtschaft). The Basic Law (Grundgesetz) of 1949, serving as the country's constitution, protects private property and establishes the main economic goals (Social Security, social equity, and social progress). Ideologically, the notion of a social market economy has its roots in the Freiburg school of neoliberalism, as developed mainly by Walter Eucken and Alfred Mullet-Armack.[7] However, it was put in practice primarily after Germany was split into the Federal Republic of Germany (FRG) (Bundesrepublic Deutschland), or West Germany, and the German Democratic Republic (GDR), or East Germany. At the end of World War II, the allied occupation forces (Britain, France, United States) put emphasis on the rehabilitation of the country and the recovery of its economy, mainly using the market system. The Democratic Republic, or East Germany, came under the control of the Soviet Union, which introduced a planned economic system that was abolished with the unification of Germany in 1990.

Economic Policy

As in all market economies, the German economy is influenced by private- and public-sector activities. The social market economy (SME) of Germany is based primarily on the private sector, the free-market mechanism, and labor–capital management or codetermination (Mitbestimmung). However, positive governmental activities are necessary to create a healthy environment for the market system, to break monopolies and cartels (through the Law Against Limitations on Competition, which is similar to U.S. antitrust legislation), and to provide Social Security and welfare.

Nevertheless, public- and union-owned enterprises play an important role in certain sectors of the German economy, such as transportation, communications, postal service, dwelling construction, and, to some extent, banking, and even mining and metallurgical operations. Union-owned enterprises, created to maximize social benefits not profits, include Gruppe Neue Heimat, a large apartment construction company; Coop-Unternehmen, the second largest retail trade firm; and the Bank für Gemein Wirtschaft, an interregional bank providing credit facilities all over Germany.

Through large holding companies, the federal government owns stocks in more than 3,000 firms. However, the waves of denationalization and decontrolization that prevail all over Europe, including the CIS (former USSR), engulfed Germany as well. Volkswagen and Veba are two companies in which privatization (Privatisierung) was carried out recently, through sales of shares to private groups, employees, and low-income persons on a preferential basis. This mixed economic system, combined with a relative harmonious labor–capital comanagement and a high rate of savings and investment, is mainly responsible

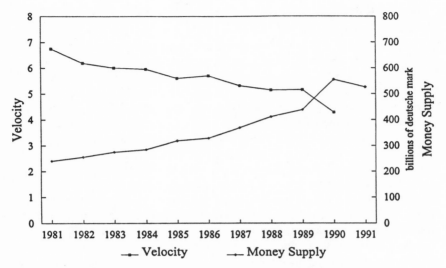

Figure 6.3 Money Supply (M_1) and Velocity of Money (GDP/M_1) for Germany
Source: International Monetary Fund, *International Financial Statistics*, various issues.

for the post–World War II German rapid growth or the so-called economic miracle (Wirtschaftswunder).

In Germany and other EC nations, labor unions are stronger than in the United States. For example, about 40 percent of the local force in Germany belongs to unions, compared to less than 18 percent in the United States. The German Federation of the Unions accounts for some four-fifths of all union membership. Wage-rate determination is made on an industry basis. Unions are entitled to strike and management can close down, or lock out, firms in reaction to strikes. Politically motivated strikes are not permitted. For a strike to be legal, 75 percent of the workers should approve it in a secret ballot. In Germany, unions exercise their influence mainly through nominating representatives in work councils,[8] but in other EC countries, they are comparatively more influential, and collective bargaining is more important, especially in Belgium and Italy and to a large extent in Britain, France, and the Netherlands, where employers press for com-anagement for gaining labor peace.

To avoid labor shortages and keep wages down, Germany allowed immigration of guest workers (Gastarbeiter) from time to time. They are mainly from Turkey (637,000 total in 1981), Yugoslavia (358,000), Italy (316,000), and Greece (132,000).

Germany's economic policy proved to be successful in achieving high rates of growth and low rates of inflation. This was due primarily to its efficient monetary policy. As Figure 6.3 shows, money supply increased in the 1980s at rates that facilitated a growing GNP and a declining velocity of money (from 6.8 in 1981 to 4.4 in 1990).

Unlike other EC countries, Germany has a federal system that allows state and local governments to have their own large budgets. France, Britain, Italy, and Spain, as well as other EC nations, have a centralized fiscal system with a strong central government budget and weak state and local public financing. Furthermore, the Social Security system, introduced first by Germany in the 1880s, is independent of the central or federal government budget.

Germany is the world leader in exports, with more than $400 billion per year, followed by the United States, Japan, and Italy. Other EC countries with a good record in exports are the Netherlands and Belgium/Luxembourg.

The unification of the German Democratic Republic (East Germany) with the Federal Republic of Germany (West Germany) in 1990 may eventually unite the rest of Europe, because Europe's division is due in large part to the division of Germany, and vice versa. The fulfillment of German aspirations for unification came not from the west but from the Soviet disengangement, the massive emigration of East Germans, and the breaking of the Berlin Wall.

Other European nations and the United States, based on historical experience and the fear of reviving nationalism, are skeptical about German unification. The slogan "ein Deutschland" reminds them of the catastrophic results of World War I and World War II. However, advanced technology in communications liquidated the old nationalistic concepts in Europe and prepared the ground for closer cooperation and even unification of neighboring countries.

Codetermination or Comanagement

Workers in Germany are represented in the firms in which they work through the works councils. Such a representation, which goes back to 1891 when consultation of labor was required for shop rules, is known as codetermination (Mitbestimmung). In 1952, the Works Constitution Act introduced an equal representation of capital and labor in the supervisory boards (Aufsichtrat) for the iron, steel, and coal industries to avoid strikes and other disturbances. In other industries, labor had one-third representation, and after 1976, one-half representation in firms with more than 2,000 workers.

To avoid a stalemate in the selection of the chairman of the board of directors, the codetermination law requires that the chairman be a neutral person selected by the stockholders' representatives in case of a tie vote. To have representation in the shop level, where the supervisory board rarely is involved, the law requires that companies employing five or more employees have an enterprise council to deal with wages, firings, and other personnel matters.

In practice, codetermination gives employees a voice in enterprise decision making, particularly in layoffs, wage determination, and profit sharing on the factory level. Industrial-level wage contracts are reserved for the unions. Nevertheless, codetermination or comanagement of capital and labor does not seem to influence the transformation of the economic system toward a workers' capitalism, as do employee ownership plans in the United States and other countries.

THE ITALIAN ECONOMY

Introduction of the Capitalist Spirit

The Italian economy from the times of the Roman Empire (31 B.C. to A.D. 476) onward has been based primarily on the free-market process. During the Roman period, efficient public administration, the construction of roads and other public works, the introduction of public or legal entities (corporations), and the use of slave labor were the main characteristics of the economy. After the fall of the Roman Empire, a large number of self-sufficient estates were created in the countryside with the feudal landlords as owners and their vassals or serfs to work for them. In the craft guilds of the cities, the master craftsmen provided food, clothing, shelter, and instructions to the apprentices in exchange for their labor. This was the manorial or feudalistic system that prevailed in Italy and western Europe in general during the Middle Ages (A.D. 476 to about A.D. 1500). With the fall of Constantinople (1453), which was the capital of eastern Rome or Byzantium, the Greco–Roman literature, the arts, and inventiveness were reintroduced by refugees from Byzantium to the west and laid the groundwork for the Industrial Revolution to start some three centuries later.

Italy is the place where the spirit of capitalism first flourished, according to Werner Sombart and Karl Marx, during the thirteenth century. Although the first beginning of capitalism could be observed early in certain Mediterranean towns, particularly in Italian ports, it became widespread in western Europe in the sixteenth century. The emancipation of the serfs from the landlords of the countryside transformed them into free laborers, competing for jobs to be provided by the capitalists of the towns. The credit system and the concept of public debt, developed mainly in Genoa and Venice as early as the Middle Ages, gave rise to bankers and financiers, joint stock companies, stock exchange markets, and the spread of capitalism not only in Italy, but in the Netherlands and other European nations.

Mussolini's economic ideology started with a corporist idea in the sense of organizing society in noncompetitive groups or guilds with the aim of supporting the national economy. This policy of the early fascist organization of the economy was successful for small independent traders, shopkeepers, and the old middle classes, which were threatened by large enterprises and strong labor-movement claims.

Economic Performance

In spite of the fact that Italy faced extensive political instability, with frequent government changes during the post–World War II years, economic performance was satisfactory. Some Italian enterprises managed to expand domestically as well as internationally.

Along with France and Germany, Italy had high rates of GNP growth in the post–World War II years, especially in the 1950s and 1960s. This good economic performance was due primarily to the migration of workers from the poor agricultural sector to the modern industrial sector.

Italy, among the worst EC nations on matters of public finance, has high annual budget deficits (about $85 billion in 1989, or 10 percent of the GNP), compared to around 5 percent for the United States. In order to compete in the unified European market, Italy must reduce budget deficits and accumulated national debt. The first steps have been already taken in that direction by raising sales taxes, cutting income taxes, controlling tax evasion, and reducing spending.

OTHER EC MEMBER NATIONS

Spain

Through exploration and conquest, Spain became a rich colonial power. Also, via diplomacy and wars, it expanded its influence to neighboring European countries during the Hapsburg Dynasty (1516–1700) and the Bourbon Dynasty (1700–1931), with some setbacks, primarily during the French Revolution (1789) and the accession to power of Napoleon Bonaparte in France.[9]

After a struggle and a civil war between the republican or liberal forces (Loyalists) and the fascists (who were supported by the then fascist regimes of Italy and Nazi Germany) in the 1930s, the totalitarian (fascist) government of General Francisco Franco was established in 1939 and remained in power for some 40 years. In the 1980s, the present socialist government of Philip Gonzalez was voted to power.

To reduce inflation and increase growth, the Gonzalez government implemented a mixture of free-market and socialist policy by encouraging competition and foreign investment, slashing subsidies to moribund companies, and imposing an austerity program. Initially, following the successful Swedish policy, it devalued the peseta, tightened money supply, and encouraged exports. Nevertheless, personal income tax rates remained high (up to 56 percent) and government expenditures gradually rose to 45 percent of gross national product. A number of state-owned enterprises left by Franco were privatized and companies could easier lay off workers.

To stimulate incentives, workers' self-management is also used. The Mondragon eighty industrial cooperatives in the Basque Autonomous Region of Spain was created in 1956 by a priest, José Maria Arigmendi. This conglomerate, which produces a number of products, from refrigerators and plastics to electronics and machine tools, provides Social Security, health care, banking services, and even college education (in engineering) for its "self-employed" workers. The workers elect the Board of Directors, which selects or hires the managers. As compared to American managers, who receive ninety-three times the average salary of workers, and the Japanese, six times, the Mondragon manager receives no more than five times the salary of the lowest paid worker.

The overall rate of investment increased (from zero or negative in 1978–84 to about 15 percent currently) and inflation declined (from around 20 percent in 1978 to 9 percent currently). However, unemployment remains high (17 percent), although reduced from its peak of 21.5 percent in 1985 and in spite of the fact that more than 1.1 million jobs were created during the last 2 years. This contradiction was due to the rapid increase of the number of women entering the labor force. Spanish policy makers argue that increases in wages lead to higher unemployment and inflation, and income and wealth redistribution and higher social welfare can be achieved through growth-oriented policies. This is what they call pragmatic or supply-side socialism.

Spain, with a socialist government, realized that there is no better alternative than joining the rest of western Europe and becoming a member of the EC. On January 1, 1986, Spain, as well as Portugal, became a member of the EC. This resulted in a flood of European investment into Spain.

Smaller EC countries

From the smaller EC nations, the Benelux countries (Belgium, Luxembourg, the Netherlands) and Denmark are more advanced than Greece, Ireland, and Portugal. The last ones face serious problems of high inflation, low rates of economic growth, and relatively low per capita income, and they receive annual aid from the EC for their development.

SUMMARY

Occasional efforts were made for a united Europe throughout history, but systematic cooperation agreements were enacted after World War II. In 1957, six western European nations established the European Common Market, which later expanded to twelve member nations and it is now known as the European Community (EC). The EC is based primarily on the free-market system with some deviations regarding government intervention among its members.

Britain, the bastion of capitalism and the largest colonial power for centuries, fell behind other countries on matters of per capita income and became a welfare state during the post–World War II years. However, its recent privatization programs tend to change social welfare programs, while the EC membership tends to reverse the path of its stagnant or declining economy. The Conservative Party objects to the creation of a central EC bureaucratic government with a central powerful bank and common currency, whereas the Labor Party favors nationalizations and EC full participation.

France, with government ownership in a number of industries, has resorted to long-term indicative or democratic planning to control the economy with indirect fiscal and monetary measures. However, because France has to follow EC directives makes the importance of these measures weak. Although French governments are influenced by socialist ideas and try to promote industrial democracy, efforts are being made to privatize previously nationalized industries, while support for industrial concentration and European unification is growing.

The German economy was primarily based on the free-market system. Bismarck, a chancellor from 1871 to 1890, raised tariffs, supported cartels, and introduced the world's first Social Security system. The Nazi party, under Hitler, introduced the fascist system based on private property and state controls regarding prices, wages, and production quotas. The capital–labor management or codetermination and the social market economy (SME) are the main characteristics of the German system. The reunification of Germany, reduced somewhat the need for guest workers. Together with France, Germany supports a stronger EC.

Italy and Spain, which had fascist regimes in the past, under Mussolini and Franco, respectively, as well as smaller EC countries, follow, more or less, the free-market system and face similar problems of budget deficits, foreign debts, and inflationary pressures. In all EC countries, there seems to be a trend toward a system of workers' capitalism, which incorporates employee ownership in Britain, Greece, Spain, and other nations, workers' consultation in France, and codetermination in Germany. All EC nations try to reduce government expenditures, which count for about 50 percent of national income, compared to lower than 40 percent for the United States and Japan.

7 Japan: A Miracle Economy

HISTORICAL ROOTS OF DISCIPLINE AND EFFICIENCY

Before the middle of the nineteenth century, Japan was an isolated feudal society. Commodore Perry, with his powerful fleet, arrived and opened up Japan in 1853 and limited trade with other nations began thereafter. During the period of the Tokugawa regime, a hereditary military dictatorship (1603–1868), transactions in silver and gold were conducted mainly with the coast cities of China. At that time, Confucianism, extolling the virtues of discipline, propriety and knowledge, was promoted. To keep the other feudal nobles (the *daimyo*) under control, the Tokugawa nobles (about 300) introduced the system of double residence. The households and professional warriors, used as personal armies of *samurai* (another ruling class), were kept at the imperial capital as residents for alternate years. An efficient network of transportation and communications and capitalistic institutions was developed as a result of the required movements of retinues and retainers from the countryside to the capital and vice versa. This was the early stage of capitalism as an advancement from feudalism.

After the overthrow of the military dictatorship and the restoration of the Meiji monarchy (1869), the Japanese government removed the power of the *daimyo*, taxed merchants passing through their lands, and removed export restrictions. A similar phenomenon occurred in the German *Zollverein* (customs union), which helped the unification of Germany at that time. At the same time, pensions were granted to the two ruling classes (*daimyo* and *samurai*) mainly in government bonds with diminishing value because of inflation. This in turn reduced the influence of these old powerful classes.

An island nation, Japan was isolated during the period of seventeenth to nineteenth centuries. Present-day hierarchical structure in the system of production has its roots in the feudal period, particularly in the institutional changes of the Emperor Meiji Restoration, after the overthrow of the House of Tokugawa, and the emphasis on modernization, patriotism, and commercial expansion.

Large family-owned conglomerates, *zaibatsu* (Mitsui, Mitsubishi, Sumitomo, Yasuda), exercised monopoly on financial and other production and trade activities, especially during the period 1868–1946. Thereafter, efforts have been made to break down these main financial cliques, increase competition, and decentralize the economy but with not much success. Since World War II, looser forms of business-affiliated groups (*keiretsu*) or cartels, with informal vertical and horizontal linkages, were advanced.[1] Thus, the Mitsubishi *keiretsu* group, which ranks first in annual sales in Japan, owns between 10 to 100 percent of stocks of more than 1,000 different firms, and the Matsushita *keiretsu* includes 200 firms dealing mainly with electronics, engineering, and management techniques.

LABOR RELATIONS AND ECONOMIC PERFORMANCE

Permanent Employment

The economic development of Japan during the post–World War II years was impressive. Its rate of economic growth was the highest in all the nations of the Organization for Economic Cooperation and Development (OECD), which includes the EC nations and the United States. The Japanese "miracle" was due primarily to a disciplined and productive labor force and the main economic and social institutions. The hierarchical organization of society, influenced by the ethical ideology of Confucius centuries ago, promotes hard work and accomplishment.[2]

Mostly, the Japanese labor unions are company unions, organized in individual enterprises. Regardless of their occupation, employees of each company form their trade union. However, there are a few loose national labor confederations with little authority. There are also a few major confederations of employers, the most important of which is the Federation of Economic Organizations (*Keidenran*), which includes about 800 industrial, trading, and financial firms.

The lifetime employment (*shushin koyo*) system of Japan, which can be traced back to the pre-Meiji period, is considered as the most important aspect of exceptional labor motivation and high productivity. Also, it keeps aggregate demand at high levels and stabilizes income and employment. Employers promise to maintain their employees, and employees, who think of their company as their family, pledge to stay in their job until retirement, regardless of better opportunities offered elsewhere. Workers consider themselves more as permanent partners than as hired hands. Although life expectancy is high (78 years), retirement age is mostly 55–60. Wages are primarily determined by seniority and by extensive bonuses, like dividends, which account for about 20 percent of the average renumeration, compared to about 1 percent in Britain and the United States.

A Share System

As mentioned previously, a proper measure to stimulate productivity and keep production costs relatively low might be to pay part of wages in the form of bonuses instead of fixed or increasing wages—a process that is gradually gaining support in the United States and the EC. Such bonuses would depend on the profitability of each enterprise and should be equal to all workers of a given age and rank. This flexible system of renumeration, which has been successfully introduced in Japan, has the advantage of reducing the fixed labor cost significantly.[3] Moreover, paying a portion of workers compensation in the form of periodic bonuses has the financial advantage of providing the enterprise with working capital for several months. Part of these bonuses may remain with a special fund for additional pension or for extra payment after a number of years of work. Along these lines, large Japanese enterprises (*zaibatsu*) decentralized ownership to achieve higher productivity. The managerial class is not aloof to personnel problems. Politeness and simple courtesy to employees and customers are also powerful weapons in Japan's managerial arsenal for efficiency.

The bonus system, which is similar to profit sharing, helps raise savings and investment and induces high rates of economic growth. In the share economy or bonus system of Japan, employees receive not a fixed wage, but a fixed share of the revenue of their enterprise. It is argued that in this system, profit-maximizing employers would expand employment to increase production and revenue till full employment. Macroeconomically, a pure share economy would reduce unemployment even in periods of recession. Labor unions, mainly in large firms, are generally flexible and workers believe mostly that they belong more to the company in which they work than to their labor union as a countervailing power. Managers put the interest of their company above their own interest and feel obliged to consult their subordinates. Wages in small firms, with up to 500 workers, are about 60 to 75 percent of large firms and this differentiation creates some conflicts from time to time.

Japan though has put emphasis on both people and machines mainly through the Ministry of International Trade and Industry (MITI). The Japan Development Bank and the Postal Savings Bank are two state financial institutions that finance domestic and mainly export industries. The Postal Savings Bank is a successful bank because of the tax-free interest on savings accounts offered by mailmen right at the door of each household. Together with MITI they encourage the establishment of new industries and promote the formation of cartels and other business expansions for achieving economies of scale and cost-saving production.

Japanese workers are distinguished for their traditional attitude of considering themselves members of a family, whether at home or at work. The same family-type relationship is true for corporations and even public enterprises and government services. Lower turnover rates, harmonious labor–management relations, a wage system based on tenure and training, and the growing revenue-sharing way of payment are the main characteristics of the Japanese industrial society. Government policy makers consult business leaders, the *zakai*, who, in turn, are involved in allocating campaign funds to politicians.

In the Japanese agricultural sector, however, there is a serious problem with built-in efficiencies of fragmented small farm holdings. The same problem can be observed in many other, particularly developing, countries. Also, there are inefficiencies from part-time farming, in which case about 15 percent of the population combine farming with off-farm work for additional income earning.

The Japanese firms rely on a horizontal coordination network in which employees participate according to their abilities developed primarily through learning by doing. Employees as a group constitute specific and internal assets to the firm and are rewarded from the value generated by the internal network of labor and capital inputs, after the payment of a fixed share of profits to stockholders. The firms are considered largely as dually controlled by ownership (financial interests) through their agents (managers) and employees. They are not much influenced by external financial controls and in case of low performance, they prefer work sharing than layoffs. On many occasions, the Japanese firm, conceived as a nexus of contracts, reduces earnings to increase investment in training for future promotions and other labor benefits. At the same time, employees, considered as assets in the dually controlled firms, are frequently willing to forgo current earnings for future promotions and other benefits. They are largely forward-looking laborers.

ECONOMIC POLICY

With a high sustained rate of economic growth and an impressive record in exports, Japan has become a major world power. Historically, the government has encouraged business investment and exports using fiscal and monetary incentives.[4] Also, indicative economic planning, similar to that of France, is used to influence and guide public and private decisions toward long-term economic objectives. Budgetary policy is exercised by the Ministry of Finance and is under the approval of the Diet (parliament).

In Japan, there are three main government agencies dealing with economic matters. The Economic Planning Agency (EPA), which involves business, labor, and government representatives, provides information and coordination, primarily in 5-year plans, regarding the different segments of the economy, and relies mainly on the private sector for implementation. The Ministry of International Trade and Industry (MITI) deals with technological innovations, priorities in industrial investment, and foreign-trade growth.[5] The Ministry of Finance takes care of financing budgetary expenditures. Through these agencies, Japan implements policies that encourage savings to finance investment and exports by providing tax exemptions for interest income, a part of income from exports and dividends, accelerated depreciation, and other measures contributing to modernization and rapid growth.

Taxation

Total tax revenue, as a percentage of gross domestic product (GDP), is around 30 percent (almost the same as the United States), compared to 37 for Germany, Britain, and Italy, 44 for France, and as high as 55 for Sweden. The share of Social Security contributions to government revenue is about 26 percent. As percentages of employees' compensations, such contributions are about the same with those of the United States (7.65 percent by employees and 7.65 percent by employers in 1990).

Special tax incentives and new financial institutions have been used to promote innovations in new products and technology. The result of such economic policies has been rapid growth in such industries as those of iron and steel, shipbuilding, automobiles, chemicals, and electronics.

The taxation system of Japan is based on personal income taxes, first introduced in 1887, corporate income taxes (since 1899), consumption (gasoline, liquor, and other commodity) taxes, and custom duties. The individual tax rates vary from 10 to 70 percent of taxable income. There are some fifteen taxable income brackets. Also, corporate income tax rates vary from 22 to 36.5 percent on profits.

Although the national government provides about half of the local government revenue, local financing, in relation to the national tax revenue (more than 20 percent), is greater in Japan than in most of other industrial countries, notably Britain, France, and Germany. The main local taxes are those of profits of enterprises and property taxes. It seems that from the standpoint of local autonomy, Japan has a system close to that of the United States, Germany, and Sweden.

Government Expenditures

General government expenditures, including central and local government spending, are around 30 percent of GDP, which for years were about the same as government revenues. However, after the rise of oil prices in the 1970s, growing deficits appeared that resulted in government debt amounting to more than 60 percent of GDP, which is more than that of the United States (which is about 55 percent).

Tax transfers to local authorities, public works spending, and Social Security and pensions absorb about 20 percent each of the general account budget. Along with rising expenditures of Social Security, growing interest payments on the national debt constitute the main items that give headaches of the policy makers. Nevertheless, defense expenditures are comparatively very small, about 6 percent of the total budget outlays, compared to around 30 percent for the United States. Official development assistance to developing countries is about 0.13 percent of GNP, compared to 0.09 for Britain and 0.06 for the United States.

Under the defense umbrella of the United States, Japan channels large amounts of expenditures, saved from military outlays, to technology-intensive and productive investments that stimulate exports. To compensate for such a protective policy, Japan pays the United States some $3 billion annually out of a total amount of $7.6 billion spent for maintaining American troops in Japan. A new agreement provides for an increase in the Japanese allotment by $600 million over the next 5 years, or 50 percent of the total amount spent, instead of the 40 percent subsidy given now, although the U.S. Congress demands 100 percent. In addition, Japan paid some $9 billion in economic and military aid for the conflict in the Persian Gulf.

Monetary Policy and Growth Financing

Monetary policy is exercised by the Bank of Japan, but it is influenced by the Ministry of Finance. The Bank of Japan manages the supply of money and credit, using the discount rate as the main tool to facilitate economic growth and keep a strong yen. It is a central bank, established in 1882, that is similar to the European banks, but less independent than the Federal Reserve Bank of the United States. In addition to privately owned commercial banks, which borrow money from the Bank of Japan, there are the following government-owned banks: the Development Bank, providing long-term loans to domestic industries; the Small Business Finance Corporation, supplying loans to small enterprises; and the Agriculture, Forestry, and Fisheries Finance Corporation, financing individual farming businesses and agricultural cooperatives. Funds for these financial institutions are obtained from the budget and mainly from private savings in the postal system. Also, the Export–Import Bank is an independent financial corporation that provides loans mainly to exporters and importers.

The question is if Japan, with a miracle economy during the post–World War II years, has peaked as a financial and industrial superpower. In other words, is Japan becoming a land of the setting sun economically, as some economists argue? It seems that Japan will remain a strong economic power for many years to come. It is true that trade surpluses are declining, real estate prices are rising, and real interest rates and, therefore, the cost of capital are comparatively high. However, the Japanese monolithic *keiretsu* system, with its peculiar binding relationships of suppliers and producers, a disciplined labor force, high savings rates, and the strategic global investments will keep Japan's economy efficient and competitive for a long period.

Japan continues to emphasize production of high-technology and industrial goods, whereas other countries and notably the United States seem to neglect productive investment in favor of financing leveraged buyouts, junk bonds, and other superficial transactions of just "changing papers." Perhaps, with a growing integrated Europe and a reorganized American economy, the comparative advantage of Japan may not last for years and a leveling off or a plateau may be reached, but not a serious decline, in the Japanese economy.

Japan's pursuit of economic gain abroad and a closed economy at home has raised concerns for its partners, notably the United States. The previous military expansionism of Japan, as well as Germany, has been thought to be replaced by economic expansionism. With the shift of international relations from the military and political power to economic and technological developments, Japan and Germany play a leading role in world affairs. From that standpoint, their economic and social systems, with workers sharing in decision making and profits, may be used as successful lessons or useful paradigms for other countries. Then, the status quo in geopolitical affairs may be replaced with a "Pax Nipponica" or "Pax Teutonica." It seems that Japan and, to a lesser extent, Germany are running a "corporatist" economy with emphasis on exports and investments abroad and regulated markets at home.

There are serious differences in Japanese and American cultural conditions, regarding employment and other labor matters. The typical salary of managers is about six times that of the average employee in Japan, whereas that ratio in the United States is as high as 93 to 1. Japanese employees have lifetime employment, get a fair share from the performance of the company, and are not laid off as soon as profits decline, as happens largely with American workers. Moreover, Japanese firms and managers in the United States are complaining that they are frequently sued and wind up in courts, paying large amounts of money in damages and litigation costs, even if they manage well on personnel matters.

GOVERNMENT PLANNING

The Japanese plans are indicative rather than imperative. They deal with certain national objectives, such as economic growth, investment targets, and sectorial and regional imbalances. Some eleven long-term plans have been enacted since the end of World War II with different durations and objectives. In addition to the economic growth rates, the plans, which are optional on the part of the prime minister, aim at such goals as price stability, stimulation of savings, countercyclical policies, and other social welfare and environmental measures.

Indirectly, fiscal and monetary policies are used to achieve the objectives of the plans, which are usually revised during their implementation, in order to achieve desirable priorities. Budgetary investment programs are also used to strengthen certain industries, improve infrastructural facilities, and stimulate exports, according to the planned targets, through tax breaks, subsidies, advice on new technology, and inexpensive loans. Antimonopoly laws are lenient and vertical and horizontal cartels or consortiums are frequently permitted among enterprises for economies of scale and foreign competition.

The plans are developed by the Economic Council, some thirty members appointed by the prime minister, and the Economic Planning Agency is responsible for the technical work, related information, and coordination of the planning process. Specialized sectorial committees on agriculture, manufacturing, housing, and so on provide data to the council for the final formulation and implementation of the plans.

FOREIGN EXPANSION POLICY: JOINT VENTURES
REDUCE SYSTEM DIFFERENCES

Japan is controlling imports and capital flow more than the United States and the EC countries. Although conditions are gradually changing, some degree of xenophobia remains. In other market economies, efforts are made to reduce cost and improve the consumers' interest through layoffs and shifts in business and labor. In Japan, the interest of the consumers comes last and this reduces the motivation to buy from abroad. Moreover, the Japanese feel that their favorable trade balance is due mainly to inborn frugality, skills, and moderation of Japanese workers, compared to most Americans and Europeans.

A continuous current account surplus in the Japanese economy intensifies the wrath of other trading countries, particularly the United States. However, recent severe competition from Japan's trade partners is decreasing its trade surplus in terms of volume. Unless domestic demand is growing, it would be difficult for Japan to sustain high economic growth.[6] Therefore, an expansionary fiscal policy, along with accommodating monetary measures to promote demand, may be needed.

Perhaps the high capacity for sacrifice of the Japanese people, their efficient work ethic, their strong nationalistic feelings, and their purely commercial vision of the world may also be responsible for the large Japanese trade surplus and the gradual American dependence on Japanese financial institutions. The concentration of financial power and Japan's role in the world markets, mainly because of large trade surpluses, and on Wall Street in particular, have not been taken seriously until now. Eight of the largest banks in the world are Japanese, and Nomura, Japan's largest security firm is twenty times larger than Merrill Lynch, with profits about equal to those of all American security firms.

In May 1989, the U.S. government cited Japan, along with Brazil and India, as unfair traders. This empowers the U.S. president to impose sanctions if negotiations within a period of 18 months or the removal of trade barriers fail. Such sanctions may include tariffs of 100 percent on selected U.S. imported products. Japan bans American semicomputers, purchases no foreign-made space satellites, and limits imports of lumber and other wood products. The Japanese argued that the United States itself maintains import restrictive measures and tries to divert attention from the major cause of trade deficit, which is the budget deficit. The solution to this problem is by way of global negotiations under the periodic rounds and forums of the GATT, where mutual multilateral concessions can solve such disputes instead of resorting to unilateral solutions that may lead to retaliations and recriminations.

In a reversal of the post–World War II trade strategy, Japan offered large tax credits for imports. Thus, companies that increase their imports of machinery, automobiles, computers, and other industrial products by 10 percent would receive a tax credit of 5 percent of the increase. As a result, it is estimated that an increase in imports by $3 billion annually would reduce the large trade surplus of more than $80 billion per year (some $50 billion of which is with the United States). However, this may increase Japan's budget deficit and government debt, which is about half of the GNP.

Globalism of Japanese companies has become a national and governmental policy. It has been built into the country's economic system. Many companies are going global in order to fight competition not only abroad, but domestically as well. Such companies include Matsushita, Sony, Mitsubishi, Majda, Kao, and many other big and small ones. Sometimes their competitive international behavior and the prospects of unfettered capitalism strike terror in the hearts of policy makers of other countries, notably the EC and the United States.

The Japanese are moving into the real wealth of America and Europe. They buy manufacturing firms, hotels, stores, land, and other property. The huge trade surpluses of Japan and the depreciation of the dollar in recent years resulted in extensive acquisitions of American companies and property by Japanese companies. The Japanese spent about $14 billion a year for mergers and acquisitions in the United States alone.

Although the Europeans, primarily the British and the French, continue to be the first in purchasing American companies and assets, the Japanese move rapidly in acquiring large and small companies and other properties in the United States. Likewise, the Japanese investors move rapidly into the European Community and the eastern European countries to take advantage of the expected integration and trade expansion.

Such purchases are related to prestige and ego for the Japanese buyers. However, for the Americans and the Europeans, the idea is that the Japanese cannot unfold and take these purchases of fixed assets home. They will still be in America or Europe in the long run, although returns on capital would be paid to Japan. The astronomical prices of real estate in Japan, compared to relatively low prices in other countries, is another reason for Japanese purchases of property abroad. For example, an apartment of about 600 square feet in Tokyo costs about $600,000 or more than ten times the average income of Tokyo residents.

Investment and Joint Ventures in the United States

Among the most important acquisitions of U.S. companies by Japanese interests are MCA Inc., a large entertainment company, for $6.13 billion by Matsushita Electric Industrial Company (in November 1990); and Columbia Pictures and CBS Records by Sony Corporation for $5 billion and $2 billion, respectively. Matsushita, known in the United States as Panasonic, competitor of Sony (with annual revenues of around $40 billion), controls close to ninety companies in Japan and many others abroad. These two giant Japanese firms control about one-fourth of the American movie market and there are fears, especially in Hollywood, concerning the growing Japanese cultural influence in the United States.[7] However, the Japanese complain that similar concerns were not raised when Italians bought MGM and Australians 20th Century Fox.

Other large U.S. companies acquired by Japanese firms include Firestone Tire and Rubber (for $2.65 billion), Inter-Continental Hotels (for $2.27 billion), Westin Hotels and Resorts (for $1.53 billion), CIT Group (for $1.28 billion), Gouls Inc. (for $1.05 billion by Nippon Mining Company in 1988), Aristech Chemical (for $860 million), and the Rockefeller Group (for $850 million). All these acquisitions and other aggressive Japanese investments are arousing alarm in America, where many people view Japan as a national security problem. In order to keep a low profile, Japanese investors are buying small American firms and new technologies and trying to avoid conspicuous purchases.[8]

There are some 240 Japanese affiliates of auto parts manufacturers operating in the United States, where about one-third of the cars sold are Japanese. Recently, the Nagoya Screw Manufacturing Company of Japan formed a joint venture with Elco Industries to supply bolts and screws to Japanese auto companies operating in the United States. Such companies include the Mitsubishi Motors Corporation and Honda Motor Company of Japan, as well as the General Motors Corporation, the Ford Motor Company, and other American companies.

Toyota Corolla Motor Corporation, which sells more than ten million cars and five million light trucks annually in the United States, has a factory in Georgetown, Kentucky (producing about 200,000 vehicles a year), and a joint venture with General Motors in Fremont, California.

The Japan Defense Agency agreed with the General Electric Company (GE) to power the FS-X fighter jet with GE engines, which are similar to the F–16 jet engines. The deal is worth more than $100 million and delivery is to start by 1999.[9]

The Industrial Bank of Japan, a large long-term credit bank, established a subsidiary in New York, after the approval of the Federal Reserve Board, to finance mergers and acquisitions in the United States. Together with other financial institutions, this bank helped to finance the huge buyout of RJR Nabisco Inc. by Kohlberg, Kravis, Roberts and Company for some $25 billion in 1988. Another Japanese financial institution investing abroad is the Nomura Securities Company, which acquired a 20 percent stake in Wasserstein, Perella and Company, a well-known mergers firm.

Investment in Europe

To solidify its position in Europe, Japan started investing into the EC, the eastern European countries, and the Commonwealth of Independent States. The highest number of Japanese investment ventures are in Britain (68), followed by Germany (53), France (38), Spain (33), the Netherlands (19), Ireland (12), and Greece (4). Some of the important investment ventures of Japan in Europe include the following.

Fujitsu Ltd., the world's third largest computer company, purchased the British International Computers Ltd. (for $1.3 billion), which is part of Europe's semiconductor research project, named Jessi. To formalize its ties with the United

States, Jessi, in which nineteen countries participate, also admitted the European unit of IBM. This buyout gives Fujitsu a foothold in the EC and makes it the second largest computer maker in the world after IBM.

The Saison Group, with some $32 billion sales a year, is involved in a number of joint ventures, ranging from Club Mediterranèe of France, Jean-Louis Scherrer (together with Hermes, the French fashion house), Thomas Cook (a British travel firm), the Sears Allstate group of insurance, and Intercontinental Hotels Corporation (bought for $2.2 billion in 1988, 40 percent stake of which was sold to Scandinavian Air Systems for $500 million).

According to Morgan Stanley Capital International, Inc., the total Japanese investment in Europe during the period 1951–90 amounted to $59.3 billion, compared to $130.5 billion for the United States and $310.8 billion total Japanese foreign investment.

SUMMARY

An island nation, Japan was an isolated feudal society before the nineteenth century. The hierarchical organization of society, influenced by the ideology of Confucius centuries ago, promotes hard work, savings, and accomplishment. Large family-owned conglomerates (*zaibatsu*) and looser forms of business-affiliated groups (*keiretsu*) or cartels exercise monopoly on finance, production, and trade activities. Labor unions are company unions and workers consider themselves more as permanent partners than hired hands. The lifetime employment, the father–children of manager–workers, the seniority system, and payment in bonuses or revenue sharing stimulate motivations and increase productivity.

Under the defense umbrella of the United States, Japan, as well as Germany, managed to sustain high rates of investment and economic growth. Special tax and monetary incentives, export subsidies, and high rates of savings encourage innovations and new technology. Indicative planning, similar to that of France, provides information for effective business operations and guides private and public decisions toward long-term objectives.

Japan's pursuit of economic gain abroad and closed economy at home results in growing exports and rapid economic development. Large surpluses in foreign trade make Japan a financial world power and a leading investor in international markets. Sometimes, the competitive behavior and the unfettered capitalism of large Japanese companies, such as Matsushita, Sony, Mitsubishi, and Majda, strike terror in executives and policy makers of other countries, notably the United States and the European Community.

8 Swedish Democratic Socialism

A BRIEF HISTORICAL REVIEW

Prior to the ninth century, details of Swedish history are obscure. Before and during the Roman period, the eastern part of the Scandinavian peninsula was inhabited by Germanic tribes, mainly the Suiones or Swedes and the Gothones or Goths, which were fighting each other. Olaf Skutkonung and Eric IX, who ruled for the periods 933–1024 and 1150–60, respectively, were the first kings who accepted and expanded Christianity, which was introduced by Frankish missionaries.

Via wars with Denmark and Poland or voluntary adherence (Estonia in 1561), Sweden entered a period of expansion in the Baltic area.

Under the rule of Bernadotte, who succeeded the throne as Charles XIV, John (1818–44), and his successors, Oscar I, Charles XV, and Oscar II (1872–1907), Gustavus V (1907–50), and Gustavus VI later, Sweden achieved significant progress politically, materially, and culturally.

Thereafter, the introduction of extensive social legislation, including the 8-hour working day, protection of working women and children, and other factory and labor laws made Sweden an exceptional welfare state. Other democratic and socialist measures taken primarily by the Social Democratic Party, which remained in power for decades, and the policy of neutrality, during World War I, World War II, and the cold war, made Sweden a respected democratic Socialist country.[1] The neutrality of the country for a long period allowed it to devote large amounts of resources away from military expenditures, to its rapid economic and social development. As a result, Sweden is among the first nations in per capita income and medical services. It follows an efficient middle way system between exploitative capitalism and repressive communism, maintaining democracy, liberty, and a free market.

ECONOMIC POLICY

Sweden has an economic system in which most resources are privately owned, but the role of government is a pervasive one, making it a system of regulated capitalism. Because of heavy taxation and the regulations on private enterprises, Sweden is considered as having a system of "democratic socialism" or "social democracy." Many social measures and reforms have been taken in order to "humanize" or "tame" capitalism.

Although there is a high level of industrial concentration with about 80 percent of the output in each industry produced by the three largest companies, widespread consumer cooperatives are reducing monopolistic power by providing low prices for basic goods. Such coops count for about 15 percent of retail stores and are based on free labor offered by the members who receive annual rebates for profits realized. Moreover, the ever-growing foreign competition is further reducing monopolistic practices in the market.

To smooth out the ups and downs of private investments, the government is using taxation as a supplementary tool to influence spending on capital formation. Business enterprises are allowed to set aside up to 40 percent of profits as an investment reserve for which no taxes are paid. Although the individual enterprises decide about the specific investment projects, the Labor Market Board determines the rate and timing of investment spending.

The annual budget of the government is divided into two parts, the current operating budget and the capital or investment budget. It has a countercyclical function in the sense of creating deficits in periods of recessions and surpluses in periods of economic upswings to be used again during consequent downswings of the economy. From that standpoint, the budget is an instrument for stability and economic growth.[2]

The current operating budget includes expenditures on defense, education, Social Security, communications, childrens' support, labor-market policies, health, housing, interest payments, and the like. On the revenue side, it includes income taxes, value added taxes, excise (gasoline, liquor, tobacco) taxes, customs duties, and other tax receipts.

The capital budget aims at the creation of government capital assets that will offer future service in a similar fashion to private enterprises. A certain amount of capital, about 10 percent, is available to the Ministry of Finance for expenditures in public projects.

To achieve harmony of interests, Sweden is using economic planning in which representatives of labor, business, and government participate in the formulation and implementation of economic policies. Significant reforms have been accepted, through consensus and cooperation, and self-regulation of the economy on the microeconomic level has been supplemented by governmental macroeconomic measures. To stabilize the economy, fiscal and monetary measures have been used even before the appearance of the Keynesian macroeconomic theory of the 1930s.

Thus, during the years 1933–37, Sweden was the first country to use deficit financing to stimulate aggregate demand and smooth out the downturn of the economy. Using the fiscal policy tools of taxation and government expenditures for countercyclical reasons, it managed to avoid the sharp decline of the economy, which other countries faced by adhering to the principle of balanced budgets. Moreover, the policy of regulating the flow of investment spending toward full employment and the enactment of social welfare programs, which cover the Swedes from "cradle to grave," made Sweden a showcase country of "welfare capitalism."

LABOR RELATIONS

Union Activities

An important characteristic of the Swedish economy is the effective cooperation of the employers and workers in wage determination and other labor issues. A system of national-level negotiations (centralized collective bargaining) is used by the Swedish Trade Union Confederation (LO) and the Swedish Employers' Confederation (SAF) to determine wages and fringe benefits, to avoid strikes and other labor disturbances, and even to teach the economic meaning and importance of union organizations and collective bargaining.

In addition to the LO, which was established in 1898 by a number of unions formed in the 1880s, and the SAF, there are three other national labor unions dealing with salaried employees, professional workers (teachers, doctors, lawyers, engineers), and state employees, respectively. The LO has more than 6,000 union branches (factory sections) that elect some 300 delegates who meet in 5-year intervals and elect the executive board (thirteen members). Also, a council of 140 members, which meets twice a year, is elected by the unions under the LO, which represents more than 90 percent of all production workers. Local unions should receive permission by the national union for important actions, which approves or disapproves wage and other agreements. In case of a strike by a union, the law requires that the union announce it 7 days in advance and at least 3 percent of the members are involved. Also, the law requires a week's notice before lockout and compulsory arbitration in cases of unresolved disputes.

In a parallel way to the labor organizations, there are many employer associations and groups of enterprises in transportation, shipping, handicrafts, agriculture and forestry, banking, commerce, and other services that aim at the protection of the employers' interests. However, they are under the concentrated power of the SAF, which approves any labor contracts on behalf of the employers and provides legal and financial assistance to the local employers' associations.

If the parties cannot reach agreement, then a government mediator intervenes. Contracts, which are concluded normally for 1 or 2 years, are automatically renewed if no notice of termination is given by either management or labor, usually 3 months in advance. During the period of the contract, no strikes or other disturbances can occur, whereas violations of the terms result in court actions.

Capital–Labor Comanagement

In Sweden, workers participate in enterprise decision making through elected work councils. The 1977 Law on Codetermination in Working Life requires companies with twenty-five or more workers and employees to have two labor representatives on their boards of directors. Subjects on which the work councils coparticipate include wage payments, working hours, hiring or layoff policies, safety rules, and other labor problems, as well as production, investment, and even mergers and acquisition matters.

The Swedish workers movement went further in acquiring more power through stock ownership. Implementing the proposal of Rudolph Meidner (the Meidner Plan), the Swedish Trade Union Confederation labor economist, the parliament approved the establishment of employee investment funds in 1982. Such funds are financed by a 20 percent annual pretax profit of the companies involved, in the form of new stocks, and a 0.2 percent increase in the payroll tax. All companies with fifty or more employees are obligated to participate in the plan. Although the funds are criticized in that they increase the power of labor unions and penalize innovative and profitable firms, moderation in wages and other labor claims reduced inflation and unemployment in recent years. Furthermore, to eliminate some disadvantages, five large funds, administered by a majority of union members, replaced those of individual enterprises. But no more than 8 percent of a company's stock can be acquired by a fund or 40 percent by all five funds together.

FISCAL POLICY

The Social Democrats have controlled the government of Sweden for 51 of the last 59 years, mostly in cooperation with the Communist Party (with about 20 out of the total 349 seats in Riksdag compared to about 160 seats of the Social Democratic Party and around 150 of three center–right parties). Its long-term policy is to guarantee full employment as the basis of a fair society in the country, but when wages rise far above labor productivity, high inflationary rates appear and austerity measures are needed to avoid economic crises. However, through centralized bargaining, employers and employees coordinate and control negotiations in a national level and labor conflicts are reduced, and efforts are made to relate wages to productivity.[3] Moreover, in order to promote equity, higher wage increases are granted to low-paid workers (wage solidarity).

Taxation

Out of a total tax revenue of 616 million kronas in 1988, income taxes on individuals were 239 million kronas, on corporation profits 32 million, and Social

Security contributions were 155 million. Taxes on property were 19 million kronas, on goods and services 149 million, 82 million of which were value added taxes, 49 million excise taxes (including 15 million on fuel, 5 million on tobacco, and 10 million on liquor), and 8 million were custom duties. The total tax revenue, as a percentage of gross domestic product, in 1989 was 56 for Sweden (41 percent excluding Social Security), 44 for France, 37 each for Britain, Germany, and Italy, 33 for Greece, 31 for Japan, and 30 percent for the United States (21 percent excluding Social Security).

Sweden is known as a welfare state in terms of health care, education, pension benefits, and other social facilities, but it is criticized as a country with high taxes. It seems that the Swedes are more tolerant of higher taxes to pay for the social programs of the government compared to other western countries, notably the United States and Japan. In addition to the main tax goal to raise revenue for welfare expenditures, the Swedish tax structure aims at the redistribution of wealth and, more important, the stabilization of the economy so that severe economic fluctuations be avoided. The "mobile income tax" and the "investment reserve system" are the main fiscal policy tools that are used to smooth business cycles.

For the first time, a progressive income tax was introduced in Sweden in 1902. It ranged from 1 to 4 percent of personal income. In the 1920s, the Swedish system, like that of the United States, relied primarily on income taxes, excise taxes, and custom duties. Indirect taxes comprised about 70 percent of tax revenue, 20 percent of which were from custom duties.

Along with other European countries, Sweden introduced the value added tax in 1969. It is a consumption *ad valorem* tax with an average rate of 15 percent on the taxable value of products and services. Transactions on machinery and other investment goods have less taxes. Luxury items are highly taxed because they do not contribute to the national interest. Liquor, tobacco, and other products, which are considered to be harmful, pay high (sumptuary) taxes. Liquor and tobacco, for which the government has a monopoly on production and sales, pay a flat rate per item and a value added tax. Total taxes on cigarettes are about 100 percent of the sales price. Furthermore, carbon dioxide emission taxes were imposed recently and other "green taxes," or rebates to producers who cut down on emission, are expected to be introduced in the near future. About 1 percent of income taxes is levied for the support of the state church.

Government Expenditures

National defense and social welfare (health, education, Social Security, family allowances, and other social services) absorb the largest amounts of government expenditures. Old-age pensions (basic and supplementary) amount to about two-thirds of the average annual earnings of the fifteen best years of the pensioners. Widow's pensions amount to 90 percent of the basic and 40 percent of the supplementary pensions. Everyone who reaches age 67 is entitled to a pension. Optionally, anyone can apply for a pension at the age of 63, accepting a reduction, or at 70, receiving more pension. Mostly, it amounts to 3 percent of the average annual earnings multiplied by the years of coverage and cannot be higher than 60 percent of earnings. Adjustments are made to the cost-of-living changes.

The basic pension is financed by a 5 percent tax on the employee's income up to a certain amount. Some 70 percent of the cost is financed by the general revenues of the central government. The employer normally contributes 10 percent of the employee's wages to the supplementary pension and nothing to the basic pension. Family allowances for children, the second largest transfer payment after age pensions, are financed totally by general government revenues.

There is a compulsory health program covering all the population of Sweden, which can be considered unique in market economies. It is financed by the employee and the employer (3 percent of payroll) up to a certain amount of income. Persons with income less than a certain amount contribute nothing, and the national government contributes a large portion to the health program. Moreover, there are generous maternity allowances for 180 days and free service of a trained midwife before and after childbirth. The health program pays the total cost of hospital treatment, three-fourths of medical fees, and part of the cost of medicine. Income lost from work because of illness is also guaranteed.[4] Unemployment insurance is administered by related societies representing labor unions and is voluntary. It is financed by contributions of the insured persons and government subsidies. Rent controls are also in effect and about 30 percent of the Swedish families receive rent subsidies.

In addition to the governmental budget, which shows the annual revenues and expenditures of the government, there is the national budget of Sweden, which presents estimates of the total national product accounts. On the one side (supply), projections of domestic production and imports of goods and services are cited, and on the other side (demand), the total consumption of the public and the private sectors is presented. On the supply side, increases in labor and other resources and their productivity are projected, and on the demand side, expected total consumption and investment are considered. Although such projections of the Swedish Planning Commissions are nonbinding, they constitute a guide for public and private decision makers.

Concerning the dilemma of unemployment versus inflation, which market economies face, Sweden managed to keep low levels of unemployment, varying from 1 to 3 percent, but relatively high inflation (around 10 percent). Compared to other European countries and the United States, Sweden has a lower rate of unemployment (about half), but a higher rate of inflation (about double).[5] The welfare system of the country is geared to a low level of unemployment even at the sacrifice of higher inflation. The idea is that it is better to have a job with somewhat inflated wages than not to have a job at all. However, measures to stimulate the economy and reduce unemployment lead to demand-pull inflation.

On the other hand, income policies for greater equality, through the improvement of low-wage categories of workers (wage solidarity), lead to cost-push inflation, as long as wage increases are higher than productivity increases.

MONETARY POLICY AND INFLATION

The banking system of Sweden is similar to that of other European countries, but different from that of the United States. The Bank of Sweden is the central bank, which is responsible for the supply of money and regulates credit and interest rates. Also, it uses the monetary policy tools of open-market operations and reserve requirements, holds foreign exchange and gold reserves, and determines official exchange rates. It is the oldest central bank in the world, established in 1668, and is a state institution responsible to the Swedish Parliament. There are seven members on the board of directors of the bank, six of which are appointed by the parliament and one by the King; these members elect the governor and the deputy governor. Although it is under the control of the government, the central bank has been given more freedom recently in exercising monetary policy.

From the commercial banks, fifteen are privately owned and one is government-owned. The four largest private banks account for about three-fourths of the total commercial banking and the largest one for about one-third. The main functions of the commercial bank are to receive savings and time deposits, to finance industrial activities and housing mortgages, to underwrite bond issues, and to participate in brokerage operations on the Stockholm Stock Exchange. In addition, there are about 400 small private, but nonprofit, banks controlled by local governments that appoint at least half of their directors. Together with the Post Office Savings Bank, they mainly finance housing mortgages and provide loans to consumers and local governments. Furthermore, there are many credit institutions that specialize in agriculture, shipbuilding, real estate, and other economic activities.[6] However, the largest credit institution is the National Pension Fund, which receives funds from old-age pension taxes and buys industrial and government (national and local) bonds, as well as bonds from the Investment Bank of Sweden, which is financing long-term industrial investment for purposes of economic growth and full employment. Industrial investment is also supported by the government through investment tax credits, so that companies can set aside a sizable amount of profits as investment reserves by not paying taxes. This is one of the countercyclical measures used by the government to stimulate investment and economic development.

The social policy of Sweden toward full employment leads to relatively high inflationary rates. Thus, the average annual rate of inflation in 1980–88 was 7.5 percent compared to 4.7 percent for the high income economies of the OECD members, 4.0 percent for the United States, 2.8 for West Germany, and only 1.3 percent for Japan. Such high rates of inflation are weakening the Swedish currency, reducing the competitiveness of Swedish products, and forcing price controls and depreciation of the krona.

The public sector of Sweden plays a significant role in the economy. Although the large majority of enterprises belongs to the private sector, some public utilities or natural monopolies are owned and operated by the government. They include telecommunications, railroads, electric power, some banks, and even a steel mill in southern Sweden. Moreover, half of Scandinavian Airlines is owned together by three Scandinavian governments (Sweden, Norway, and Denmark). On the other hand, public consumption is approximately half of private consumption and government (central and local) investment is about equal to private investment.

Sweden, with a population of 8.4 million and a per capita GNP ($19,300 in 1988) almost the same as that of the United States, is known as a welfare or egalitarian state with a better distribution of income than other market economies. Nevertheless, the income share of the lowest 20 percent of households in 1988 was 8.0 percent compared to 8.7 for Japan, 6.8 percent each for West Germany and Italy, 6.3 percent for France, and 4.7 for the United States. Again, according to World Bank statistics, the income share of the highest 10 percent of households, for the same year, was 20.8 for Sweden, 22.4 for Japan, 23.4 for West Germany, 25.0 for the United States, and 25.5 percent for France.

SWEDEN AND THE EC

In 1960, that is, 3 years after the formation of the European Community (EC), the European Free Trade Association (EFTA) was created in Stockholm. In addition to Sweden, it included Austria, Britain, Denmark, Norway, Portugal, and Switzerland. EFTA, or the "Outer Seven," and the EC, or "Inner Six," were formed to gradually reduce tariffs and encourage investment. However, EFTA permitted the retention of individual external tariffs and, in the process of closer cooperation, it was not as successful as the EC. Britain and Denmark, along with Ireland, joined the EC in 1973, and Portugal, along with Spain, also joined the EC in 1986.

Sweden, Switzerland, and Finland face the dilemma of maintaining individual neutrality or joining the EC for more trade and investment, and Austria and Norway contemplate membership of the EC. It seems that Sweden and the other remaining members of the EFTA will soon join the EC as their preferential trade relations are approaching the end. Through bilateral agreements with the EC, Sweden and other EFTA members already export their products duty free to the EC, and vice versa, without contributing to regional or agricultural programs and EC budget expenditures. Moreover, the largest amount of Swedish foreign trade is with the EC.

The Swedish economic model of extensive welfare programs faces an identity crisis. The long-run neutrality of Sweden lost importance, as east–west tensions ceased to exist, while its sizable public sector becomes more and more uneconomical as it generates inflationary pressures and lower incentives. To avoid further economic isolation, Sweden hopes to join the European Community soon. Similar hopes are expressed not only by Austria, which has already applied for EC membership, but by other neutral countries, notably Finland and Switzerland. Also, Norway is moving toward applying for EC membership, which it rejected in 1972.

Instead of negotiating tariff reduction with the EC, Sweden and the other EFTA members think of joining the EC in the near future. In addition to the two conservative opposition parties, the Swedish Social Democrats, seeing its popularity declining, proposed a new look to EC membership. This will stop the flight of Swedish capital into the EC to escape restrictions and heavy taxation, thereby stimulating domestic investment and real economic growth. With the dissolution of the Warsaw Pact and the eastern European nations moving toward EC membership, it will be unwise for Sweden and the other neutral countries not to pursue urgently joining the EC. Already, in order to synchronize its economy with those of the EC countries, Sweden reduced its top income tax rate to 50 percent.

On December 12, 1990, with an impressive vote of 198 to 105 and 26 abstentions, the Swedish parliament decided to apply for EC membership. With the collapse of communism, there is no need of neutrality for Sweden and other nonaligned European countries. The severe loss of industrial competitiveness is an important reason for Sweden to achieve full EC membership, which is expected before the end of 1994.[7]

Under the pressure of businesses and the fear of being left outside the single European market, Sweden applied for membership in the twelve-nation European Community on July 1, 1991. The dissolution of the Warsaw Pact military alliance of the Soviet Union and the eastern European nations accelerated the time of application for membership.

SUMMARY

Historically, Sweden went through wars and other disturbances that affected its course of economic and social development. Extensive social legislation, dealing with working conditions and welfare measures, was introduced primarily during the twentieth century. The neutrality of the country allowed it to devote large amounts of resources to economic and social development and to be among the first nations in per capita income, free education, and medical services.

The Swedish system of "democratic socialism" is primarily based on private ownership but with heavy taxation and government regulations. To reduce monopolistic power from the existing industrial concentration, widespread consumer cooperatives have been established. Great emphasis is placed on public and private investment (mainly through the employee investment fund). The governmental budget is divided into the operating budget and capital or investment budget, which was used for countercyclical purposes even before the appearance of Keynesian theory. The effective cooperation of employer associations and labor organizations, as well as work council controls and the policy of full employment and social welfare from "cradle to grave," made Sweden a showcase of welfare or egalitarian capitalism.

Nevertheless, heavy taxation and inflationary pressures from large government expenditures are gradually forcing a change in policy toward less government and more private initiative. The Social Democrats, who controlled the government for more the half a century were recently voted out of power in favor of less socialist parties. Moreover, the dissolution of the Warsaw Pact and the reforms in eastern Europe make neutrality unnecessary and Sweden more interested in joining the EC. Together with the other EFTA countries, it became a member of the expanded EC, known as the European Economic Area (EEA).

9 The Soviet System and Its Collapse

A BRIEF HISTORICAL REVIEW

As described by Greek and Roman writers, the vast territory of Russia was sparsely inhabited by nomadic tribes in ancient times. In the north, there were the Slavs. In the Crimean peninsula of the south, known as Scythia, there were Cimmerians, Scythians, Sarmatians, and other Asiatic peoples. Many settlements and trade posts were established in the Crimea and other Black Sea areas by the Greek merchants, remains of which exist even today.

Migrations and successive invasions occurred mainly by the Goths of Scandinavia, who established the Ostrogothic Kingdom, the Huns of Mongolia (fourth century A. D.), the Avars (or Tatar people), the Magyars (a Hungarian people), and the Khazars (until the eleventh century). During that time, the Slavic tribes dwelled in the northeastern Carpathian mountains. The western Slavic groups eventually evolved as Poles and Czechs, those of the south as Serbs and Bulgars, and those of the east as Russians.

The first linkage of Russian city–states occurred in the tenth century around Kiev, which became the capital and the commercial center of the country. The adoption of the Eastern Orthodox religion and the schism from the Catholic Church, as well as the development of new commercial routes of western Europe via Constantinople and Venice, made Kiev a less important trade and cultural center, especially after the Fourth Crusade (1204).

On the other hand, the occupation of Russia and the destruction of Kiev and other cities by the Mongols (1237–1452) cut ties with the west, forced people back to agriculture, and made them subservient to the autocratic Mongol rulers. As a result, the economic development of the country was held back. With the independence of the country (1452), the capital was moved from Kiev to Moscow.

Developments During the Era of Peter the Great and Later

Realizing that Russia remained backward compared to western Europe, Peter the Great, who reigned from 1689–1725, initiated drastic reforms introducing technical training, sciences, and new technology. Also, he moved the Russian capital from Moscow to St. Petersburg, a new city closer to the western world that he took from Sweden. To implement his program of westernization, he resorted to autocratic repression. He even ordered the death by torture of his son (Alexis Petrovich, 1690–1718). In addition to the development of industry and trade, Peter achieved successive territorial expansions from the Baltic Sea to the Crimea and from Central Asia to Byelorussia.[1]

Westernization policies and expansion continued thereafter, especially under Catherine the Great. Also, through successful wars against the Ottoman Turkish empire, Russia achieved virtual control of the Dardanelles (1833). To block Russia from eventual mastery of Constantinople, and the straits of the Bosporos, France and Britain attacked and defeated Russia in the Crimean War (1853–56). In spite of the westernization policies and the nominal abolition of serfdom, Russia remained largely a feudalistic and backward country.

With the emancipation of the serfs (1861), about half of the land was assigned to the tilling peasants, but the more productive land remained with the gentry. The peasants, who were obliged to pay redemptions, formed communes that assigned plots for cultivation in rotation, which Marx appraised (1882) as an effective measure of common ownership. However, this communal system was not successful, mainly because of the low incentives of production in rotated plots scattered in different places.

To pay for redemption and taxes, the peasants increased production to the point that Russia became the first country to export grain toward the end of the nineteenth century. This enabled the country to import needed machinery and other materials for the development of railways and other infrastructural facilities that helped increase the output of coal, oil, cloth, and other vital products.

The Bolshevik Revolution

Before the Bolshevik revolution of 1917, there were serious but unsuccessful socialist movements in 1903 and especially in January 1905, when a massacre against the protesting workers occurred in St. Petersburg (Bloody Sunday). The Mensheviks advocated the overthrow of the tsarist regime by democratic means, but the Bolsheviks believed in violent revolution and split from the Mensheviks in 1912. The reforms introduced by the established parliament (Duma) from 1906–10 and later, including the release of the peasants from the communes and the cancelation of their debts, did not have major results. World War I, which started in Europe in 1914 and engulfed Russia, made things worse, as corruption continued and repression was intensified. In February 1917, riots took place in the capital, the czar was forced to abdicate his throne, and the moderate pro-

visional government of Alexander Kerensky proceeded with slow and unsuc-
cessful economic and other reforms until the Bolsheviks took power in the
Russian capital on November 6–7 (October 24–25 in the then prevailing Old
Julian Calendar).

WAR COMMUNISM AND THE NEW ECONOMIC POLICY (NEP)

War Communism (Mid–1918 to Early 1921)

Although Marx predicted communism would be established first in advanced
capitalist countries, it arrived in Russia instead, a backward country with limited
industry and some 80 percent of its population illiterate and working in the rural
sector under oppressive conditions. Under the leadership of Vladimir Lenin
(1870–1924) and other revolutionaries, the Russian people (mainly peasants,
soldiers, and workers) revolted against the oppressive socioeconomic system that
prevailed under the tsarist regimes. Under the slogan "Peace, Land and Bread,"
the Bolshevik revolutionaries overthrew the provisional government of Alexander
Kerensky of the Labor Party and established the worker councils (Soviets) to
supervise the transformation of the economy to the new socialist system.[2]

All the land of aristocrats, the Church, and the landlords was confiscated and
distributed by local committees to the peasants for private use. The right to
private property in the land was annulled forever without any indemnity. Selling
of land and hiring outside labor were not permitted. Factories were taken over
by the workers employed in them, who elected their own managers and equalized
wages. Nationalization, however, involved heavy industry, communications,
transportation, oil, grain trade, and banks.

Because the Bolsheviks signed a separate World War I peace treaty with
Germany and because other countries did not want the establishment of the
communist system, expeditionary forces from Britain, France, Poland, Greece,
Japan, and the United States invaded Russia. The Red Army, commanded primarily by Leon Trosky and Joseph Stalin, was fighting not only these invading
forces, but the tsarist White Armies as well. Trotsky was in favor of interna-
tionalization of the revolution, while Stalin was not. Also, Stalin was known
for the tricks he used during the war, negotiating with the enemy troops during
the day and wiping them out at night. All over Russia, from 1918–21, there
was a civil war and a military type of economic organization to establish communism (War Communism).

Lenin, making his first appearance in the second Congress of Soviets, on
November 8, 1917, declared: "We shall now proceed to the construction of the
socialist order." A manifesto was adopted appealing to all warring peoples to
open negotiations for a democratic peace. Also, a resolution demanded that the
use of land must be equalized, that is, divided among the toilers on the basis of
labor or consumption, whereas the Council of People's Commissars proclaimed

the rights of self-determination of the different nationalities forcibly included in the tsarist empire. Also, some 37,000 firms were nationalized during the period of War Communism.

The liberal printing of money to finance purchases from the peasants led to hyperinflation and a barter economy that some of Lenin's followers considered as a "naturalization" of the economy. This was expected to lead to the destruction of the bourgeois market economy and the establishment of the moneyless society with common ownership and selfless citizens that Marx envisioned in his last stage of ideal communism. However, severe shortages forced Communist Party activists and the police to go to the rural areas to collect badly needed food for the urban centers. As a result, many peasants reduced or concealed production and slaughtered their cattle, while a rationing system was introduced in the cities to avoid widespread starvation. Low incentives for work, mismanagement, and lack of coordination caused a severe decline in the agricultural and industrial production and forced Lenin in 1921 to enact his New Economic Policy (NEP) that lasted till 1928.

New Economic Policy (NEP)

To avoid the collapse of the Russian economy, significant changes were introduced. They included the denationalization of retail trade and small-scale industries; the replacement of forced requisitioning of farm products by a fixed tax in kind; permission for the employment of up to twenty persons by private entrepreneurs, who could also lease previous nationalized enterprises; and the determination of wages by the market. Also, many enterprises became independent (except for certain strategic industries), labor mobility and profit making were allowed, and collective bargaining was permitted. In a sense, this policy was considered as a strategic retreat from communism to capitalism, a step backward to stabilize the economy and prepare it for two steps forward, as Lenin said, toward full communism.

As a result of these measures of "capitalism under communism," work incentives were restored, peasants were producing more than what they were consuming, and a surplus of food and raw materials supported the development of industry. Production in 1925 was restored to the pre–World War I level. The performance of the private entrepreneurs and small farm owners or the class of "petty bourgeois" restored the economic growth of the country under the system of what may be called "market socialism."

The relatively good performance of the economy during the period of the NEP encouraged some party functionaries, mainly Nikolai Bukharin and Mikhail Tomsky (the right-wing members) to argue in favor of the continuation of this new policy. The idea was that successful peasants (kulaks) would continue to produce more than they consumed and their savings would finance new investment for further growth. At the same time, with their surpluses, they would buy industrial products and provide food and raw materials to the urban centers and all the sectors would grow simultaneously (balanced growth). Production incentives would increase, worker controls and responsibilities would improve industrial performance, and labor productivity would increase.

Trotsky, Evgenii Preobrazhensky (an economist), and other left-wing party members favored a rapid industrialization or a big push toward heavy industry even at the neglect of the consumer sector (unbalanced growth). They argued that continuation of the NEP would bring back the capitalist system, and heavy industry would modernize the Soviet economy and strengthen the military for the protection of the country from its surrounding enemies. Also, they were against workers' control of enterprises and in favor of strict controls by the state through national plans. They emphasized goals or quick end results (teleologists), in contrast to the gradual changes based on past experiences, in which the right-wingers (geneticists) believed.[3]

COLLECTIVIZATION

The debate on gradual or rapid industrialization or balanced versus unbalanced growth was terminated by Joseph Stalin through forceful collectivization of agriculture and the introduction of the central planning process. Although, initially, he was supporting the right-wing arguments of not suppressing the peasants and not interrupting Lenin's NEP, problems of grain procurement turned him against the peasants. In the meantime, using shrewd political activities, he had removed the left-wingers and, finally, adopting the forceful program of the left, he removed the right-wingers as well. Then he initiated a drastic program of collectivization and central planning in 1928. The massive agricultural collectivization involved the transition from the small, backward, and scattered peasant farmers to amalgamated, large-scale socialized farms.

Many farms were pooled together to form large collectives (kolkhozy) that included livestock holdings and capital equipment of the peasants. This forceful collectivization was supposed to be "voluntary." The peasant–members were to elect democratically the management boards and other executives and to decide on production plans. However, the Communist Party determined the single slate of nominees who were responsible not to the "voting" members, but to the government for the implementation of the central plans and the delivery of the quotas assigned.

Responding to forceful collectivization, the peasants resorted to extensive slaughtering of livestock and the destruction of buildings and inventories. But Stalin responded with more force and purged resisting peasants, union leaders, and others who were not carrying out his policy of quick industrialization and development of the backward Soviet economy.

The substantial subsidies paid by the government to the agricultural sector have not produced good results from the standpoint of production. The Soviet Union, which was the largest grain exporter years back, became the largest importer in spite of the efforts of the Soviet leaders after Stalin, primarily Khrushchev, Brezhnev, and Gorbachev, to give high priority to agriculture.

THE PLANNING PROCESS

Central Imperative Planning

The main feature of the Soviet economic system was the formation and implementation of central planning. The first Five-Year Plan (FYP) of 1928–32 was introduced by Stalin and was followed by the second FYP of 1933–37 and consequent plans thereafter. In all the plans, emphasis was placed on producer goods (inputs for inputs) at the neglect of consumer agricultural goods.

The Third Five-Year Plan of 1938–42 was not completed because of World War II. The planning process was suspended and the economy was directed toward war material production. The Fourth Five-Year Plan of 1946–50 was formulated for the restoration and the development of the economy, as was the Fifth Five-Year Plan of 1951–55.

Thereafter, the planning process became problematic because of the difficulties of coordinating the Comecon planning (of Czechoslovakia, East Germany, Hungary, and Poland) with the Soviet planning. That is why the Sixth Five-Year Plan, 1956–60, was changed and a new Seven-Year Plan, covering the period 1959–65, was formulated in 1957. Another, more practical, five-year plan, the eighth in number, was implemented in 1966–70, and a long-term 20-year plan, 1961–80, was adopted. The latter set production goals primarily, which proved difficult to achieve, as were the goals of a similar program, formulated in 1986, that aimed at a double output by the year 2000. To a large extent, these plans were ambitious and unrealistic and were modified by annual plans that were more practical.

The procedure of resource allocation and output apportioning was followed by the State Planning Commission (*Gosplan*) that formulated the plans and passed them down to ministries, regional units, and finally to individual state enterprises. After reviewing the plans, responsible officials suggested modifications and sent the plans to their superiors all the way back to Gosplan for adjustment and final revisions. After the approval by the Supreme Soviet (parliament), the plans had the force of law and were sent back to enterprise managers for implementation.

Incentives and Inefficiency

For a better coordination and fulfillment of the plans, there were material incentives (bonuses) and moral or nonmaterial ones, including appraisals for serving fellow citizens and driving out selfishness, attractive vacations, usually on the shores of the Crimea, and receiving medals such as the "Order of Lenin" or becoming "Heroes of Socialist Labor." Unsuccessful managers and workers, though, might lose bonuses, be demoted, or might be given undesirable vacations on the steppes of Siberia.

Concerning quality, if the plans asked, for example, for so many tons of steel, the managers might turn out heavy sheets of steel to overfulfill the plan's targets and collect bonuses. If the plans demanded meters of steel, thin sheets of steel might be produced, as happened in some cases. The same thing could occur with the production of shoes, glasses, and many other categories and subcategories of products. Similar cases might be observed in services such as plowing shallowly to increase the number of acres plowed per unit of time, or in transportation, and so on. In order to provide the necessary materials on time, managers used *tolkachi* (special suppliers) and *blat* (personal influence to obtain favors).

In such cases, it was difficult for the planners to specify sizes, weights, strengths, and times required for the production of the plethora of goods and services projected in the central plans. As a result, severe shortages and long lines outside retail stores became common. From that point of view, useless products were produced, consumers were unsatisfied, exports suffered, and disequilibria of supply and demand were frequent.

ADMINISTRATIVE ORGANIZATION

After the death of Stalin and the end of his cruelty in 1953, economic reforms were introduced, mainly by Nikita Khrushchev until 1964. Also, the rate of economic growth was relatively high (5 to 7 percent a year), and the prestige of the country was high after the launching of Sputnik (the world's first satellite) in 1957. These events inspired Khrushchev to proclaim that the Soviet Union would "bury" the United States economically.

Khrushchev introduced decentralization reforms by transferring managerial authority from the center to the newly created Regional Economic Councils of the several republics to bring leadership closer to production, reduce bureaucracy, and avoid duplication. However, technological progress was not enough and the rate of industrial productivity was falling. Then new reforms were introduced in 1965 by Aleksei Kosygin, the successor of Khrushchev. A number of decision-making councils, including the Regional Economic Councils, were dissolved. These reforms, introduced mainly by Yevsey Liberman, Professor at Kharkov University, enhanced the role of centralized planning management, but allowed the attainment of profits or surpluses to be used by enterprises for technological improvement and payment of bonuses for efficient labor performance.

Later, however, during the presidency of Leonid Brezhnev (1965 until the early 1980s), economic growth declined, in spite of the emphasis on agricultural investment.[4] Also, income inequalities increased, with Brezhnev earning forty times the salary of an office clerk. The economic decline continued during the Twelfth Five-Year Plan (1986–1990) and thereafter.

During the 1970s, Soviet planners started moving away from collective farms toward a more industrialized agricultural system, which combined crop growing and harvesting with storage and processing and saved about 50 percent production costs compared to nonspecialized collective and state farms.

Up to the political reforms of 1989, the locus of power rested with the Communist Party. The Communist Party Congress was elected by the Party organizations throughout the country. It met every 5 years to elect the Central Committee (several hundred members), which, in turn, met twice a year to elect the Politbureau (some thirteen members). This body set the economic, social affairs, and foreign policies, while the Secretariat (headed by a powerful general secretary, assisted by a large staff) ran the daily affairs of the country.

On the other hand, the government, which followed the Party's directions, consisted of the Supreme Soviet of the USSR (Union of Soviet Socialist Republics), a nominal Parliament elected every 5 years. It met twice a year to approve legislation and to select the Council of Ministers (consisting of the prime minister and a number of ministers) and the Presidium of the Supreme Soviet (consisting of a chairman and some deputies).[5]

DRAMATIC CHANGES AND THEIR MEANING

During the presidency of Mikhail Gorbachev (1985–91), and especially after the decision of the Communist Party Central Committee in June 1987 to introduce reforms and to decentralize the Soviet economy, gradual changes started taking place, but at a slow pace. More radical economic and political reforms were accepted by the national conference of the Communist Party from June 28 to July 1, 1988. The 4,991 delegates of the party's first national conference in 47 years decided to increase efforts toward social and economic restructuring (*perestroika*) and political and sociocultural openness (*glasnost*).[6] Two major reforms introduced in the conference were to shift authority from local Communist Party bureaucrats to local government councils and establish a more powerful president by indirect election. The tenure of all elected officials, including the chairman of the party or the president would be for 5 years, with a limit of 10 years at most. As Mikhail Gorbachev said, ''We are introducing a pluralism of opinions, rejecting the intellectual monopoly . . . a new human image of socialism as the goal of *perestroika*.''

It seemed that piecemeal reforms were not leading to the free-market mechanism and the equilibrium of supply and demand. More drastic reforms that would lead to price decontrols, elimination of subsidies to inefficient enterprises, more freedom of business entry, easier investment credit to the private sector, currency convertibility, and encouragement of competition were needed.

The unanticipated economic and political changes, introduced primarily by Gorbachev in the late 1980s, surprised or fascinated many economists and politicians the world over. The dismantling of the Berlin Wall, a symbol of the cold war, and the withdrawal of the Soviet troops from eastern Europe led to the dramatic changes of the economic and political systems of all these countries.

The main questions are: Why did all these revolutionary and dramatic changes of our century occur in a short period of time and with not much resistance? Why were the peoples of the former Soviet republics and eastern Europe ready and eager to embrace such drastic changes and reforms? As the author observed during his research trips to Russia and other republics, people complained and asked: "Why have we been left far behind, economically and technologically, from other people of so many countries?" They seemed to realize that their economic and political system was responsible for bureaucratic inertia, oppression, apathy, neglect, and inefficiency. The saying that "they pretend to pay us and we pretend to work" could be concluded from many conversations. Such neglect and lack of incentives in production were primarily the result of common ownership, a principle that Aristotle pointed out some twenty-five centuries ago in criticizing Plato's ideal state of communism that "common ownership means common neglect."

THE DISINTEGRATION OF THE USSR

A New Commonwealth of Independent States

After the Bolshevik revolution, a number of neighboring republics formed the USSR (Union of Soviet Socialist Republics) in 1922, which incorporated more republics later, voluntarily or through annexation. Before its disintegration in 1991, the USSR included the Slavic part of the Union, that is, Russia (the largest republic with 77 percent of the USSR), Ukraine (the second richest republic), Byelorussia, and Moldavia; the Caucasus (Azerbaijan, Armenia, and Georgia); Soviet Central Asia (Uzbekistan, Kazakhstan, Kirghizia, Turkmenistan, and Tadzhikistan); and the Baltics (Lithuania, Latvia, and Estonia).

Table 9.1 shows the size of the fifteen republics of the former USSR in terms of population, land, GNP, GNP per capita, and joint investment ventures. The first republics to become independent (on September 6, 1991) were the three Baltic states (Lithuania, Latvia, and Estonia), which were occupied in 1940 by the Soviet Army as a result of the secret Hitler–Stalin pact.

On December 8, 1991, the republics of Russia, Ukraine, and Byelorussia created a new "Commonwealth of Independent States" and declared that the USSR ceased to exist. The remaining republics, except Georgia, joined the Commonwealth later.

Most of the radical economic measures were promoted by Boris Yeltsin, who was elected president of the republic of Russia in June 1991, which contains half of the population and three-quarters of the land mass of the former Soviet Union. He enjoyed great popularity and had the wealth of the republic behind him. Nevertheless, he was criticized as an unpolished and autocratic leader, who rules by decree, ignoring the Parliament.

Regarding the efforts of the former Soviet republics to form a confederation, there is the danger that in a political and economic confederation of the Com-

Table 9.1
Economic Indicators of the Former Soviet Republics, 1990

Republics	Population Millions	%	Land %	GNP %	GNP Per Capita($)	Joint Ventures (with foreign cos)
Russia	147.0	51.4	76.6	61.1	5,810	620
Ukraine	52.0	18.0	2.7	16.2	4,700	113
Uzbekistan	19.0	6.9	2.0	3.3	2,720	18
Kazakhstan	16.0	5.7	12.1	4.3	3,720	11
Byelorussia	10.2	3.5	1.0	4.2	5,960	33
Azerbaijan	7.0	2.4	0.3	1.7	3,750	1
Georgia	5.4	1.9	0.3	1.6	4,410	30
Tadzhikistan	5.0	1.8	0.7	0.8	2,340	0
Moldavia	4.5	1.5	0.2	1.2	3,830	19
Kirghizia	4.1	1.5	0.9	0.8	3,030	0
Lithuania	3.7	1.3	0.3	1.4	5,880	0
Turkmenia	3.4	1.3	2.2	0.7	3,370	0
Armenia	3.4	1.2	0.2	0.9	4,710	5
Latvia	2.6	1.0	0.3	1.2	6,740	61
Estonia	1.5	0.6	0.2	0.6	6,240	116
Soviet Union	284.8	100.0	100.0	100.0	5,000	1,027

Sources: "The Soviet Union's Unequal Parts: Diverse and Restless," *The New York Times*, September 1, 1991, E2; and "Ta Dekapente Kommatia tou Sovietikou Pazl" (The Fifteen Pieces of the Soviet Pazl), *To Vima*, Athens, September 1, 1991, A16.

monwealth of Independent States (created in December 1991), each independent republic may want its own army, its own money, or its own customs service. In the final analysis, the states may turn against each other, as happened with the republics of Armenia and Azerbaijan. Even in the Russian federation, two out of the twenty main subdivisions, the oil-rich Chechen-Ingush and Tatar republics, did not sign a federal agreement on March 31, 1992. Moreover, Russia wants back the Crimean peninsula, which was given as a gift to the Ukraine by Nikita Khrushchev and his "Ukrainian Mafia" (Brezhnev, Podgorny, Chernenko, and others).

Financial Considerations

To keep the same monetary unit for all the republics and to make it convertible, it is suggested that a new "hard" ruble with the full backing of a foreign reserve currency be issued and backed by gold reserves ($20 billion) and loans ($20 billion). A similar system was introduced during the Russian civil war, when troops from Britain and other allied nations invaded Russia in the spring of 1918. With the proposal of John Maynard Keynes, who was a Treasury official at that time, the British established a National Emission Caisse that issued "British ruble" notes that were convertible into pounds at a fixed rate. This convertible ruble was to replace more than 2,000 separate "fiat" rubles used and backed by nothing. When most of the allied troops withdrew from Russia in September 1919, the system was abandoned.

Also, Alexander Hamilton in the United States in the late 1780s introduced a similar system, using gold and the property of the state as collateral for government bonds.

The Moscow Narodny Bank Ltd., which was first established in London in 1915 as a cooperative bank, is currently acting as an investment bank and helps arrange joint ventures. It tries to attract western companies to invest in Russia and to exploit its vast resources, mainly oil, gas, and forest products.

Some of the deals arranged by the Moscow Narodny Bank include a joint venture with a British company producing commercial vans, a hotel near Moscow's airport involving French and Belgium companies and banks, and a furniture factory in St. Petersburg financed by Finnish banks.

The establishment of an expected stock market in Moscow would promote initially the sale of notes and bonds and eventually stocks. Some banks in St. Petersburg (Leningrad) are already selling notes, which can become tradeable, with an 11 percent interest rate. Expectations are that the New York Stock Exchange would cooperate with its counterpart in Moscow for the sale of bonds and other financial instruments, as happened years back (1905) when the first Russian bonds were traded in New York.

For the reestablishment of a stock market (similar to the one operated in St. Petersburg from 1703 to 1917), the New York Stock Exchange conducted seminars in Moscow in 1990 on regulating financial markets, raising capital, and stock speculation. Moreover, the first commodities exchange since the 1917 Bolshevik Revolution opened in Moscow in September 1990. A seat on the Moscow Exchange, which is like the Chicago Mercantile Exchange, costs about 100,000 rubles.

WORKERS' OWNERSHIP AND PRIVATIZATION

Privatization Cases

To change the system of the monopoly of the state ownership and to stimulate production incentives, the former Soviet Parliament, with a vote of 350 in favor, 3 against, and 11 abstentions, on March 6, 1990, cleared the way for the creation of worker-owned and private enterprises. The new legislation allows citizens to own property, to open businesses, and to create stock-owning societies. It permits property to be leased for life with the right of inheritance.

These measures, which resemble Lenin's New Economic Policy (NEP) implemented in 1921–28, were not bold enough to transform the planning system into a western type of mixed economy with mainly private ownership of the means of production. Moreover, to a large extent, local governments thwarted such measures as they wanted to keep control of the means of production. Nevertheless, the formation of new cooperatives with prosperous entrepreneurs and the spread of stock-holding workers and companies were growing through time, in spite of the ideological and bureaucratic inertia. Workers could buy or lease state enterprises, and were entitled to a share of after-tax profits. To make privatization more effective, vouchers, worth 10,000 rubles ($62), were given to every Russian, from babies to Babushkas, to buy shares in state enterprises.

The Moscow Low Voltage Equipment Factory, producing electrical equipment, was one of the first state enterprises to be transformed into a shareholding company. Some 1,600 employees and workers of the company put up 500 rubles each to hold 25 percent of the shares. The rest was sold to other individuals and investors, including local government committees, a bank, and an Italian company. Because of its efficient operation, the company, with permanent losses in the past, realized sizable profits and paid higher wages. The factory first became a worker-owned cooperative in 1988, when a related law was introduced in the former Soviet Union, and became a western-style shareholding company. To improve quality and productivity, the workers were and still are responsible for repairing defects themselves or losing bonuses under a piecework system.

Some 45,000 workers of the Uralmash machine tool works in Sverdlovsk demanded, through their Workers Committee, not simply to have a voice in running the state-owned company, but to own it. They wanted to have property and to be masters of the factory, not hired labor, and thereby to increase productivity and wages.

After the failed putsch of August 1991, *Pravda*, long the voice of Communist Party ideology, came under the management of its staff and became the voice of civil liberties. In August 1992, a Greek entrepreneur (Yannis Yanikos) acquired 55 percent of *Pravda*. In addition, the mayor of Moscow (Gavriil Popov) and other economists proposed plans of transferring restaurants, factories, and other stores to their workers for faster privatization and higher efficiency.

Management Buyouts

A serious problem currently is the privatization of state enterprises at the factory level. An effective way of transferring ownership and control to the private sector is to sell plants to their managers and key employees. Such a restructuring of state enterprises can take place by splitting them into viable and competitive firms under middle managers or interested employees with work experience and operational skills. The responsible government agencies can determine margins of realistic values of the assets to be sold and ask managers, employees, and other individuals, including foreign investors, to submit their proposals. These agencies or banks can provide working capital and facilitate the sale of plants by acting as bondholders.

By establishing management buyouts (MBOs) and market-oriented companies, work incentive would increase, apathy would be reduced, and widespread ownership would be fostered. Moreover, the distribution of raw materials and products would be improved, through decentralization, and business experience would be enhanced. Microeconomic managerial reforms or changes at the company level, through business training regarding production, distribution and marketing, are needed to transform state firms into innovative and competitive economic units. Macroeconomic policies can support such restructuring. American and EC business schools and consultants, as well as joint ventures, can help the development of MBOs and the process of smooth transformation of state firms into free-market companies.

In many cases, small enterprises, such as restaurants, retail stores and the like, are sold to the managers and workers of the enterprises or to individuals at auction. On the other hand, large firms are turned into corporations with shares that are sold to the public. Some 25 percent of the shares are usually offered to the employees and workers free or at nominal prices, 5 percent to top executives, a certain percent to suppliers, and the rest is sold to individuals and foreign investors. Because of lack of money or interest on the part of the private sector, the majority of stocks is normally held by the state, which sells them gradually to individuals.

Many state enterprises are converted by their managers into corporations owned by stockholders, a proportion of which is held by the managers themselves. Thus, the managers of the Elecropribors, a Ukrainian state enterprise, would buy around 5 percent of the shares, the workers would acquire a part, and 30 percent of them would be kept by the government. In this case, the managers expect the workers to be passive stockholders in managerial decision making.

The privatization process, including the transfer of state-owned firms to workers and employees, in eastern European countries and the former Soviet Union is reinforcing the system of "people's capitalism." Selling state enterprises to individuals and making workers total or partial owners of the firms in which they work, with special discounts, seem to be effective alternatives to public- or private-sector monopolies.

COOPERATION IN TRADE

During the post–World War II period, world trade has been growing year after year and at rates higher than the growth rates of output. The largest percentage (about 90 percent) of trade has been conducted among market economies and to a limited extent with the former USSR and other planned economies. This is another element promoting the expansion of the market vis-à-vis the planning system.

International trade leads to specialization and cheaper production, thereby generating economic benefits to the countries involved. Reduction in tariffs and other restrictions, which stimulate trade and increase prosperity, can better be achieved by countries with similar economic systems. From that standpoint, economic cooperation and integration of different nations lead to lower cost of production, cheaper prices, higher growth, and more trade.[7]

Foreign trade by planned economies and mainly by the former USSR had been exercised mainly through state agents and on a bilateral rather than multilateral basis. It had been largely an extension of the domestic trade system in which tariffs and exchange rates have played a limited role, if at all. In this form of barter-type monopolistic transactions, exports had been used to finance imports.

In their trade with the market economies, planners resorted to dumping operations, that is, selling abroad at lower prices, covering the difference with subsidies.

INVESTMENT AND JOINT VENTURES

In order to attract foreign investment and modern technology, the former USSR allowed joint ventures with up to 99 percent foreign ownership in April 1989. More than 400 such joint enterprises have been registered and more than thirty of them are in operation. Among the benefits offered are reductions in tariffs for imported production goods, a 20 percent tax reduction on exported profits, and freedom in hiring, firing, and personnel appointments.

To facilitate economic transactions and to exploit the opportunities created in the area, the Deutsche Bank A.G., Germany's biggest bank, led a consortium and arranged a credit line of $1.6 billion. The credit was extended to help Russia modernize its consumer goods industry and also to benefit the textile and shoe industries of Germany. About 30 percent of the total $16 billion loans to Moscow since 1984 was from Germany, 40 percent from Japan, and only 2 percent from American banks.

In addition to the credit package of $1.6 billion from Germany, Italy provided the former Soviet republics with $775 million export credits in 1988 and more credit and investment continue to flow into all the ex-Soviet republics from the west. Also, the main seven industrial nations announced a $24 billion aid package to former Soviet republics in April 1992.

Although EC firms are more aggressive in pursuing joint ventures in eastern Europe and the ex-Soviet republics, compared to American firms, U.S. companies, especially their subsidiaries in Europe, moved rapidly in establishing joint ventures in the area. Moreover, EC firms financed a gas pipeline to link Siberia to western Europe.

Some forty nations agreed to allow the newly created European Bank for Reconstruction and Development (on May 29, 1990) to provide loans not only to the private sector, but also to the public sector of the ex-Soviet republics and other east European nations. Such loans to projects like roads, telecommunications, and other infrastructural facilities would help revive these economies. Other loans and credit lines are extended by the United States, mainly for food imports, medical products, and distribution facilities, as well as by the World Bank and the International Monetary Fund.[8]

As these republics prepare for a system of free-market forces and promote private ownership, they also want to integrate their economies to the international community by joining the International Monetary Fund (IMF), the World Bank, and other world institutions. As a result, they expect credits from the IMF of up to $12 billion over 3 years to help reform their economies. Initially, though, they have to transfer about $1 billion for membership to the IMF, which is expected to bring discipline to their economies as they move to a market system.

With a gross national product of more than $1 trillion, Russia, the largest ex-Soviet republic, is entitled to about 6 percent of the total voting power and the right to appoint one of the twenty-two directors of each institution.[9] On March 31, 1992, the IMF endorsed the Russian plan for economic reforms and opened the way for loans, full membership, and eventual integration of the Russian economy with the west.

SUMMARY

Russia, the largest republic of the Soviet Union with a vast territory rich in oil and other resources, was inhabited primarily by Slavs, Scythians, Sarmatians, and other Asiatic peoples. Although Peter the Great and Catherine the Great achieved territorial and trade expansions and followed westernization policies, the country remained feudalistic and backward.

The Bolshevik revolution and the War Communism (1917–21) introduced a Communist system in which private property was abolished and factories were taken over by worker councils (Soviets). Because of low work incentives, mismanagement, and lack of coordination, production declined and a number of capitalist measures was reintroduced by Lenin (New Economic Policy, 1921–28).

Thereafter, a drastic program of collective farms (*kolkhozy*) and state farms (*sovkhozy*), as well as central planning, was initiated by Stalin and the Communist Party. Responding to forceful collectivization, the peasants resorted to the destruction of inventories and the slaughtering of livestock. But Stalin responded with more force and purged resisting peasants and others who were not carrying out his policy of quick industrialization, particularly during the 1930s.

The First Five-Year Plan (FYP) of 1928–32 and the consequent long-term and annual plans, supervised by the State Planning Commission (*Gosplan*) and the central bank (*Gosbank*), emphasized industrialization at the neglect of consumer goods. Although material (bonuses) and nonmaterial incentives were given for plans' fulfillment, serious problems appeared regarding quality and quantity of production, as well as bureaucratic inertia. Moreover, false reporting, favors and corruption on the part of managers and supervisors or party members were widespread, and severe punishments were enacted to reduce or eliminate them.

The dramatic transformations of the Soviet system, after 1985 when Gorbachev came to power, were expressed primarily by the terms economic restructuring (*perestroika*) and democratic openness (*glasnost*). Changes from the slow pace of reforms to more radical measures toward privatization and the market economic system occurred mainly after the failure of the military coup in August 1991 by hard-liners of the Communist Party, which was subsequently abolished by Gorbachev, Yeltsin, and other architects of Soviet changes. As a result of the reforms toward western capitalism, foreign investment and joint ventures, as well as financial support, are entering the former Soviet republics. Nevertheless, the conflicts and splits of these republics slow foreign investment and retard growth. A commonwealth of eleven republics was created in December 1991, when Gorbachev was removed from power, mainly by Yeltsin, who was elected president of Russia and continued the privatization of the economy.

10 Reforms of the Eastern European Economies

INTRODUCTION

Eastern European nations, mainly Poland, Czechoslovakia, Hungary, Romania, and Bulgaria, were liberated from Nazi Germany by the Red Army in 1945 and came under the political and economic influence of the Soviet Union. From a military point of view, they, together with East Germany and Albania, became members of the Warsaw Pact (1955), a counterpart of the North Atlantic Treaty Organization (NATO). Economically, these countries formed (in 1949) the Council for Mutual Economic Assistance (CMEA), or Comecon, a similar but less effective organization than the Common Market of Western Europe, or the European Community (EC). Both organizations, the Warsaw Pact and CMEA, were dominated up to 1990 by the Soviet Union. Yugoslavia was loosely associated with both economic organizations and Albania; after 1961, it was associated with neither. As mentioned previously, from the other Balkan nations, Greece is a full member of the European Community since 1981 and Turkey an associated member since 1964. Recently, both Communist organizations, the Warsaw Pact and CMEA, were dissolved.

Although trade and investment among the CMEA member nations had not advanced as much as that among the EC members, some cooperation on matters of production and long-term economic development had been achieved. The low level of cooperation and advancement in foreign trade in CMEA was primarily due to duplications in industrial production. Trade among the CMEA members was primarily conducted on a bilateral basis. Each nation planned its own development and included a growing trade with the other partners.[1] There was not an integrated planning organ or a common economic policy for multinational allocation of resources and to take advantage of specialization and economies of large-scale production.

Western ideals of freedom, democracy, and laissez-faire economics inspired, to a large extent, the recent revolutionary changes in eastern Europe and in the former Soviet Union in particular. As the Berlin Wall that confined such ideals collapsed, the ice of the cold war has gradually been melted and suspicions that prevailed for decades have been evaporated. These changes are challenging established defense organizations, such as NATO, which has begun to be re-modeled accordingly.

During the post–World War II period, western and particularly American policies were built on fears of war between the foregoing two opposite defense organizations and the question was how to overcome that long legacy of suspicion and mistrust. The support for rapid reforms to shifting these pre-Communist countries into market economies, with privatization and "people's capitalism," by a consortium of the trilateral powers (EC, United States, Japan) would lead to mutual economic and geopolitical gains.[2]

FISCAL AND MONETARY POLICY

All the economies of eastern Europe have moved rapidly toward smaller public sectors and serious efforts have been made to reduce bureaucratic inefficiencies. Because these countries are currently facing high rates of inflation and high rates of unemployment, policy makers have a rough time to reverse this trend using fiscal policy measures.

Government expenditures, as percentages of gross domestic product (GDP), were relatively high during the last decade, but declining, recently, in almost all east European countries, as Figure 10.1 indicates. In 1989, when drastic reforms to reduce the public sector were enacted, government expenditures varied from 40 percent of GDP for Romania, almost 50 percent for Poland and Czechoslovakia, and 55 percent for Hungary. Thereafter, such expenditures began to decline, due primarily to austerity measures and the privatization of a number of inefficient state enterprises, the deficits of which were covered by the governmental budget.

With the ideological walls dismantled in eastern Europe and the evolution of western Europe toward a unified market, less government spending, greater competitiveness in production and distribution, and sustained economic growth for higher standards of living are the objectives of all these national economies.

To finance budget deficits and to cover other expenditures in their economies, under reforms, east European countries resort to an increase in the money supply. Given that real growth is not increasing much and the velocity of money, that is, the ratio of gross domestic product (GDP) over the money supply, is relatively constant or growing, printing new money leads to inflation.

For example, if the velocity of money (V) increased by 4 percent and the increase in money supply (M) were 10 percent, then the increase in prices (P),

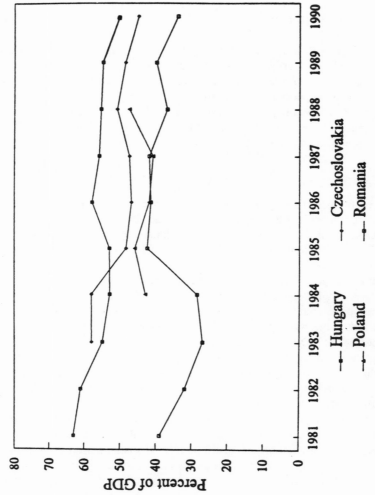

Figure 10.1 Government Expenditures as Percentages of GDP for Poland, Czechoslovakia, Hungary, and Romania

Source: International Monetary Fund, *International Financial Statistics*, various issues.

or inflation, would be 12 percent, assuming 2 percent real output (Q) growth. That is,

$$\Delta M/M + \Delta V/V = \Delta P/P + \Delta Q/Q$$

or

$$\text{Inflation } (\Delta P/P) = 0.10 + 0.04 - 0.02 = 0.12$$

Tax revenues in the declining economies of the east European countries are not sufficient to cover public-sector expenditures. Also, government domestic borrowing from the general public, by issuing bonds and other securities, is not normally used in these countries. Therefore, an increase in the money supply is the main source of financing public-sector deficits, but this measure is related to high inflationary rates. Policies to mitigate inflation, via demand stabilization and restrictive credit ceilings and factor costs, are not much effective, primarily because of inflationary expectations.

In all these countries, financial markets are imperfect and transmission of savings to productive investment is largely ineffective. Such market deficiencies and the endemic financial instability undermine the confidence of savers and investors, as well as the mobilization of savings and the allocation of funds to productive ventures.

The crucial questions facing post-Socialist countries are: What is the optimal exchange rate regime for these countries? How can they hold a constant relationship of their currencies with other hard currencies? They struggle to reduce or avoid price controls, repress inflation, and achieve currency convertibility. However, supply constraints, overvalued currencies, and import substitution make their stabilization and growth policies difficult.

ECONOMIC GROWTH

As Table 10.1 shows, the initial results of economic transformation in east European countries have been serious disruptions and steep declines in output. This is particularly so for Bulgaria, Romania and Poland. Although data from these economies in transition should be interpreted with caution, there is no doubt that the region is in a major economic decline. Fixed investments, which are needed for retooling or replacement of inefficient plants, dropped severely and industrial production declined by 16 percent in 1991. Inflation and unemployment have reached levels not seen in the postwar years and are expected to worsen in the medium run, as non-essential labor and inefficient firms will be eliminated. The small private sector has not been able to absorb the unemployed people. Trade among these countries plummeted, while trade with the former Soviet Union fell about 60 percent. Investment confidence remains low and exports to western countries for hard currency are slowly adjusted.

Table 10.1
Rates of Growth of Gross Domestic Product for Eastern Europe

	1970-80	1980-87	1988	1989	1990	1991
Albania	6.2	3.2	N.A.	N.A.	N.A.	N.A
Bulgaria	6.4	3.9	2.6	-1.4	-11.8	-22.0
Czechoslovakia	4.5	2.1	2.6	1.3	-4.7	-12.0
Hungary	4.9	1.3	-0.1	-0.2	-4.0	-6.0
Poland	5.7	1.7	4.4	0.2	-12.0	-8.0
Romania	9.2	5.2	-0.7	-3.9	-8.2	-15.0

Note: For 1991 estimates.

Source: United Nations, *Yearbook of National Accounts Statistics: Analysis of Main Indicators* (New
     York: United Nations, 1987), Table 5; and United Nations, *The World Economy at the End
     of 1991* (New York: United Nations), December 1991, Table 4.

According to International Financial Statistics, Poland, the most populous
eastern European country (38 million), had a surplus in the current accounts of
$3.1 billion in 1990, while former Yugoslavia (24 million) had a deficit of $2.4
billion, as did Romania (23 million) and Czechoslovakia (16 million) with $3.3
billion and $1.2 billion deficits, respectively. Hungary, with a population of 11
million, had a small surplus in current accounts ($0.4 billion) in 1990.

POLAND

A Brief Historical Survey

Poland, which falls within the Great Plain of Europe, is bordered by Russia
in the east, Czechoslovakia in the south, and Germany in the west. It is rich in
mineral resources, primarily coal, iron, zinc, and copper ores, potassium salts,
sulfur, and related products. Also, more than half of its land is arable. In addition
to agricultural and metal products, chemicals, fertilizers, cement, textiles, beet
sugar, paper, machinery, glass, and textiles are the main manufacturing goods
produced in the country. Coal, clothing, steel, and sugar are the main products
exported, primarily to neighboring countries.

During World War I, Poles, conscripted into the armies of Russia and the
Central Powers, fought each other. With the collapse of the Central Powers, the
Republic of Poland was formally established in November 1918 and Joseph
Pilsudski, a prominent politician, became the leader of the country. By the terms

of the Treaty of Versailles (1919), Poland received substantial territorial grants, including a narrow belt along the Vistula River to the Baltic Sea (Polish corridor). Also granted were significant economic rights in the Free City of Danzig, which Nazi Germany claimed later. This claim was used by Hitler as a reason for starting the war against Poland in September 1939.

On September 17, 1939, the Red Army invaded Poland and a partition treaty gave half of the country to Germany and half to Russia. The eastern part of Poland, which was under Russia, was occupied by Germany on June 1941 when Hitler invaded Russia.

Post–World War II Development

The Polish people, as other occupied people of Europe, suffered heavy casualties under the Nazi armies (5 million civilians and 600,000 soldiers), especially the Jewish section of the population for which a policy of extermination was pursued. By March 1945, the German invaders were driven out of Poland by the Red Army aided by contingents of Polish troops and resistance groups.

After the purging of "national Communists," who favored Yugoslav leader Tito's defiance of Stalin, the pro-Stalin Communists became dominant. Even Wladyslaw Gomulka, secretary general of the party was jailed. A Soviet chief of the Polish army was installed and Poland became a satellite of the Soviet Union. In 1949, the Council for Mutual Economic Assistance, or Comecon, was established as a counterpart of the European Recovery Program, a U.S.-sponsored plan for the rehabilitation of Europe that was created in 1948.

Collectivization of farms, nationalization of industries, and economic planning, similar to the Soviet model, were enacted. A 6-year industrialization plan (1950–55), which gave emphasis on heavy industry at the neglect of the consumer sector, achieved good results regarding production of coal, steel, and other goods useful for capital formation and industrialization. In 1956, and as a result of the Soviet reconciliation with Yugoslavia, the "national Communists" and Gomulka were exonerated. Gomulka, who was elected as the chief of the Polish Politburo, moved to dissolve inefficient collectives and to democratize the country. However, he declared that as long as the NATO maintains troops in West Germany, Soviet troops would remain in Poland.

The measures of rapid industrialization led to workers' hardship and riots, especially in 1956. Similar riots in 1970 initiated some reforms based on western markets and technology. This policy and the oil crisis of the 1970s forced Poland into heavy foreign debts without much economic improvement in the exporting sector.

The dismal conditions of the economy and severe shortages forced price increases and other austerity measures in 1980 that touched off workers' strikes at the Gdansk shipyard. Then the Solidarity Labor Union, which was created by Lech Walesa, negotiated with the Gierek government and achieved increases in wages, freedom of political prisoners and the press, reduction of the work week from 6 to 5 days, and other economic and political concessions.

Many workers demanded a self-management system similar to that of Yugoslavia and free elections, but the government of General Wojciech Jaruzelski imposed martial law. In the free elections of 1990, Walesa was elected president of Poland, and drastic economic reforms began.

Privatization and Employee Participation

Although Poland appeared to lead in transferring its economy to capitalism, the snail's pace of privatization of state-owned enterprises remains disappointing, mainly because the people are poor and cannot afford to buy stocks. On the other hand, there are questions regarding the power of the employees and workers in the process of privatization of the firms they work in and the possible discounts in selling shares to them. Because workers and individuals do not have money, scrip or coupons are given to them to acquire stocks, which happens in Czechoslovakia as well.

Nevertheless, a few large firms have been converted into shareholding companies, including Exbud, a building enterprise; Slaska, a cable company; Norblin Metal Rolling company, which makes copper wire and cable; and Prochnik, a textile manufacturer. Although these companies remain state-owned, they are run under commercial or market rules. Only profitable companies can be privatized easily, and the money-losing ones, which cannot be nursed back to healthy operation, are liquidated and their assets are sold at auction.

Under a new Polish law, employees can elect one-third of the boards of directors. They are also entitled to buy up to 20 percent shares of their company at half the flotation price. However, managers of firms controlled by employees complain that they face limitations on making decisions for which responsibilities rest primarily on them. They think that it is better to be supervised by professional directors than employees' councils.[3]

In Poland, employees' councils were established first in 1956 and were supported, to a large extent, by Solidarity economists in the 1980s. In 1990, the Polish Parliament permitted the employees councils to fire managers and replace them with new ones. As a result, hundreds of managers were dismissed.

Although employee councils and privatization gained more importance since the fall of communism in Poland, state-run firms still account for a large percentage of industrial production. The main question that remains in this transformation stage is what shape capitalism will take and how to deal with overstuffed enterprises. Workers want higher wages under capitalism, but they also want to maintain their jobs, which were guaranteed under state or Communist control.

Poland tried gradual, *perestroika*-type, reforms for a couple of years before 1990, but with not much success. It was the "shock therapy" of January 1990, which, although painful initially with hyperinflation and massive shortages, stabilized the economy later. It seems that a gradual transformation from communism to capitalism proved to be ineffective, not only in Poland, but primarily in the former Soviet Union. This was so mainly because it combined the worst elements of both systems by trying to create a market system but keeping predominantly state ownership.

On the other hand, the new economic plan of Solidarity-led government incorporated, among other reforms of transferring state ownership to private ownership, the setting up of ESOPs. In addition, the plan set up a stock market where the stocks of the employees and other individuals and institutions can be exchanged. Other East European countries are expected to introduce similar measures in their economic reforms.

In its effort to create a competitive economy and an investment market, the Polish government sells state-run enterprises to private investors and the workers. More than 7,000 state firms or about 80 percent of the economy are expected to be transferred to the private sector. Already, many companies, dealing with various activities from construction to textiles, glass works, and cable and audio equipment, are being privatized and many others are on the way to liquidation. Normally, up to 20 percent of the shares are reserved for the workers and employees of the companies involved at lower prices. Also, a limited portion is being sold to foreigners and some are retained by the government. The shares are mostly held by national banks until they are transferred to the buyers or until stock markets are established to facilitate such exchanges.

The transformation of socialism to capitalism in Poland did not materialize without turbulence. A serious case of corruption was revealed recently involving PKO BP, the largest public savings institution of Poland, and the Art-B, a private company that supervises scores of Polish firms.

CZECHOSLOVAKIA

A Brief Historical Review

Czechoslovakia lies in a strategic location between eastern and western Europe, as well as between the agrarian regions of the Balkans and the more industrialized areas of Europe. It comprises the previous provinces of Bohemia, Moravia, Silesia, and Slovakia. It came into existence in October 1918 as a result of the defeat of the Austro–Hungarian Empire in World War I and the union of Czechs and Slovaks. Other sizable minorities are Germans and Magyars. The first president, elected by the National Assembly in 1918, was Tomás Masaryk, who held office until 1935.[4]

On March 15, 1939, German troops occupied the country, except Carpatho–Ukraine, which was annexed by Hungary. The Nazi occupation was marked by ruthless exploitation of resources and brutal oppression of the people. Underground resistance by the Czechs led to savage reprisals, as the extermination of the male population of the town of Lidice in 1942, a familiar Nazi behavior in

Kalavryta (Greece) and other towns occupied by the Germans. In 1945, the Red Army liberated the country.

During the post–World War II period, the main economic policies followed by Czechoslovakia, as was the case with other eastern European countries, were similar to those of the Soviet Union. In the process of sovietization of the economy, the government initially established state-owned cattle raising and fruit-growing enterprises, and, later, nearly all industry, wholesale, and foreign trade had been nationalized.

The economic reform movement that began in 1963 reached its highest point in 1968 when Alexander Dubcek replaced Antonin Novotny and the so-called "Prague spring" arrived. Centralized physical planning was, to a large extent, replaced by a market economy guided by economic regulations involving monetary, fiscal, and income policies. Workers were permitted to strike and elect their managers through their established councils, as in Yugoslavia. Enterprises were to decide on their inputs and outputs, and profits, after tax, could be allocated for bonuses or for developmental investment.[5] However, Dubcek and his colleagues offended the Soviet leaders by introducing not only economic reforms, as the Hungarians did in 1968, but moving into political reforms as well. Then, implementing the Leonid Breshnev doctrine that socialist states must intervene to protect other socialist countries from revisionism, the Warsaw Pact, mainly Soviet troops and tanks, invaded Prague on August 20, 1968, to save Czechoslovakia from the "capitalist wolves." Dubcek was replaced by Gustav Husak, a hard-liner, who remained in power until 1987, when he was replaced by Milos Jakes. Under both rulers, no substantial reforms were conducted, production incentives declined, and productivity growth slowed down.

Czechoslovakia, following the example of Hungary and Poland, achieved a peaceful anti-Communist revolution in December 1989, electing Vaclav Havel, a novel writer in opposition, as President. Havel proposed that Hungary, Poland, and Czechoslovakia can work in unison to return to a friendly community of stable Europe, after some four decades of Soviet domination. Thereafter, military organizations such as NATO should be dissolved and an all European integration be pursued. A joint action to rejoin Europe would avoid rivalry among individual East Bloc countries as they try to have more trade and joint ventures with the EC and other western countries.

Transition to Capitalism Problems

As a result of the recent economic and political reforms, the Czechoslovak government ended subsidies on food and other farm products (worth about $1.1 billion), and prices rose substantially, especially of bread, meat, cheese, and other dairy products. To counterbalance the effects of price increases on the consumers, the government distributed about $5.50 per month to each person and a further increase of assistance to mothers of young children. Further price increases occurred in home appliances and other products until free competition was restored.

Czechoslovakia, along with Hungary and other eastern European countries, faced a serious energy problem as the Soviet Union drastically cut oil supplies. In 1989, such supplies were reduced by 16 percent and in 1990 by 65 percent. Moscow announced that it cut 7 million tons supply of oil to eastern European countries because of difficulties in oil production. Czech oil imports from the Soviet Union were about 16 million tons annually for previous years, at lower prices than those in the international markets. In exchange, low-quality machinery was exported to the Soviet Union. To meet domestic oil demand, Czechoslovakia turned to other oil-producing nations, particularly Libya, Algeria, Syria, and Iran (through a pipeline via the former Soviet Union).

There is a serious problem for Czechoslovakia, and for other eastern European nations, regarding the bumpy transition to capitalism and the previously nationalized enterprises. Pre–World War II owners or heirs of such enterprises demand compensation for nationalization or transfer of ownership without any payment.

The privatization program of Czechoslovakia proved to be a successful example for other ex-Communist countries. The vouchers or coupons, given to the adults for only $37, can be exchanged for shares in state-owned companies. About one-third of some 1,450 state firms have already been transferred to the private sector. After the separation of Slovakia, as a result of the elections of June 6, 1992 and the resignation of President Havel, the Czech republic (with about 10 million people, compared to 5 million of Slovakia) is likely to be beneficial for the Czech reforms from the standpoint of investment and growth, because the pro-union Slovak leaders are not in favor of quick privatization of mainly ornament industries located at their territory.

Foreign Investment and Joint Ventures

As a result of the political and economic changes of the country toward a free-market economy, foreign investment ventures have begun to be formed in Czechoslovakia as well. Thus, a European Community bank is projected to be established in Prague to offer financial and other services in the newly democratized eastern European countries. Also, Czechoslovakia and Bulgaria applied and were accepted as members of the World Bank in 1990.

Among other foreign ventures, Bell Atlantic Corporation and U.S. West Inc. agreed to form a joint venture enterprise with the Czechoslovak Ministry of Posts and Telecommunications, in which 49 percent belong to the American companies and 51 percent to the Czechoslovak agency. Anheuser–Busch, the American brewer of Budweiser beer, agreed to settle longstanding trademark differences with the original Czech producer of the same name beer since the sixteenth century for expansion of sales all over Europe. At the same time, Pilsner Urquell brewery, a 158-year-old famous company, is in the process of transforming into a dynamic profit-making private firm of international importance. More investment capital enters the country from the EC, particularly from Germany.

HUNGARY

A Brief Historical Review

The Hungarian people are considered as belonging to a branch of the Finno–Ugrian peoples who appeared in the area between the Ural Mountains and the river Volga about the first century B.C. Being a nomadic people known as Magyars and under the pressure of other tribes, they gradually moved westward. They crossed the Carpathian Mountains and under Prince Arpad occupied the territory around the Danube and the Tisza rivers at the end of the ninth century. Later, the Magyars extended their rule to Slovakia, Slovenia, and other surrounding areas.

From 1526 to 1686, Hungary came under the Turks, whereas the north and the west came under the control of the Habsburg Empire. More than half (2,700) of the villages were destroyed by the marauding Turks, and people were forced into slavery. Also, heavy taxes were imposed by the Ottoman Turks, as well as in all occupied Balkan nations. After the Turks were finally routed by the armies of allied Christian powers, the Habsburgs, who were also Holy Roman Emperors, extended their rule all over Hungary, which became dependent on their policies for four centuries. As a result of the Turkish and the Habsburg oppression, Hungary fell economically and culturally behind contemporary Europe.

A reform movement in the 1840s grew into a struggle for independence that was suppressed by the Habsburgs with the assistance of Tsar Nicholas I of Russia. In the following two decades, the Viennese government kept tight economic and political control of Hungary. But Austria's defeat in the war with Prussia (1866) forced a compromise and the creation of the Austro–Hungarian dual monarchy (1867) that lasted for 50 years. In 1873, the three separate towns (Buda, Pest, and Óbuda) were united and formed Budapest. Its present population is 2.2 million, about one-fifth of Hungary.

With World War I, the Austro–Hungarian monarchy collapsed and a period of political turmoils and economic setbacks occurred during the interwar period. About two-thirds of the country was handed over to its neighbors. In June 1941, Hungary entered World War II on the side of Nazi Germany and a Hungarian force was sent to help Hitler fight the Soviet Union. In March 1944, Hitler's armies officially occupied Hungary until April 1945, when the Soviet army came and the system of communism, with a centrally planned economy, was established. Collectivization of agriculture and nationalization of industry were begun by the Socialist Workers' Party (Communist Party) in 1948.

Post–World War II: Democracy Movements

In the First Five-Year Plan (1950–1954), ambitious economic targets were forwarded under Premier Matzas Rakosi, a hard-line Stalinist. After Stalin's death in 1953, Rakosi was replaced by Imre Nagy and more moderate policies, with emphasis on consumers' industries and less oppression, were followed. Nikita Khrushchev, who replaced Malenkov as a Soviet leader in February 1955, put Rakosi again in power. A peaceful demonstration in October 1956 and the escalated violence against the oppressive regime of Rakosi brought Soviet tanks into Budapest. Nagy was restored again by the Soviets. He introduced new economic reforms, including the establishment of enterprise workers' councils similar to those in Yugoslavia, disbanded the security police, and declared Hungary's neutrality. Hostilities were escalated with the Soviets, and Warsaw Pact tanks crushed the Hungarian revolution on November 4, 1956. Close to 3,000 people were killed, 20,000 left for the west and Nagy and many of his associates were executed.

Thereafter, the Soviets installed Janos Kadar, who abolished the workers' councils, but used cash incentives, not force, to attract farmers into cooperatives. Farm managers were not appointed by the Party, but by free peasant voting. Profitability and innovations were encouraged in industry and the market mechanism was slowly restored.

New Economic Reforms

After related discussions on reforms throughout eastern Europe, the Kadar administration introduced more comprehensive economic reforms in 1968, known as the New Economic Mechanism (NEM). These reforms aimed at the abandoning of physical imperative planning and using financial means to achieve projected targets. Also, enterprises were free to purchase their inputs and to produce according to the orders of the consumers. However, regarding profitability and financial considerations, they were guided by the central government. Further economic reforms were initiated in 1979 onwards.

In addition to small private firms, free contracts for groups of individuals with enterprises were permitted for overtime work with extra pay, using their own equipment or that of the enterprises. Also, more autonomy and democracy were allowed in the appointment or election of management and representative councils.[6] A market for bonds was established, bankruptcy laws were introduced, the National Bank of Hungary became responsible only for money supply and interest rates, and new taxes on income and sales were imposed, while those on enterprise profits were reduced.

In spite of the drastic economic and political reforms in Hungary and other eastern European countries, one can still observe severe controls on passports at airports and other entrances, as well as on commodities at customs houses.

Moreover, in restaurants and other shops, most of which are state-owned, some relaxation and laziness can be seen in services offered, and management is not eager to satisfy customers as they are responsible to government bureaucrats on whom their salaries and promotions depend.

Moreover, the establishment of an institution to support small enterprises and to reduce state bureaucracy is in progress. Hungarian and other international economic experts, mainly from Germany, Sweden, the United States, and Canada, would supervise the institution, which is expected to set up advisory bureaus for enterprises all over Hungary.

Joint Ventures

Up to 1990, registered joint ventures in eastern Europe were limited. The largest number of such joint ventures was in Hungary (628), followed by Poland (170), Bulgaria and Yugoslavia (41 each), Czechoslovakia (20), and Romania (5). EC and especially German companies have formed far more joint ventures in eastern Europe than U.S. companies.

Among the first foreign companies that invested in Hungary, after the democratization of the late 1980s, was the General Electric Company, which acquired a light bulb manufacturing firm. Also, the General Motors Corporation continues to buy automobile components in Hungary in order to increase its car sales in that country. However, later investment and joint ventures increased not only in Hungary, but in other eastern European countries to take advantage of their untapped markets.

In August 1991, Burger King, the American fast food chain, opened a large store in Budapest with the slogan "Come to taste the new world." There is a problem, though, of price adjustment because of high inflation and small devaluations of the forint, which results in losses of joint ventures.

Hungary, which had a stock market from the 1860s until 1948, permits foreigners to buy shares up to 100 percent of public and private enterprises. The Budapest stock market is the only one in the planned economies where bonds are sold. Moreover, a new bankruptcy law was introduced recently in Hungary to take care of enterprise failures in a fashion similar to that of the west. However, foreign owners cannot shut down or transfer their enterprises overseas. Many western brokerage and investment firms also help raise funds for purchasing shares of Hungarian enterprises.

THE BALKAN TRIANGLE

The winds of freedom and democracy of eastern Europe are blowing through the Balkan region as well. However, the Balkan area, which was under Turkish occupation for about 5 centuries and experienced four costly wars during the first half of this century, is troubled again by ethnic conflicts.[7] The Greek minority in Albania, the Turkish minority in Bulgaria, and the Albanian minority in

Yugoslavia are the main ethnic groups involved in serious disputes. To improve neighborly relations, the Foreign Ministers of the six Balkan countries (Albania, Bulgaria, Greece, Romania, Turkey, and Yugoslavia) gathered in Tirana, Albania, in October 1990 for better cooperation on trade, art festivals, fighting terrorism, human rights, pluralistic democracy, and ethnic problems. A similar conference took place in February 1988 in Belgrade, as well as in 1930 in Athens and some other unsuccessful ones after World War II, toward creating a Balkan Federation.

After the drastic changes in eastern Europe in 1989, ethnic rivalries, which were suppressed under Communist rule in Albania, Bulgaria, Romania, and Yugoslavia since World War II, surfaced again. All these countries gradually and painfully move toward democracy and a market economy while they pursue closer relations with western Europe.

Yugoslavia

The economic history of Yugoslavia is related to the expansionary trends of neighboring powers and the efforts of the native peoples to absorb and unite with each other. In ancient times, the Illyrians, then the Greeks under Alexander the Great, and later the Romans and Byzantines occupied the area. Around the seventh century, the Slavs came and settled permanently. Together with other Balkan countries, most of the area was occupied by the Turks from the fifteenth to around the beginning of the twentieth century.

The kingdom of Yugoslavia was formed in 1918 from parts of the Turkish and the Austro–Hungarian empires. Marshall Tito, who united the long embattled ethnic groups against the occupation forces of Germany and Italy and became president for about four decades, introduced the Soviet model of central planning in the immediate postwar years.

After the break with the Soviet Union (1948), Tito replaced the Soviet model of centralized planning and monocentric "state capitalism" with a polycentric "social" or "indicative" planning, which was characterized by worker-managed enterprises and market-incentive socialism. In this new form of socialism, the property of the enterprises was not owned by the state or individuals, but was held in trust for society.[8] Small firms with fewer than five employees were primarily run by the workers themselves on an equal-shares basis, so that "exploitation of man by man" can be avoided.

Since the reforms of 1965 and the 1970s, the country moved further toward the self-management system with the Basic Organizations of Associated Labor (BOALs) in each enterprise and self-supporting communes or local communities. Taxes were collected primarily by the republics and the communes, but also by special funds, such as "public roads," "waterworks," and "joint ventures." Trade agreements were signed with the EC, particularly in the 1970s and 1980s.

The growing resentment against the Communist system in former Yugoslavia added an ideological divide to the historical, cultural, and religious differences of the most prosperous republics of Croatia and Slovenia with Serbia. Out of the six republics (Serbia, Bosnia and Herzegovina, Croatia, Slovenia, Macedonia, Montenegro) and two provinces (Voivodina and Kosovo), Serbia was the most populous (with 9.3 million people) and exercised political and economic controls upon the others. The Catholic Croatians (4.8 million) and Slovenians (2.0 million), who were under Austria until 1918, did not want the hegemony of the Christian Orthodox Serbs, who threw off Turkish rule in the nineteenth century. Moreover, since 1981, the Albanians of Kosovo (about 1.6 million) have been agitating for separation from Serbian control.

In a referendum in 1990 both republics, Croatia and Slovenia, voted to install a non-communist system, whereas Serbia chose to keep its Communist government, later named Socialist, under hard-line President Slobodan Milosevic. The ethnically divided republics met in Sarajevo (where World War I began with the assassination of Austrian Archduke Franz Ferdinand in 1914) in March 1991 and later in other places for a compromise, but without success.

In addition to political differences among the republics and provinces, there were economic differences as well, which intensified the movement of disintegration. Thus, average monthly net wages per worker in 1990 varied from $167 for Kosovo, $229 for Montenegro, $299 for Serbia, $348 for Croatia, and $413 for Slovenia. The more prosperous westernized Croatia, which earned 90 percent of former Yugoslavia's tourist income, and, Slovenia, which produced more than 30 percent of the country's exports to the west, complained that they shared proportionally more for government programs in support of the poor regions of the south.

The parliaments of the republics of Croatia and Slovenia overwhelmingly passed declarations of independence on June 25, 1991, that led to full secession from Belgrade, after ethnic fighting, thousands of deaths and significant property destruction. Similar independence was declared by Bosnia and Herzegovina (with 4.1 million people, about 40 percent Muslims, 33 percent Serbs, and 18 percent Croats), as well as Macedonia (1.9 million of Slavs, Albanians, Greeks, Bulgarians, and Turks).

Greece, along with other nations, did not recognize "Macedonia," for historical and geopolitical reasons, because the name "Macedonia," the country of Alexander the Great and Aristotle, was deliberately given to the republic by former President Tito in 1945 for expansionary reasons into the Greek region of Macedonia and the Aegean Sea.

The Christian Orthodox Serbs of Bosnia and Herzegovina objected and did not participate in the election of President Alija Izetbegovic, a Muslim, and his government and a severe ethnic and religious war broke out with thousands of deaths, mainly in Sarajevo, and the involvement of the United Nations for the supply of food and medical aid.

Although the former Yugoslav republics became independent, the worker self-management system, which prevailed for four decades, seemed to remain largely in operation. However, as a reaction to the influence and the controls of one party (the former Communist, renamed Socialist, Party) and the undemocratic process of decision making, the pressures for changes and abolishment of the system increased. This was so, particularly for the advanced republics of Croatia and Slovenia, which began to adjust their economic system to that of the European Community, particularly that of Germany, as they expect an association status and eventually full membership to the Community.

Nevertheless, the European Community itself has adopted measures of workers' participation in enterprise decision making and, to some extent, employee ownership. Moreover, Germany has a system of codetermination or comanagement of capital and labor.

In any case, Serbia, the largest republic, and Montenegro, which decided to remain federated under the old name Yugoslavia, as well as the provinces of Voivodina and Kosovo and to some extent Bosnia and Herzegovina, maintain a system of self-management. However, the economic and sociopolitical system of the republic of Bosnia and Herzegovina became doubtful because of the ongoing destructive civil war.

An effective policy may be to support an associated and even full membership of the former Yugoslav republics and other neighboring countries in the European Community. This would reduce ethnic conflicts, giving hope for economic and sociopolitical improvement and increasing trade and investment with other countries.

Romania: Recent System Changes

On December 22, 1989, Nicolae Ceausescu, the Communist dictator since 1965, resigned and was executed together with his wife Elena on December 25, 1989, by the revolted army. This was the result of demonstrations and the massacre in Timisoara and Arad (Transylvania) of rioting people, mostly from the Hungarian minority and other anti-Communist revolutions in other cities and in other eastern European countries. The Front for National Salvation, with Ion Iliescu as president, which took power on December 26, 1989, won the elections of May 20, 1990 (the first free elections since 1937) with 66 percent of the popular vote. Romania, in its efforts to turn the state-owned economy into a free-market economy, faces severe problems, although it has a small foreign debt, compared to other eastern European countries. The process of selling state assets to the private sector, including foreign investors who can have full ownership of companies, continues with priorities in housing construction, food processing, tourism, and trade services. Also, free prices are gradually introduced for almost all commodities and services and economic hardship remains a serious problem for the 23 million Romanians.

Bulgaria

In the postwar years, Bulgaria has experienced an unprecedented period of peace and progress, mainly because it has not had to confront any external threat and, unlike Romania, did not lose territory to its neighbors. Moreover, it does not suffer from internal disunity, as does Yugoslavia, or the political instability of Greece and the internal turmoil of Turkey.

As in other East Bloc countries, the Bulgarian Communist dictatorship of more than 40 years was overthrown, together with the long-tenured President Todor Zhivkov, on November 10, 1989. Thereafter, anti-Communist demonstrators dismantled reminders of Communist rule, including the mausoleum of Georgi Dimitrov (father of Bulgarian communism), burned the Communist Party head-quarters, and eliminated other Communist sacred symbols. Free elections on June 10, 1990, though, gave a reformed Communist (called Socialist) Party 57 percent of parliamentary democracy. However, Bulgaria faces serious economic problems from reduced supplies of cheap Russian oil and gas, food shortages, and a heavy foreign debt of about $16 billion. Also, severe problems appear in the process of privatization of the economy, especially in land ownership. The drastic reforms and the austerity measures introduced recently will suppress the living standard of the 9 million Bulgarians for some time to come.

Albania: Reforms

Seeing the tide of European changes, Ramiz Alia, the Albanian leader after Enver Hoxha (the iron fist leader from 1945–85), introduced limited reforms. They included price changes to reduce the gap between supply and demand, bonuses for key workers, and decentralization in decision making. Local orga-nizations can appoint all but the most senior officials and experts. Directors of enterprises, hospitals, and other institutions can be appointed only with the approval of workers who can remove them if they fail to perform. Albania remains the poorest country of Europe and many people want to emigrate to other countries, particularly to Italy and Greece.

In the free elections of March 22, 1992, the Democratic Party won 92 of Parliament's 140 seats. The Communists, renamed Socialists, who controlled the 3 million poor Albanians for almost half a century, won 38 seats. President Sali Berisha, a heart surgeon, and Prime Minister Alexander Meksi started moving rapidly toward privatization and free-market reforms.

SUMMARY

After many wars and disturbances throughout history, eastern European coun-tries, primarily Poland, Czechoslovakia, Hungary, Romania, and Bulgaria, came under the political and economic influence of the Soviet Union, during the post–World War II years. They became members of the Warsaw Pact defense group, a counterpart of NATO, and the Council for Mutual Economic Assistance (CMEA), or the Comecon economic group, both dominated by the Soviet Union. Both organizations were dissolved after the revolutionary changes in eastern Europe in 1989 and later.

For centuries, Poland faced disastrous wars with Germany, Sweden, Russia, and Turkey that led to its economic deterioration. After World War II, the Soviet system of central planning, with collectivization of farms and nationalization of industries, was imposed. The pressure for reforms led to a number of riots since the 1950s with the formation of the Solidarity Union in 1980 and the movement for workers' control in industry. After the "shock therapy" of the economy and the election of Lech Walesa, the Solidarity leader and a Nobel Prize winner, in 1990, capitalism and the privatization of state enterprises gained importance.

Czechoslovakia, which lies between the agrarian regions of the Balkans and the industrialized areas of Europe, came into existence in 1918 as a result of the union of Czechs and Slovaks. Occupied by the Nazi troops (1939–45) and liberated by the Soviet Army, Czechoslovakia came under the Soviet influence and, like Poland and Hungary, it followed the system of central planning and state control of the economy. Some reforms implemented by Dubcek in 1968 ("Prague spring") were reversed by the intervention of Soviet troops to save the country from "capitalist wolves." A peaceful anti-Communist revolution in 1989 enacted drastic reforms toward the market economy, denationalization, and foreign investment.

As a result of wars and oppression, mainly by the Turks and the Habsburgs and lately the Soviets, Hungary fell behind contemporary Europe. After World War II, the Communist system was introduced. Although economic changes were reversed with the crush of the revolution of 1956 by Soviet and Warsaw Pact tanks, Hungary managed to implement a number of reforms, especially after the introduction of the "New Economic Mechanism" in 1968. More changes toward the free market and joint ventures were enacted after 1989.

The poor Balkan countries (Yugoslavia, Romania, Bulgaria, Albania), which have been for centuries under Turkish occupation and internal conflicts, introduced reforms similar to those of the other eastern European nations. Yugoslavia, which practiced a self-management system for the last four decades, was split into independent republics after severe ethnic conflicts.

11 The Chinese Experience

A BRIEF HISTORICAL REVIEW

China, a country of radical transformations, has the largest population in the world (1.2 billion) and a relatively poor land. Although its land area is third in the world, after the Soviet Union and Canada, only about 15 percent of it is arable. This contrast makes per capita production and income low (about $300 per year) and presents pressures for population control. Imperial conquests, drastic political and economic transformations, and unification movements throughout history made China a big and important nation.

The early Chinese civilization, a neolithic culture characterized by the cultivation of rice, the domestication of animals, and the making of pottery, developed in the bend of the Yellow River before 3000 B.C. Monetary units in the form of metallic forks, knives, and similar instruments were used in China in ancient times.

The first emperor, as the Chinese maintain, was Fu Hsi, who is considered the founder of China. He was the ruler during the period about 3000 B.C. in which hunting and fishing were the main activities of survival, whereas, during the rule of Shen Nung (2737 B.C.) agriculture became important. However, Scuma Ch'ien, the great historian known as the "Herodotus of China," begins with Huang Ti, the "Yellow Emperor" (2704–2585 B.C.), as well as Yao, Shun, and Yu, as the heads of Confucius' extract and originators of wisdom and prosperity. During the Shang dynasty (1766–1122 B.C.) and the Chou dynasty (1122–255 B.C.), agricultural production and the arts flourished, while the feudal system was developed.

The Ch'in dynasty (255–206 B.C.) abolished the feudal system, drove the Hun Tatars back, and continued building the Great Wall for the defense and the unity of China; the Han rulers (202 B.C.–A.D. 220) drove further back the Tatar hordes and opened trade, mainly of silk, with the Syrian and Roman markets. At that time, Buddhism infiltrated China from India. Thereafter and particularly during the Sui dynasty (589–618), the great T'ang dynasty (618–907), the Sung era (960–1280), and the Ming dynasty (1368–1644), China achieved, to a large extent, unity and expansion. Also, iron and bronze tools and weapons, as well as gunpowder (sixth century), woodblock printing (ninth century), mathematical theorems, and other inventions were developed in China some 300–500 years before similar discoveries in Europe.

Nevertheless, during the period of the Mongol (Yuan) domination (1234–1368), China lost its technological, cultural, and economic vitality. However, under Kublai Khan (1280–1294), the empire was extended from the Dnieper River in Russia to the Pacific Ocean and from the straights of Malacca to the Arctic Ocean. Khan repaired and completed the Grand Canal that connected the north with the south. Marco Polo traveled through the canal and used a passport and paper money, which were not known in Europe at that time. The highway into Europe and trade with the Arabs made the Mongols in Central Asia embrace Islam. Under the Ming dynasty (1368–1644), Portuguese and Spanish traders settled in various ports in China.

After a period of prolonged struggle, the Manchu rule (1644–1911) from the northeast, the last royal dynasty, established harmonious relations among the people of China for some time. Population increased rapidly while the more European and American traders, as well as Catholic and Protestant missionaries, entered the country. The East India Company of England (1645–1834) was one of the most aggressive foreign firms operating in China, mainly in Canton, trading silk, tea, porcelain, ginseng root (with medical properties), furs, and even opium from India (a British colony).

Because of the abuse of opium and widespread addiction, the Chinese government prohibited the importation of the drug. This led to the Opium War (1839–1842) in which the victorious British forced China to cede the island of Hong Kong (1842) to pay an indemnity and to open more ports to western trade. Further concessions to the west, mainly to England and France, were made after the Second Opium War (1856–1860). Growing imports and domestic cultivation of opium instead of grain reduced food supplies and increased the number of addicted people,[1] and corruption and colonialism worsened the economic plight of the country.

Many Chinese resented the increasing western influence over their country and, when coupled with serious economic problems, uprisings began arising throughout the country, especially in Canton and Shanghai. In fact, in the period from 1850 through 1900, a number of uprisings occurred.

The reaction from the empire was to crack down uprisings and centralize power in Peking. To do this, they took out more loans from the west, which was now better organized to maximize its profits.[2] This further indebtedness to foreigners was construed as the Manchus selling out the ethnic Chinese for their own interests.

This spurred a rash of revolutionary activity under the leadership of Sun Yatsen, who was educated with western ideals. Although most of his initial efforts were unsuccessful, in 1911, the rebels seized Wuhan with the help of many turncoats in the military. In 1912, the empire was finally over after 2,000 years of uninterrupted leadership and a republic was formed. As it turned out, the successful rebellion was not much of an improvement in the short run. Warlordism and anarchy took the place of a genuine republic. Nevertheless, the vast significance of an end to the dynastic system should not be belittled. The combination of foreign dominance and domestic discontent changed China's history to a great degree.

CHINA IN TURBULENCE: THE COMMUNIST MOVEMENT

The rise of Communist thought in China began soon after World War I. The Chinese people were extremely upset with the Treaty of Versailles and how it addressed China's relationship with Japan. As a result of their threat to leave the newly formed League of Nations, Japan was allowed certain rewards in China, much to the chagrin of the Chinese people. The government of China gave in to public pressure and refused to sign the treaty. After this incident, some Chinese sought to discover political process for their country. To this end, they formed study groups to examine different political theories.

The leaders of these groups were Li Dazhao and Chen Duxiu. One of their students, who would later play the most prominent role in the Communists' rise to power, was Mao Tse-tung. These groups functioned under the guidance of the Communist Internationale (Comintern) and gained strength from the Bolshevik victory in Russia in 1917.

In order to expand the cause of communism, its leaders decided that it was necessary to ally with progressive bourgeoisie to encourage a bourgeois revolution. This was in accordance with Marxist theory that capitalism had to be realized before true communism could set in. The Communists sought to do this by approaching the Guomindang, Sun Yatsen's Nationalist Party. Together they formed the United Front.

The Nationalist (Guomindang) Party, which formed a government in Canton under Sun Yatsen in 1917, received support from the Soviets (1923) against the government of the north at Peking (later named Beijing). After the death of Sun in 1925, Chiang Kai-shek took control of the Party and in alliance with the Communists marched to the north against the warlords.

Large segments of the Nationalist Party were not trusting Communist "friends." These suspicions became exacerbated, however, as the movement succeeded further and philosophical differences became more important. This problem culminated in what is known as the Shanghai Massacre of workers and the Communist forces in 1927. Then, the nationalist leaders declared the establishment of a national government under their control and banished the Communists. The Communists were forced underground as Mao Tse-tung and other leaders fled into the mountains.

The Communists were saved from complete extinction at this time because of more pressing problems that China was facing. The ruling nationalists were preoccupied with the fact that the economy was a shambles. As if economic worries were not enough, Japanese aggression toward China increased at this time as well. Japan successfully invaded Manchuria and remained in control there despite international condemnation.

In his continued efforts to wipe out the Communists, Chiang Kai-Shek launched his encirclement campaigns in the early 1930s. As a result, by 1934, the Communists were once again on the verge of annihilation when Mao Tse-tung, who became their leader, decided to give up the base area and the headquarters established in southern Jiangxi province. The Guomindang chased after them relentlessly from 1934 to 1935 in what is known as the "long march," covering some 6,000 miles, to Yanan, a desolate outpost in the Shaanxi province. Only 10 percent of the Communist members that started the march completed it.

In the meantime, while Chiang Kai-Shek was concentrating on the Communists, Japan was in a position to overrun most of China, and that is just what they did, controlling the eastern two-thirds of China by 1939. However, in September 1940, Japan's alliance with Nazi Germany made the Chinese problem a part of World War II. U.S. intervention then occurred as President Roosevelt allocated large amounts of money for aiding China.

The Guomindang, plagued with continuing economic problems and corruption, lost the last of its popular support while the Communists were continuing to increase theirs with proposals for land reform. At the end of 1948, the Communist Party went on its strongest offensive and defeated the Guomindang in the north. Chiang Kai-Shek gave one final effort in an immense battle from November 1948 to January 1949, and was destroyed. On October 1, 1949, Mao Tse-tung proclaimed that China was now free, independent, and Communist, and established the People's Republic of China on the mainland, while the Nationalists were driven to the island of Taiwan.

ECONOMIC PLANNING

Before Mao Tse-tung and the Communist Peoples Liberation Army took over, China was in a dismal economic condition. Beggars were prevalent in all cities and dead bodies of starving people could be seen drifting in the rivers. Foreign privileges in the form of exclusive clubs and private parks, with such insulting signs as "no dogs or Chinese," were common, especially in Shanghai. Mao used moral appeals for self-sacrifice, equality, and changes in the stubborn Chinese tradition of a patriarchal way of life to achieve rapid growth.

After the Communists took power in 1949, their main problem was the reconstruction of the Chinese economy after years of wars and a runaway inflation. In a short period, they restored production, reduced inflation, and introduced honesty and hard work among the people. Using the experience of the Soviet Union, Mao Tse-tung and his party moved to the rapid industrialization of the country. In 1950, China signed a treaty with the Soviet Union for technical assistance and economic aid. By 1952, the prerevolutionary level of production was achieved.

Drastic agrarian reforms in which about half the farm land was distributed to peasants, during 1950–52, at the expense of rich landowners and the "compradore" bourgeoisie, considered as agents of imperialism. About two-thirds of industrial capital of domestic and foreign ownership was nationalized. Some other industries of so-called "capitalist-roaders" were nationalized in 1955–56.

New laws protected women from "tyrannical husbands," imposed heavy penalties for consumption of opium, and introduced mass education. Severe penalties were imposed to village and town exploiters in mass trials. To provide foodstuff for the cities, a tax of 17 to 19 percent of the harvest was levied. However, to avoid the Soviet experience of peasant resistance, farm collectivization was postponed.

With the help of the Soviet specialists, the First Five-Year Plan for the period 1953–57 was formed. The ambitious targets of double industrial production and a 25 percent increase in agricultural output were overachieved, while per capita income increased by 100 percent compared to that of 1949. Soviet equipment and machinery, as well as advisement and financial aid, helped achieve these impressive goals.

During the first decade of Mao's rule, China performed well economically. Investment reached about 25 to 30 percent per year of national output. About half or more of total investment was going to industry. An impressive record of output growth could be observed in such products as steel, petroleum, and cotton cloth. Comparative studies showed that China did considerably better than India with regard to both economic and social development.

Emphasis was given to heavy industry and self-sufficiency for such needed industrial materials as steel, coal, machinery, chemicals, and tractors and other farm equipment. As in the Soviet model, priority was given to industrialization while consumer needs were largely neglected. To reduce reactions of consumers and peasants to severe shortages, ideological campaigns and sociopolitical propaganda were used. Also, collectivization was gradually developed to higher forms of cooperation.[3]

Nevertheless, the bureaucratic hierarchical Soviet model of planning with one-man management and quota-system production generated some opposition in China. Even bonuses and other material incentives were criticized as creating privileges and reducing initiative. Moreover, in overpopulated China, the pressure for agricultural production was heavy, not only to satisfy the needs of the poor peasants, but to create surpluses for the rapidly growing cities. Therefore, a new policy of balanced growth between agriculture and industry was needed to replace the Soviet model of unbalanced growth in favor of industry. Then, Mao Tse-tung proclaimed a policy of having the economy "walking on two legs," that is, based on the development of industry and agriculture, simultaneously. He introduced an extreme leftist program, the so-called Great Leap Forward, with the establishment of people's communes. It was a bold move toward a utopian Communist state, a communal way of life, and a drastic socioeconomic change introduced for the first time in human history.

PEOPLE'S COMMUNES

The Great Leap Forward

Collectivization and communization were considered necessary in China, where the land used to be cultivated by peasant families in very small plots that were often scattered in different places. The average size of each plot was no more that 3 acres. In 1949, when the new regime (Communist) took over, the landlords were compelled to confess publicly about the sins they had probably committed during the operation of their land. The land then was gradually expropriated from the landlords, individual farming was replaced by mutual-aid teams, and then by cooperatives or collectives, where the income was distributed first on the basis partly of labor contributed and partly on ownership of land. Later on, it was based entirely on the contribution of labor. An increase in farm size for greater specialization and a more effective utilization of manpower were the main reasons for collectivization.

The agricultural transformation from ownership by peasants to that of collectives of the state took about 12 years in the Soviet Union and involved violence and extensive losses in cattle and other agricultural products, whereas in China, it took less than 6 years, was smoother, and was accompanied by smaller losses.

By 1958, when the Second Five-Year Plan was put into operation, more than 750,000 collective farms, comprising 123 million families, had been created. This plan introduced the Great Leap Forward, which was to be carried out through the establishment of communes.

The success of the Great Leap Forward was to be accomplished by the dismantling of the Chinese family and the introduction of a new form of human organization, the commune. This transformation from a family-centered society to one centered around a commune broke the ties of the peasants with the past and initiated a military way of life similar to that of ancient Sparta. Some 26,000 communes were organized to accommodate the rural population. Similar communes were organized for a large part of the urban population. Each commune was subdivided into regiments, battalions, and companies in a military fashion. The members of each commune varied from 4,000 to 5,000 households. Men and women were assigned to separate jobs, and children were sent to nurseries— a model that is reminiscent to Plato's ideal state in ancient Greece and Charles Fourier's plan in France (in the 1830s).

Commune mess halls provided meals for people all over China. More than 120 million rural women were released to join the work force. Sometimes people were kept at work as many as 20 hours a day in order to accomplish certain operations. Communes were largely self-sufficient, producing the necessary agricultural and small-scale industrial commodities for their own use. In the beginning, a large part of consumption was supplied freely by the commune. In a typical commune, people freely obtained a good number of goods and services, such as food, clothing, housing, medical protection, and even free burial arrangements, with the provision of being buried 10 feet deep so that orchards could be planted above. The average city family had one combined living room and bedroom. Illiteracy had been drastically reduced. (In 1950, more than 90 percent of all Chinese adults were illiterate, compared to 24 percent in 1982.)

Greater attention was given to ideology and revolutionary goals than to production incentives and economic efficiency. Egoism was to be eradicated. Some communes distributed income according to needs and not according to work or productivity of each worker. People were motivated to work for the good of their fellows. They implemented the doctrine of common ownership even to cooking pots and other personal property. Millions of small-scale industrial firms and so-called backyard furnaces for the making of iron and steel were established, mainly to absorb part of the extremely high supply of labor. Huge armies of labor were used in irrigation, flood control, and other large projects and in myriads of small-scale projects.

The Failure of the Communes

In spite of some initial success and the herculean efforts with the mass mobilization of peasants and workers, lack of economies of large-scale production, organizational and managerial inefficiencies, and lack of proper equipment and raw materials led to problems in coordination, poor quality, and waste. It became obvious that, in order to avoid chaos in the economy and to promote industrialization, a more cautious policy of balanced growth among the different sectors of the economy with emphasis on material incentives was needed.

Moreover, the Sino–Soviet rift and quarrel of Mao with Nikita Khrushchev let to the withdrawal of Soviet advisors and other economic and technological assistance and to further deterioration of the economy. By the 1962, real GNP was just equal to that of 1957, that is, the Great Leap Forward produced zero economic growth and, given the continuing growth of population, severe food shortages appeared and the country faced a potential disaster.

The drastic movement in the communization of society went too far in institutional changes, asking too much too soon from a social and economic point of view. Productivity was sharply reduced and the commodities produced were of very poor quality. The shift of plan making and plan supervising to local authorities eroded management and reduced efficiency. Bad weather conditions also brought about severe agricultural failures during the years when communes were introduced. All these elements led the Communist leadership to change its policy, reestablishing individual work incentives on a large scale and shifting investment to agriculture.

Nevertheless, the autonomy and freedom-of-production teams on matters of management of production and distribution is still well respected. The communes and production brigades may make adjustments only in the spirit of coordination without compulsion. Furthermore, pooling small plots together and allocating each crop to the area best suited to it have obvious advantages. But when a thousand or more workers are sharing their joint proceeds from very large co-operatives, incentives for conscientious work are not strong.

A retreat from the Great Leap Forward was followed by restoration of small private garden plots and reintroduction of a rural free market—a policy that resembled the New Economic Policy (NEP) introduced by Lenin in the Soviet Union in 1922. Communes were split into smaller production teams of sixty to eighty households, but the socialist nature of agricultural production remained largely unchanged. Capital formation in heavy industry was to be reduced in favor of agriculture. Skilled, technical, and managerial labor was to receive greater returns than ordinary labor. Improvement in quality of commodities produced and higher labor productivity were to receive high priority. Instead of building new plants, the technology of old ones was to be modernized. In other words, by 1962, the Chinese planners seemed to have embraced, at least temporarily, a strategy of balanced growth, recognizing the close interdependence of the agricultural and the industrial sectors.

EFFECTS OF THE CULTURAL REVOLUTION

The failure of the Great Leap Forward forced the Chinese leaders, mainly Chairman Mao Tse-tung and Premier Zhou Enlai, to change strategy and to restore centralized planning and a steady industrialization process. However, this calm of balanced growth process of development had not lasted long. In 1966, Mao Tse-tung decided to create a new human being and called upon the youth and the pure (ideologically) to deny themselves as individuals in favor of higher social goals and to eliminate counterrevolutionaries, landlords, and rich peasants, rightists, criminals, and other bad elements (lazy people). This was the Great Proletarian Cultural Revolution.

By the end of 1967, and under the pressures of the Cultural Revolution developed by the young Red Guards, the government announced its intention to abolish again private garden plots and free markets and to return to some type of agricultural–industrial communes. In such communes, the dislocation of rural population and industrial regional concentration could be avoided.

After the chaos that existed in China during the 1960s, the Chinese government attempted to restore order through a variety of measures. The final result, however, was a continuous conflict between government factions, which too often led to inconsistency in policy, inefficiency, and corruption.

The 1960s in China were characterized by a collapse of formal administrations in favor of Revolutionary Committees. Just before the turn of the decade, the return of the formal apparatus began to emerge. This was evidenced by the formation of the May Seventh Cadre School, "barefoot doctors," and a total reformation of the educational and the economic systems.

The May Seventh Cadre Schools were designed to combine manual labor with serious indoctrination. Many urbanites and other intellectuals were sent to villages, often to their dismay, to learn how difficult manual labor really was. In this way, they could be less likely to look down on people who always worked with their hands. Unfortunately, many "sent-down youths," as they were called, resented this program and many fled while others simply developed an increased dislike for village life. The "barefoot doctors" program was somewhat more successful. Here, peasants were given very basic medical training and were sent back to their villages to take care of the village population with low expenses. Thus, for the cost of training one specialized surgeon, the government could train a great number of these "barefoot doctors," who probably did more good for people than a surgeon could.

The result was a series of conflicting orders and flip-flopping policies that threw villages into confusion over what to do as left and right battled for control at higher levels. Also, corruption rose drastically as many used "back door" techniques to avoid harsh leftist policies. For example, children of prominent people were able to avoid being sent down to villages for long periods of time, while others felt as "idealistic dupes." Additionally, many continued to buy and sell in private underground markets to get around Communist controls. So, the time period of the 1970s in China was one of constant conflict, confusion, and corruption, far from the utopia envisioned by the Communists.

In the self-sufficiency movement, the quality of products produced in small plants was so bad that the production teams did not want to spend money on it. Of course, they were forced to do so by the government, showing once again how they placed ideological goals ahead of practical ones.[4]

Yet another example of this was the lack of economic incentive for workers. In keeping with their policy that selfishness would not be tolerated, the government sought to limit economic incentives for harder work. Consequently, the hardest workers slacked off in their work rather than let themselves by taken advantage of. As a result, production did not increase much.[5]

When the villagers saw the corruption, inefficiency, and continual flip-flops in government policies, many became very weary of Maoist ideology. There was confusion and dissatisfaction for working people, as the government had gone from a period of chaos in the 1960s to a period of conflict and turmoil in the 1970s.

NORMALIZATION AND THE POST-MAO ERA

With the removal of Chen Pota, the leader of the fanatical Red Guards, in 1968, and the appointment of Lin Biao, the designated successor of Chairman

Mao at the 1969 Party Congress, order was restored and economic development began. During the Cultural Revolution, real output declined by 20 percent, but in the early 1970s, expansion resumed. Organization and control became less rigid and output kept pace with population growth. Lin, who attempted to assassinate Mao in 1971, died in a mysterious plane crash in Mongolia. Zhou Enlai, who remained in power, held talks with President Nixon at that time in Beijing and brought China in the United Nations.

After the death of Mao Tse-tung and Zhou Enlai in 1976, and the arrest of the "Gang of Four," including Mao's wife Jiang Qing, economic policy changed. Deng Xiaoping, who previously served as Chief of Staff, Minister of Finance, and had other positions, and was purged twice for his pragmatic policies and repudiated in the streets of Beijing, became the leader of the country. Then the Cultural Revolution was repudiated and modernization was emphasized. From 1977 to the present, managerial efficiency, technological improvement, and economic growth (ranging from 6 to 8 percent per year) were favored. Responsibility was shifted from the communes first to the production teams (villages) and later to families. Workers' participation in decision making was subordinated to production efficiency and enterprises were permitted to retain 5 percent of the planned profits and 20 percent of any excess. Efforts were made to implement a self-management system, similar to that of Yugoslavia, that combined planning and the market mechanism in price determination.

Under Deng Xiaoping more economic reforms and liberation movements were enacted. He encouraged or tolerated such innovative posters as "The suffocation of democracy produced bad results" and "Marxism has become just another religion . . . why should we believe in Marxism?" and "Capitalism and Socialism are just names. The important thing is we want happiness, freedom, and an advanced economy. Whichever system achieves that, that's what we want."[6] With the market-oriented reforms, Deng wanted to make China strong and rich through a long-term development plan.

In agriculture, communal work and equal sharing were abolished and the "household responsibility system" was introduced. Initially, ownership of land remained with the commune, but households were given plots to cultivate for up to 50 years. The households signed contracts with the production teams to deliver a certain quota at fixed prices in the form of taxes or rental fees and to sell the rest of production to free markets and bazaars. The team signed similar contracts with the brigade and the brigade with the commune. Peasants could hire up to 100 workers and sell their land utilization rights so that small pieces of land could be gathered for economies of scale. Almost all peasants joined this new responsibility system and production increased dramatically, particularly for cotton, oil seeds, and wheat.

The market-oriented reforms that started in agriculture in 1968 were gradually extended to industry. The "contract responsibility system," which prevails even today, gives managerial autonomy to enterprises and local governments for decision making on investment, prices, composition of output, wages, and other policies.[7] Enterprise management, in turn, has to meet government targets regarding output, profit levels, and taxes. Typically, contracts usually of 3 to 5 years are signed and the enterprises are expected to sell a certain amount of output to the government at regulated prices, and additional output can be sold at market prices. Local governments are mainly responsible for the negotiations of contracts with firms in their jurisdiction.

Individuals can set up their own farms and fire employees or can jointly establish cooperative enterprises. They can borrow, use their own funds, or sell bonds and stocks, mainly through the recently established stock markets in Shenyang, Shanghai, and Beijing. In case of poor performance, enterprises can go bankrupt. This measure made the workers less demanding and more productive as they were afraid that they may lose their jobs. As a result of the decentralization and liberalization measures, millions of private farms have been created.[8]

Moreover, emphasis is placed, more and more, on local self-reliance. Firms buy most of their intermediate inputs from organizations located within the same province and sell their own output there as well. Such a local self-reliance may eliminate a good number of bureaucratic bottlenecks or white elephants in the process of resource allocation.

NEW TRENDS AND POLICY CHANGES

Fiscal and Monetary Policy

As in many other countries, budget deficits became a serious problem in China also. Due mainly to decentralization policies, government revenues are falling faster than expenditures and deficits reached about 2 percent of the GNP and are growing. Before 1979, all profits of the enterprises were remitted to the budget and the government, in turn, provided them with working capital and investment. Now, many of firms retain a portion of profits for investment and for bonus payments to managers and workers. A portion of the profits is paid for taxes in addition to indirect taxes paid by each firm. However, contractual taxes are fixed and when the economy grows, taxes, as a proportion of total national output, decline, making countercyclical policy difficult. With the greater autonomy they gained, local governments, which collect almost all major taxes, remit less and less to the central government.[9] This is an additional reason for growing deficits.

Presently, there are a few major banks that specialize in different sectors (agriculture, industry, commerce, etc.), in addition to two universal banks that can operate in any sector and compete with the specialized banks. Also, there is a large number of credit cooperatives and nonbank financial institutions. Before the reforms of 1978, all commercial and central banking activities were handled by the People's Bank of China (superbank), except for the foreign exchange operations that were and still are the responsibility of the Bank of China. Not only the central bank, but specialized banks and even some enterprises are issuing their own bonds. Monetary policy is implemented by the People's Bank of China through its own lending to banks, control on interest rates, reserve requirements, and credit ceilings. However, money supply and credit policies are coordinated by the State Planning Commission and approved by the State Council (related ministers).

As a result of Chinese market-directed reforms, a number of enterprises sell shares of ownership to raise capital for investment. Such shares were originally offered to the workers who worked in the enterprises and were not transferable, but eventually they were issued to the general public. With the development of stock exchanges and future markets in a number of cities, primarily in Shanghai and Zhengzhou, shares are sold by collective and other (except state) enterprises in textiles, furniture, and other industries. Usually, a basic interest (around 7 percent) is guaranteed and an additional dividend per year (up to a certain percentage) is paid depending on the performance of the enterprises involved. For example, the Shanghai Yanzhong Industrial Company recently issued 100,000 shares for 50 yuan each (around half of the average monthly salary).

Shareholders above a certain number of shares, say, 100, can vote the board of directors who elect the general manager without much intervention of the party or the government. Employees of the companies are normally offered a certain portion of the shares with or without preferential terms. Although such stock ownership is criticized as a new path to capitalistic exploitation and inequality, this measure is praised as creating more employment, increasing incentives of production, and absorbing excess savings. As Prime Minister Li Peng said of a state-run inefficient firm, "Share ownership is the only way out." Already, close to 50 percent of industrial production is privately run.

The Chinese economy is too large to be run through commands from the center. To turn back to central controls is like rowing a boat upstream. Freeing the financial system, allowing banks to make their own lending decisions, and opening futures markets, such as the wholesale grain market in Zhengzhou, would help price determination and commodity distribution.

As expected, velocity of money, that is, the ratio of GNP over the money supply, is constant and small (around 2.5 a year). Therefore, increases in money supply finance economic growth and feed inflation. The annual growth of money supply is mostly 20 percent. Table 11.1 shows velocity of money, per capita GNP, population, exports, and other variables.

Economic Growth

In the 5-year plan of 1991–95, economic stability is emphasized and problems of employment are addressed. Industrial production is expected to increase by more than 7 percent a year, inflation to be reduced, and unemployment to be suppressed to levels lower than 4 percent. China's planners aim for sustained and balanced but moderate economic growth during the 1990s and not exceedingly high industrial growth to outstrip agricultural growth and overtax the dis-

Table 11.1

Population (millions), Per Capita GNP ($), Total GNP, Government Expenditures, Exports, Money (M; billion yuan), Velocity (GNP/M), and Exchange Rates (yuan/$) for the Peoples Republic of China

Years	Population	GNP Total	GNP Per Capita $	Gov't Expend.	Exports	Money	Velocity	Exchange Rates
1980	996	426	252	121	27	93	2.9	1.5
1981	1,008	463	224	111	37	107	2.6	1.7
1982	1,021	504	218	115	41	116	2.7	1.9
1983	1,033	563	230	129	44	137	2.8	2.0
1984	1,046	676	231	155	58	245	2.8	2.8
1985	1,059	833	246	184	81	302	2.8	3.2
1986	1,074	946	238	233	109	386	2.5	3.7
1987	1,090	1,118	277	245	147	457	2.4	3.7
1988	1,106	1,401	342	271	177	549	2.6	3.7
1989	1,122	1,591	302	304	195	583	2.7	4.7
1990	n.a.	1,740	n.a.	333	293	701	2.5	5.2

Sources: International Monetary Fund, *International Financial Statistics,* various issues; and United Nations, *Yearbook of National Accounts Statistics,* various issues.

tribution system of the country. The average annual growth rate of GNP per capita for 1965–88 was 5.4 percent and that of inflation for 1980–88 was 4.9 percent. Life expectancy at birth is 70 years and adult illiteracy is about 30 percent.[10]

Traditional Conditions and Reforms

To preserve unity and stability, the Confucian mandarins of the Chinese bureaucratic government try to keep people passive toward their inward-looking political leaders. Although they call for foreign trade and investment, they continue to warn against western capitalist and imperialist goals of economic domination and cultural contamination. They emphasize the Marxist–Leninist–Maoist ideology to explain the needs for economic equality, moral superiority, and cultural independence. The strong family and clan tradition, the "iron rice bowl," and the work unit in present-day China preserve the hierarchical structures of society and the subordination of individual interests to those of the group and the state.

The authoritarian political tradition of China, which prevailed for thousands of years, was abruptly replaced by communism in 1949. However, thereafter, the Chinese leaders cling to similar elitist traditions and continue, more or less, the same hierarchical behavior. Power and economic gains stay with the hierarchy and the government is isolated from the public. To counterbalance criticism, the controlled Chinese media argue that even the American model of democracy of the two political parties is questionable as the difference between the two parties "lies in which fat cats they represent."[11] That is why so many Americans do not even bother to vote, as the difference between the two parties is that between Coca-Cola and Pepsi-Cola.

As a result of the economic reforms from 1979 to 1989, the "responsibility system," which had proved so successful in agriculture, was imitated in the dual pricing system as well. Planned inputs and outputs became small fractions of the total inputs and outputs of firms, while the rest can be traded freely among firms.[12] Moreover, rewards of managers are based not on their success in meeting physical output targets, but on the firms' tax payments and accounting profits. Likewise, workers share in the accounting profits.[13] In practice, more than three-fourths of retained profits went to the managers and workers to increase efficiency. On the other hand, the Chinese started to experiment with auctioning the job of manager every 5 years and the departing manager receives bonuses based on the bid price of the new manager, which depends on the future prospects of the firm.

The reforms of liberalization and decentralization that started in 1978 were interrupted by the crackdown against the democracy movement on June 4, 1989, at Tiananmen Square in Beijing, where hundreds of students were killed. There seems to be a setback or postponement of the reform measures after the 1989 crackdown and the ousting of Zhao Ziyang, the then Communist Party leader. Although Deng Xiaoping, the pragmatist, called for cooperation and not fighting among Party factions, a small group of octogenarians emerged from retirement to order suppression and keep tight control of the country. There is speculation that among the dozen or so old leaders, "the gang of elders," who are the policy makers, Deng still favors liberalization, but he is antagonized by Chen Yun, an old architect of central planning. Experts of Chinese politics are confused and wait for all or some of "the gang of elders" to die to determine political and economic trends.

POLICIES ON FOREIGN INVESTMENT

Oil exports, about 500,000 barrels a day, provide a sizable amount of foreign exchange. Although China relies heavily on coal, and oil accounts for about 20 percent of energy consumption, new drilling on China's coasts by such companies as Chevron, Texaco, and British Petroleum is expected to increase production, which is now about 3 million barrels a day. After the extension of the most favored nation trade status by the United States and improved relations with Japan, foreign trade and investment will rise. In 1991, exports to the United States amounted to $19 billion. However, there are U.S. claims that China does not open its markets to American goods, and tariffs, up to 100 percent, are threatened for certain Chinese goods.

To attract foreign capital, technology, and know-how, a law passed in 1979 permitted foreign firms to invest up to 25 percent of capital in joint ventures. Moreover, foreign credit and technology are pursued. Special economic zones, with low rents and taxes, for export-oriented investment and close ties with Hong Kong (a free-market center in Asia that will be returned to China by Britain in 1997) were established. Since 1984, almost the whole of coastal China opened to foreign investment for the introduction of new technology and the utilization of plentiful cheap labor.

As a result of the post-Mao open policy, more than 2,500 joint ventures were made, mainly by Japan and western Europe and to some extent by the United States (notably in hotels). Moreover, with the open-door policy, cultural and even political contacts were established.[14] Foreign languages were introduced in the schools and Chinese students were sent to study abroad. Some enterprises can deal directly with foreign traders instead of having to deal with the monopoly of the Ministry of Foreign Trade. Also, China became a member of the International Monetary Fund, the World Bank, and other world institutions some 10 years ago.

SUMMARY

China, an overpopulated country, came through many radical transformations in its historical development. The first monetary units in the form of metallic forks and knives appeared in ancient times, and the philosophy of Confucius originated wisdom and prosperity for a long time. However, wars, foreign dominations, and uprisings spurred revolutionary activities that culminated in the establishment of Mao's communism in 1949.

During the period 1949–58, moral appeals for self-sacrifice, central planning similar to that of the Soviet Union, and pressure for rapid industrialization were used to stabilize and develop the economy, with rather good results. In 1958, the Second Five-Year Plan introduced the Great Leap Forward and people's communes. It was a military-type organization with men and women assigned to separate jobs and commune mess halls providing meals all over China. In spite of herculean efforts of mass mobilization of peasants, lack of economies of large-scale and managerial inefficiencies led to disastrous results in 1958–60. A retreat from this policy was followed by restoration of small private plots and firms and rural free markets.

In 1966, Mao Tse-tung introduced the Cultural Revolution and called young Red Guards to favor higher social goals, destroy egoism, and eliminate counterrevolutionaries. Confusion, inefficiency, and corruption prevailed until the death of Mao in 1976. Thereafter, market-oriented reforms, with more reliance on households, were enacted by Deng Xiaoping, about a decade before the Soviet *perestroika*. Enterprises started selling shares initially to their workers and later to the general public, and a number of stock markets have been established.

Foreign investment and technological dissemination are encouraged and more than 2,500 joint ventures have been made. However, there is a slow pace of joint ventures and foreign investment after the crackdown against the democracy movement in June 1989 at Tianamen Square. There are speculations, though, that when old leaders, "the gang of elders," pass away, more liberalization measures will take place.

12 Development Strategies, Convergence, and Integration

CHALLENGES TO DEVELOPING COUNTRIES

There are some seventy-seven developing or third world countries with great diversity among them, regarding the stage of development, per capita income, traditional conditions and institutions, and public- versus private-sector activities. Some of them are small, some large, and almost all of them overpopulated. Many of them had been under colonial rule for many years. All of them struggle to convert their economies from a poverty level to a more advanced stage through rapid industrialization and growth. Although many developing nations have achieved political independence, some economists and politicians think that economic domination of the former colonies still exists and that monopoly capitalism will selfishly continue to exploit them.

The main problem of these poor countries is how to alleviate the poverty, hunger, and illiteracy of their people. Economic development, that is, growth and structural change, requires new institutions, new industries with modern technology and skills, and sociopolitical changes. Economic growth and change, in turn, require investment in plant and equipment, as well as investment in human beings. But developing countries have a high propensity to consume, because of high rates of population growth and low per capita income. This leads to a low level of investment and low productivity, so that it is difficult for these countries to escape from the vicious circle of poverty,[1] regardless of what economic system they follow.

Moreover, lack of entrepreneurial and labor skills, large inequalities in income and wealth, high rates of unemployment and inflation, political instability, and varying cultural conditions make exclusive reliance upon the market or the planning mechanism for the development of poor nations doubtful. Developing countries such as Mexico, Argentina, Brazil, India, Thailand, Egypt, and Kenya combine market arrangements with government policy. However, as these countries mature, their economies would converge toward western market economies and the institutional characteristics and main system differencies would gradually disappear. At the same time, government intervention would be reduced and private enterprises would grow.

Developing nations face such complicated economic, social–cultural, and political problems that are difficult to solve no matter what system (laissez-faire, Keynesian, or Marxian) is used. From an economic viewpoint, non-Communist India is not performing better than Communist China, and capitalist Philippines is in a far worse position than capitalist Japan and semi-Socialist Israel. It is doubtful that many developing countries in Africa, Asia, and Latin America can create the same economic institutions and policy instruments used by industrial countries.

State Capitalism and Free Markets

Many developing nations, mainly in Latin America, make efforts to change their economic system from state capitalism with heavy government intervention, which was popular in previous times, to free-market capitalism. The idea is to increase national wealth and improve the standard of living of their population, preserving political freedom at the same time. However, the question remains: Can classical capitalism, and the marketplace alone, where millions of people are operating for profit, solve the problem of extensive unemployment and rising poverty? Can the American free-market capitalism be considered as a successful model, a buccaneering system for developing countries? Or, can a system of "democratic capitalism," with diffused ownership, bring about a balance between free markets and social welfare?

Although such questions concern developed countries as well, they are more urgent and imperative for developing poor countries, which search for viable alternative systems to raise income and eradicate poverty.

Two major characteristics of the modern American system, regarding corporate management, are important for developing countries. The first is that numerous stockholders delegate authority to nonowner executives. The second is that there is a growing number of companies in which employees participate in decision making through ESOPs.

On the other hand, the German system of codetermination is primarily based on labor sharing in corporate decision making. This system is successful in using an apprenticeship program, which creates new jobs and careers for young people, and it should be considered by other countries, including third world countries.

Another successful system, which developing countries can imitate, is the Japanese employee revenue-sharing system, as well as that of the owner–manager executives in a number of companies, forming groups in which the members are owners of each other.

Depending on the peculiar characteristics of developing nations, they can choose elements of one of the foregoing systems or a combination, a synthesis of them. Each developing country can choose, from the experience of other economies, such economic institutions and policies that best fit their stage of development, sociocultural conditions, and future objectives. From that standpoint, the review of the advantages and disadvantages of different economic systems helps developing countries to select the best possible combination of government and private activities that can work together to promote rapid development.

According to dependency theorists, private-sector capitalism is largely associated with colonialism, imperialism (through multinational corporations), class tensions, and income and wealth inequalities. Nevertheless, in a number of developing countries, such as India, and, to some extent, Nigeria and Mexico, socialism is preached, but capitalism is practiced.

Privatization and Employee Ownership

In previous years, nationalizations were popular, particularly in public utility industries. Even banks were nationalized in India in 1969 and Mexico in 1982. Presently, sales of publicly owned assets and government disengagements in general occur in a number of low-income nations. With such measures, these nations try to emulate reformed capitalism.

The waves of privatization and employee sharing have engulfed developing countries as well. Thus, Argentina, in its effort to modernize public utilities and improve efficiency, is in the process of denationalizing state enterprises by selling them, totally or partially, to the private sector. Such enterprises include the state-owned telephone company (Entel), Argentina's airlines, gas, electricity, railroads, and other transportation and port operations. In Aerolineas Argentinas, the government will retain 51 percent control, and 9 percent of the shares will be distributed among employees and the rest 40 percent will be sold to Scandinavian Airlines. More of less, the same arrangement will occur with Entel, 40 percent of which will be sold to Telefonia de Espana, a Spanish state company, for $900 million. This move was necessary to reduce the losses of public enterprises, which count for more than 50 percent of Argentina's budget deficit, to reduce inflation, and to implement austerity measures suggested by the International Monetary Fund (IMF) because of the heavy external debt of the country.

On the other hand, the state of Sao Paulo in Brazil sold 60 percent of shares of Vasp Airlines to employees and other private groups (Canhedo).

Moreover, Viasa, a Venezuelan state-owned carrier, offered 20 percent of the airline's stock to its employees and 60 percent to Iberia, the Spanish state-owned airline, in partnership with Venezuela's Banco Provincial group.

RELATIONSHIP OF LABOR AND PRODUCTION IN OVERPOPULATED COUNTRIES

Overpopulated nations, such as India and other poor nations, face serious problems of surplus of labor and shortages in food and other products. As Figure

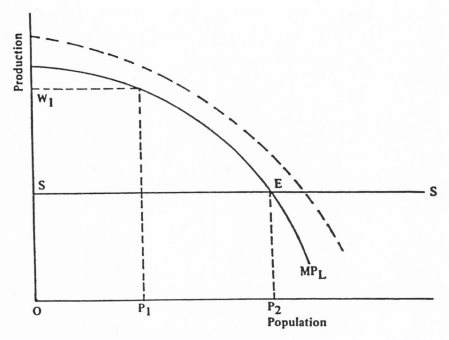

Figure 12.1 The Relationship of Population and Production

12.1 shows, when population is relatively small, say, OP_1, wages, determined by the marginal product of labor (MP_L) will be W_1. Note that the MP_L curve indicates that there will be diminishing returns because of the fixity or relatively smaller increase in natural resources. With actual wages above the subsistence level (OS), population will increase, the supply of labor will increase, and wages will decline to the subsistence level at the equilibrium point E (the classical stationary state) or below. Technological improvement will shift the MP_L curve outward (broken curve) and make possible a temporary increase in wages until a new rise in population eats away the gains.

A common characteristic of the overpopulated poor countries is the existence of surplus labor in the subsistence or agricultural sector. The reallocation into industry of these surplus workers, whose contribution to agricultural output is zero or negligible, is a necessary condition for further economic development.

MARKET MECHANISM AND DEVELOPMENT PLANNING

Regional Inequalities

According to the neoclassical principle of comparative advantage, existing sectoral, regional, and sociocultural differences can be diminished through trade and factor mobility. They are a temporary phenomenon attributed to market imperfection. Economic development, through trickle-down and spread effects, will eventually eliminate such differences and inequalities. However, such differences and income inequalities are facts of life and tend to increase instead of decreasing and narrowing the disequilibrium gap.

The concentration of economic activities, through resource movement from the village to the town and the metropolis, is not geographically or chronologically rhythmical. Unemployed or underemployed resources, especially labor, may move from poor rural areas to provincial cities or big centers in equal proportions or, as is more customary, in higher proportions to the large industrial cities. This depends on the demand for these resources in each particular area, which, in turn, depends on the availability of the cooperant factors, market conditions, and governmental policies.

Two important questions are associated with this transformation process:

1. Does the operation of the free-market mechanism increase or decrease regional inequalities?
2. Is this trend, with its backwash or polarization effects on underdeveloped areas, expected to come to an end or will it be reversed through the spread of trickle-down effects?

The unhampered operation of the market mechanism enlarges the gap of regional inequalities by stimulating migration and capital movement into the lucky regions, where remuneration is relatively higher, while retarding and backwashing the unlucky regions by draining their productive resources.

Interregional inequalities are expected to be gradually reduced when the reverse process starts, that is, when the spread effects (the growth diffusion from the rich to the poor areas) begin. When a country reaches a stage in which prosperous regions are congested with industries, the spread effects will eventually overwhelm the backwash effects, and the development of the poor regions will start speeding up again. It will probably take many years for this reverse process to occur, although development plans may speed the process.

Development Planning

Because of poor transportation and other infrastructural facilities, the operation of the market system in many developing countries is inefficient and in some cases primitive. From that standpoint, governmental policies and comprehensive development, not necessarily imperative, planning is used to coordinate resource allocation, investment priorities, foreign trade, and sectoral and regional economic growth. Such plans may use incremental capital output ratios (ICORs), that is, the ratio of investment to additional production, to project capital requirements, not only in a national level, but sectoral and regional levels as well.[2]

For many developing or third world countries, private savings and investment are limited. Depending on the tax and borrowing ability of governments, public investment may provide needed capital formation for development projects. However, the reliability of development plans, more and more on such public investment, may lead to gradual expansion of the public sector, at the expense of the private sector, and eventual governmental controls on many or all sectors of the economy.

Through imitation of the known techniques used in rich countries, combined with population control, developing countries can accelerate their rate of development, provided that the necessary capital is available. Along these lines, any ambitious development program favoring high rates of growth, through rising public and private investment, would be expected to increase income substantially. However, output might not keep pace with high demand, and the result would probably be inflation. For macroeconomic equilibrium, total demand must be equal to total supply and total income to total spending.

Assuming other things the same, the equilibrium level of national income requires that total savings, that is, domestic savings (S_d) and foreign savings (S_f) or borrowing, plus imports (M) must equal total investment, that is, domestic (I_d) and foreign (I_f) investment plus exports (X), or

$$S_d + S_r + M = I_d + I_f + X$$

Using a simplified version of the Harrod–Domar–Tinbergen model, without gestation lag, we can calculate the rate of economic growth. Thus,

$$g = \frac{j}{v}$$

where g is the annual rate of growth of output (DQ/Q), j the investment-to-output ratio (I/Q), and v the incremental capital output ratio (ICOR, or DK/DQ). Here we assume surplus labor and constant ICOR, particularly in 5-year intervals, a period normally used in economic planning.

For an annual growth rate of per capita income (g') of 3%, assuming an annual rate of population growth (r) of 2%, and a present national income or output (Q) of \$100 billion, national income or output in 5 years ($t = 5$) must be \$128 billion. Or

$$Q = Q(1 + r)^t (1 + g')^t = 100(1.02)^5(1.03)^5 = 128$$

The expected rate of economic growth (g) may be determined by the average propensity to save (s), the expected difference in foreign trade (exports − imports) as a percentage of national income (f), and the capital/output or income ratio (v):

$$g = \frac{s + f}{v}$$

By assuming $s = 0.15$, $f = 0.03$, and $v = 3$, the rate of economic growth would be 6 percent of the national income. Also, s is assumed to be equal to j.

$$g = \frac{0.15 + 0.03}{3} = \frac{0.18}{3} = 0.06$$

The ICOR for a 5-year period can be calculated as follows:

$$\text{ICOR} = \sum_{t=1}^{t=5} I_t / (Q_{t+5} - Q_t)$$

Future output can be estimated with the following equation:

$$Q_{t+n} = Q_t + \sum_{t=1}^{n-1} I_t / (\text{ICOR})$$

Balanced and Unbalanced Growth Strategies

Considering the two main sectors, agriculture and industry, which one must be given more emphasis, if any? Should the allocation of investment and other resources be equiproportional to produce balanced growth or nonproportional, following an unbalanced growth policy in favor of one or the other sector?

Many economists and politicians support the argument of unbalanced growth, according to which development at best can be achieved through a deliberate unbalancing process in the economy in accordance with a predesigned strategy. Development can be initiated by emphasizing a few leading sectors of the economy at the expense of others, through government planning.

In a similar fashion to the Marxian stages theory, Walt Rostow launched his stage schema with emphasis on investment and technological progress. He distinguished the "traditional society," with an hierarchical social structure with a high proportion (75 percent) of the working force involved in the production of food; the stage of the "preconditions for takeoff," where the rate of capital accumulation is higher than the rate of population growth, which is characterized by the appearance of the entrepreneurial class and the development of national governments; the "takeoff into self-sustained growth" stage with a few leading sectors growing most rapidly (cotton industry in England, railroads in the United States and Russia, timber in Sweden); and a net rate of investment growing from 5 to more than 10 percent. Thereafter comes the stage of "technological maturity," with more populations moving from the rural areas to the urban centers having higher industrial skills; and the stage of "mass consumption," in which mass production of durable goods, such as automobiles, television, videos, refrigerators, and other household gadgetry, as well as Social Security and welfare benefits are provided. In spite of the criticism of these stages regarding their duration and aeronautical resemblance, they present perceptive suggestions of changes for countries moving from traditional to technical advanced economies.

Moreover, as the argument goes, the main reason for backwardness is the lack of entrepreneurial decision making. The development process can be set in motion by generating a chain of unbalanced growth sequences in order to induce decision-making through tensions and incentives for private entrepreneurs and state planners. Initiation of development in those sectors that present maximum backward and forward linkages with other sectors is advisable. The development of these sectors, upon which other sectors depend through technical and demand relations, would provide the necessary inducement and would apply to the lagging dependent sectors, thus stimulating and further accelerating the economy. For rapid growth, emphasis must be given to an industry with extensive linkages. Such an industry may become the prime mover, the leading economic unit, in creating demand that will stimulate innovations, thereby supplying other industries with needed input. Development or indicative planning is largely used to coordinate such growth policies.

Governmental Spending

Central government expenditures are comparatively less in developing or third world countries than in developed countries. They vary from around 12 percent of GNP for Peru, 18 percent for India and Zaire, and 31 percent for Brazil, as Table 12.1 shows. In developed or industrial countries they vary from 35 percent for Britain, 43 percent for France, 48 percent for Italy, and as high as 54 percent for the Netherlands.[3] Countries with a federal form of government have relatively low central government expenditures, but high general (federal, state, city) government expenditures. Thus, the United States, for example, has about 23 percent central, or federal, government expenditures, but close to 40 percent general government or public-sector expenditures. The same thing can be said for Canada and Yugoslavia.

It would seem then that higher stages of development are related to higher public-sector expenditures. As third world countries gradually move toward higher per capita incomes, they are expected to follow the same pace rich countries followed in the past, that is, to have growing public-sector expenditures. Historically, the same thing occurred to the industrial countries, as World Bank statistics indicate. Thus, the percentage shares of government expenditures in GNP or GDP in 1880 were 15 percent for France, 10 for Germany, 11 for Japan, 10 for Britain, 8 for the United States, and only 6 percent for Sweden. But, gradually they increased to 52 percent for France, 47 for Germany, 33 for Japan, 48 for Britain, 37 for the United States, and 65 percent for Sweden.

Regarding income distribution, there is no great difference between developing

Table 12.1
Economic Indicators of Some Developing Countries with Mixed Economies, 1989

Countries	Population (millions)	Per Capita GNP U.S.$	Per Capita GNP Growth (%)	Inflation Average Annual (%), 1965-89	Central Govt. Expenditures (% of GNP), 1980-89
India	832.5	350	1.8	7.7	17.7
Indonesia	178.2	500	4.4	8.3	20.6
Brazil	147.3	2,540	3.5	227.8	30.6
Nigeria	113.8	250	0.2	14.2	28.1
Pakistan	109.9	370	2.5	6.7	21.5
Mexico	84.6	2,010	3.0	72.7	21.2
Philippines	60.0	710	1.6	14.8	15.7
Thailand	55.4	1,220	4.2	3.2	15.1
Turkey	55.0	1,370	2.6	41.4	23.7
Zaire	34.5	260	-2.0	59.4	18.4
Kenya	23.5	360	2.0	9.0	28.0
Peru	21.2	1,010	-0.2	160.3	11.6

Sources: World Bank, *World Development Report*, various issues; United Nations, *Yearbook of National Accounts Statistics*, various issues.

and developed countries. According to World Bank statistics, the share of the lowest 20 percent of households in GDP (1990), in percentages, was 8.1 for India, 8.8 for Indonesia, 4.4 for Peru, and only 2.4 for Brazil, compared to 8.7 for Japan, 6.8 for Germany, 6.3 for France, 5.8 for Britain, and 4.7 for the United States. The share of the highest 20 percent of households in GDP, varied from 41.4 percent for India, 51.9 for Peru, and 62.4 percent for Brazil, compared with 41.9 for the United States, 38.7 for Germany, 37.5 for Japan, and 36.9 percent for Sweden.

Moving away from government intervention toward greater reliance on the marketplace is one of the most important trends of our days. Markets instead of controls are guiding developing countries to new economic policies. Old traditions and cultural conditions are rapidly changing under the pressure of policy coordination and cooperation among countries and between economic blocks. The heavily regulated economies of many developing nations are moving toward privatization, deregulation, and other microeconomic measures that embrace the market mechanism and the decentralization process of decision making.

On the other hand, competition in the marketplace is teaching many people in poor countries the harsh laws of economic growth and its relationship to population growth. Being under conditions of overpopulation and low per capita income for decades, they began to abandon fatalistic theories and old taboos that lead to low performance and economic stagnation. People in developing countries started questioning old social philosophies of welfarism and equality in poorness and prepared for a dramatic rise in domestic and world competition.

The fall of communism as a viable competitor of capitalism leaves many developing countries with the problem of rapid adjustment to free-market economics according to their peculiar conditions. As the twentieth century runs its course, the dilemmas of overpopulation and environmental protection are forcing economic congruence and sociopolitical cooperation.

The Use of Technology

To avoid unemployment, developing countries use labor-deepening technology (L) per unit of output (O), although modernization may require mechanization and capital-deepening technology (K). For this reason, subsidies or other fiscal and monetary measures are used to support moribund enterprises and keep them in operation. Depending on the availability of factors of production, capital-widening technology can also be selected. In that case, the capital–labor ratio remains the same along the expansion line ($OO_1O_2O_3$) as output moves up the hill to higher levels of production (isoquant curves), as Figure 12.2 shows.

For the selection of development projects in economic planning, the following ratio can be used:

$$\frac{B}{C} = \frac{\sum_{t=1}^{n} B_t/(1 + r)^t}{\sum_{t=1}^{n} C_t/(1 + r)^t}$$

Where B_t and C_t are benefits and costs, respectively, in year t, n is the life of the projects, and r is the rate of discount. Projects with benefit–cost ratios greater than 1 are expected to improve social welfare and deserve approval, whereas projects with a ratio less than 1 should be abandoned. Such projects may include irrigation and other water works, transportation, health, and educational programs.

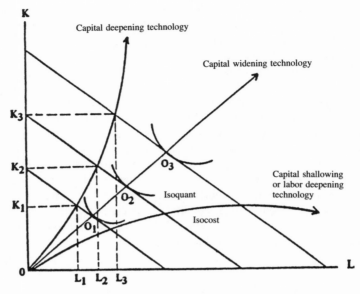

Figure 12.2 Technological Change and Project Selection

CONVERGENCE AND ECONOMIC INTEGRATION

Synthesis of Opposites

In previous historical reviews, we briefly discussed arguments relative to ideological differences between capitalism and communism. The supporters of each system argued that the disadvantages and the resultant crises of the other system would eventually lead to its downfall.

The main Communist criticisms of capitalism include economic instability or business cycles, unemployment, income and wealth inequalities, and what is considered as the "exploitation of man by man," or the economic "dictatorship" of the capitalist system; and the major capitalist criticisms of communism, as practiced in China, Cuba, Vietnam, and other Communist countries, include restrictions on economic and political freedoms, lack of work incentives and entrepreneurial initiatives, political and economic dictatorship, and widespread laziness or negligence due to common ownership.

Both systems have learned from experience how to overcome their own weaknesses. The strict individualism of the capitalistic system gave way to private collectivism through the distribution of stock ownership and corporate decision making. Capitalism has become more collectivist and more stable by introducing social welfare measures and encouraging the growth of the middle class. Communism, on the other hand, has become more individualist, putting more and more emphasis on the market and incentives for profits.

Perhaps, the Hegelian dialectic approach of thesis–antithesis–synthesis, which Marx used to explain the development process, may very well be used to explain the gradual evolution of the two systems, capitalism and communism. Such a socioeconomic evolution may take place not through a conflict between the two opposites, as Marx predicted, but through a process of peaceful synthesis of the two ideologies, a method used by Plato in his *Dialogues* and later by Scholastics to modify and reconcile two opposite arguments into a new emerging view that incorporates elements of both.

The movement toward the integration of eastern Europe and the EC into a pan-European economy and the economic reforms on trade and investment in the region are expected to be the major preoccupations of international economics in the forthcoming years. The implications of the drastic reforms toward the market economy and the problems of currency convertibility are among the important variables that need further investigation. These reforms indicate that there is a subvergence of a Communist to capitalist system and a trend toward economic and political integration.

Effects of Multinational Corporations

The industrial system of advanced countries is not a terminal phenomenon and the growth of autonomous giant corporations will continue while the entrepreneurial corporation will decline. The new industrial systems, in both market and planned economies, exercise power over beliefs and ideologies and are convergent in their development. Large-scale organization requires autonomy from the controls of bureaucracy, of both the capitalist and the state. Such autonomy gives the corporation authority over market or planning mechanisms. In both systems, capitalism and socialism, the state tends to become subordinate to giant corporations, acting as their servant in providing full or nearly full employment demand, sufficient training and education for the required manpower, and price–wage stability. Fortunately, Galbraith argues, in his *New Industrial State*, the convergence between the two industrial systems is occurring rapidly and the concept of inevitable conflict, which Marx predicted, will gradually be steamed out and replaced by the principle of peaceful cooperation.[4]

The growth of international trade and investment, the drastic improvement of transportation and communications, the increase in consumerism, currency convertibility, sports activities, and tourism, as well as the expansion of multinational corporations, dismantle national and ideological barriers and bring countries and people closer together. Thus, Citibank has operations in more than 100 countries and IT&T in about 70. The same thing can be said for Coca-Cola, IBM, Exxon, Mobil, Mitsubishi, Matsushita, Nippon, Namura, Volkswagen, Nestlé, Fiat, and scores of other giant companies.

NEW FORMS OF CONVERGENCE

There may be a distinction among international, national, or inner-country and inner-industry convergence. International or worldwide convergence involves the movement of different economic and political systems, mainly capitalism and communism, toward a hybrid system. It had some plausibility when it was first advanced and up to the 1970s, but gradually it lost steam, mainly because of its emphasis on the political aspects of convergence. In any case, what happened recently in the former Soviet Union and the eastern European countries is evidence of the triumph of capitalism over communism rather than their convergence into a middle-of-the-road system.

National or macroeconomic convergence may be considered as the hybrid of the public and the private sector into a mixed system in which there are mostly private companies, but a number of government enterprises primarily in public utilities, such as the post office, transportation services, space administration, energy, and the like. Moreover, the use of fiscal and monetary countercyclical policy by the public sector, which absorbs some 40 to 50 percent of GNP in most market economies, aims at the support of the private sector to keep, among other things, an equilibrium between the two sectors for the sake of economic stability and growth.

Inner-company or microeconomic convergence can be referred to as the movement toward the mixture of management and labor in enterprise decision making. The system of comanagement or codetermination that prevails mainly in Germany, the share economy that prevails, to a large extent, in Japan, and the growing Employee Stock Ownership Plans (ESOPs) in the United States, the EC and other market economies, as well as the partial split of ownership of government enterprises to citizens and workers in Poland and other ex-Communist countries (democratic capitalism) may be considered as belonging to this type of microeconomic convergence.

EMPLOYEE SHARING UNDER A TRIPOLAR COMPETITIVE WESTERN WORLD

As nations or groups of nations move from cold war to trade war, a tripolar competitive world is expected to dominate economic and political relations in the 1990s, and later. In this tripolar competitive world with the European Community, the North American Community (United States, Canada, and Mexico), and the Pacific Rim (Japan, Korea, Taiwan, and other neighboring nations) would be the main players in the international economic arena. In the process of competition among corporations of these groups, new industrial organizations with employee participation and advanced technology would prevail, whereas international labor and trade-promoting institutions, such as the ILO and GATT, might be dead.

In this type of democratic free enterprises and large multinational corporations with capital-intensive methods of production, the old fashion contravening power of labor unions would be largely diminished and eventually disappear. In such a growing business world, worker ownership and participation in decision making would enhance labor benefits and incentives by sharing in the performance and the profits in the companies in which they work.

Nevertheless, ethical consideration and the use of the carrot before the stick on matters of labor remuneration and wealth distribution should not be ignored. Otherwise, what occurred in the 1980s in the United States and other countries, in which the rich got richer and everyone else paid the price, would occur again, perhaps more vigorously. Moreover, redistribution of wealth to other nations would continue for countries with deficits in their international transactions. According to the Congressional Budget Office, average incomes of the richest 20 percent American families increased from $65,000 in 1980 to $93,000 in 1992, whereas for the lowest 60 percent after-tax income dropped since 1977. For the lowest 20 percent bracket, it dropped from $10,000 to $8,000.

FUTURE EXPECTATIONS

Trends Toward the Market System

Market economies are basically characterized primarily by private ownership of the means of production and a competitive market mechanism. Enterprises belong mainly to the private sector, and decisions are taken by individual entrepreneurs or boards of directors who are representatives of the stock owners. Planned economies, on the other hand, are based primarily on the centralized process of production and distribution. Enterprises are managed by governmental appointees and all the economic activities are coordinated by the overall national plan.

As mentioned previously, market economies move gradually away from extreme individualism toward more collectivism. The public sector, which includes central and local government and public enterprises, has already grown to about half of the entire economy in many market economies. On the other hand, previous planned economies have gradually been moving away from strict state controls.[5]

Federations and International Economic Cooperation

It seems that the future belongs to economic and political federations. This verifies what Pier-Joseph Proudhon predicted in 1863, that "The twentieth century will initiate the era of federations." This can be seen in the former USSR and other eastern European countries where there is a trend toward voluntary or democratic, not imposed, federations. The need for economic cooperation in a growing world economy is forcing reduction or elimination of trade and investment barriers and eventually the establishment of economicopolitical federations, which liquidate nationalism and promote socioeconomic integration.

In addition to the old federations of the United States and Switzerland, similar federations of one form or another can be observed in Australia, Canada, Latin America, and Central America (Argentina, Venezuela, Brazil, Mexico), Africa (Nigeria, South Africa), Asia (Malaysia, United Arab Emirates), and primarily in Europe (Germany, Austria, Belgium, Czechoslovakia, and the new Commonwealth of Independent States) with the EC at the forefront.

Although the future remains unknowable and reliable predictions are difficult, one can imagine and hope that future societies would be more democratic with more openness, less oppression, and more cooperation. The information-processing revolution and the drastic improvement of transportation and technology or the vast accumulation of knowledge would help people to communicate easier and to cooperate more effectively on socioeconomic and geopolitical matters. If we were transported in time to the last century and we imagined about economic and political developments at the present time, we could see the eventual betterment of societies, although with some serious setbacks.

In eastern Europe and the former USSR, the economic system of the future would probably be that of a social market economy. Mutual understanding would make the economies of the area more positive and less politically controlled regarding alternative choices in sociopolitical, individual, and corporate matters. Existing planned economies, such as China and North Korea, are expected to reform their economies toward the market mechanism with more cooperation in international trade and investment.[6]

Trade cooperation and joint investment ventures among countries liquidate lingering nationalism and reduce regional conflicts, which have plagued many nations for decades. Congruence, then, may bring an economic and sociopolitical synthesis through peaceful cooperation and mutual trade and investment.

Furthermore, there are certain realities facing the world today that are expected to prevail over dogma, whether of the liberal or conservative variety. They include economic and political justice, respect for the environment, as well as concern for the world community in the present nuclear age. All these elements point to the need for socioeconomic and even political cooperation on a worldwide basis.

On the other hand, a middle way with respect to property acquisition, justified by the anxiety about livelihood was recommended by Aristotle. The pursuit of wealth in excess of this limit was considered a corruption or an unnatural form of acquisition.

A successful experience of economic convergence may be followed by groups of countries such as the European Community (EC) and other advanced countries. Also, other developing and uncommitted nations that are anxious to avoid extreme capitalism or communism can search for such a converging system that combines the best elements of the two extremes.[7] Although it is difficult to expect an optimum combination of the public and private sectors in both systems in the near future, it is equally or even more difficult to accept what extreme apologists of either system suggest: "convergence" is a camouflage for subversion. However, there is always the possibility of serious setbacks of congruence by the short-term strategies and the long-term goals of the big powers. As Victor Hugo said, though: Nothing is more powerful than an idea whose time has come.

SUMMARY

A major problem of overpopulated developing countries is lack of savings, which limits investment. This leads to low productivity and the vicious circle of poverty. Because of the weakness of the private sector to accumulate capital and to foster development, the role of the state is deemed important in many poor countries.

Although the trend is toward the free-market mechanism and the emphasis on entrepreneurial activities for long-term industrialization, it is difficult for developing countries to copy institutions of industrial capitalism or centrally planned socialism.

Mostly, macroeconomic or development, not necessarily imperative, planning is used to coordinate aggregate economic activities. In such planning, fiscal and monetary policies, similar to those of developed market economies, are used to support the private sector and achieve desirable growth targets. Moreover, the growing employee ownership and worker participation in enterprise decision making correct some of the disadvantages of capitalism and communism and tend to support a labor–management convergence through privatization.

The recent trend of regional convergence or integration, through economic cooperation and creation of common markets, mitigates private–public-sector differences and tends to increase trade and investment among nations. Moreover, joint ventures by multinational corporations liquidate ideological differences and national barriers and improve international transactions and socioeconomic cooperation.

Notes

CHAPTER 1

1. Ernest Barker, *The Political Thoughts of Plato and Aristotle* (New York: Dover, 1959), 143.

2. Adam Smith, *An Inquiry Into the Nature and Causes of the Wealth of Nations*, ed. by E. Cannan (New York: Modern Library, 1937), 423.

3. Frederick Hayek, *The Road to Serfdom* (Chicago: University of Chicago Press, 1944), 72–82; also Milton Friedman, *Capitalism and Freedom* (Chicago: University of Chicago Press, 1962).

4. Louis Putterman, *Division of Labor and Welfare: An Introduction to Economic Systems* (New York: Oxford University Press, 1990), chap. 2; and Moris Borris, *Comparative Economic Systems: Models and Cases*, 6th ed. (Homewood, Ill.: Irwin, 1989), chaps. 25–26.

5. Robert B. Reich, *The Work of Nations: Preparing Ourselves for 21st-Century Capitalism* (New York: Knopf, 1991); and his "Secession of the Successful," *The New York Times Magazine*, January 20, 1991, 17, 42–45.

6. Vilfredo Pareto, *Cours d' Economie Politique*, vols. I and II (Lausanne, 1896–97).

CHAPTER 2

1. Hicks calls this type of economy a revenue economy or nonmarket economy. John Hicks, *The Theory of Economic History* (New York: Oxford University Press, 1969), 24. Also Gerhard Lenski, *Power and Privilege: A Theory of Social Stratification* (New York: McGraw-Hill, 1966).

2. Plato, *Laws*, in B. Jowett, trans., *The Dialogues of Plato* (New York, 1876), 736. The argument of eliminating desires to increase happiness is used in modern times by zero-growth economists against the extensive use of natural resources and in favor of environmental protection.

3. More information in R. H. Tawney, *Religion and the Rise of Capitalism* (New

York: Harcourt, 1926) chap. 3; and Max Weber, *The Protestant Ethic and the Spirit of Capitalism*, transl. by Talcott Parsons (New York: Scribner's, 1958), chap. 2.

4. The term physiocracy, a compound Greek word meaning the "rule of nature," was first used by Du Pont de Nemours (1768) to signify the similarities of the natural order in the harmonic movements of the planets and stars to economic activities.

5. Adam Smith, *An Inquiry Into the Nature and Causes of the Wealth of Nations*, ed. by E. Cannan (New York: Modern Library, 1937), 3.

6. John Stuart Mill, "Principles of Political Economy," in *Masterworks of Economics*, vol. 1, ed. by Leonard Abbott (New York: McGraw-Hill, 1973), 162.

7. *Ibid.*, 164.

8. John E. Cairnes, *Some Leading Principles of Political Economy Newly Expounded* (London, 1874).

9. John M. Keynes, *The General Theory of Employment, Interest and Money* (New York: Harcourt, 1936), 96.

10. Such predictions are developed in Joseph A. Schumpeter, *Capitalism, Socialism and Democracy*, 2d ed. (New York: Harper and Brothers, 1947).

11. Alvin Hansen, *Economic Issues of the 1960s* (New York: McGraw-Hill, 1960), 44–45.

12. As John K. Galbraith argues, "Production creates the wants it seeks to satisfy, or . . . the wants emerge pari passu with production." *The Affluent Society*, 2d ed., rev. (Boston: Houghton Mifflin, 1969), 147; also *The New Industrial State*, 2d ed., rev. (Boston: Houghton Mifflin, 1971), chap. 19.

CHAPTER 3

1. Adam Smith, *An Inquiry into the Nature and Causes of the Wealth of Nations*, ed. by E. Cannan (New York: Modern Library, 1937), 50.

2. John Stuart Mill, "Principles of Political Economy," in *Masterworks of Economics*, vol. 2, ed. by Leonard Abbott (New York: McGraw-Hill, 1973), 135–136.

3. Karl Marx, *Capital*, trans. from the 3d German edition by S. Moore and E. Aveling (New York: Modern Library, 1906), 652.

4. Vladimir I. Lenin, "Imperialism, The Highest Stage of Capitalism," in E. Varga and L. Mendelsohn, eds., *New Data for V.I. Lenin's Imperialism* (New York: International Publishers, 1940), 206.

5. Paul Baran, *The Political Economy of Backwardness* (New York: Monthly Review Press, 1957).

6. Input–output analysis, which is reminiscent of Quesnay's input–output tables (in the Physiocratic School) is largely the creation of Wassily Leontief. See his *Input–Output Economics* (New York: Oxford University Press, 1966).

7. Ludwig von Mises, "Economic Calculation in the Socialist Commonwealth," reprinted in Friedrich A. Hayek, ed., *Collective Economic Planning* (London: Routledge, 1963), chap. 3.

8. Oskar Lange, "On the Economic Theory of Socialism," in Benjamin E. Pillincott, ed., *On the Economic System of Socialism* (Minneapolis: University of Minnesota Press, 1938), 80–84. A number of related articles were reprinted in Oskar Lange and Fred J. Taylor, *On the Economic Theory of Socialism* (New York: McGraw-Hill, 1964), 39–142.

CHAPTER 4

1. Adam Smith, *An Inquiry into the Nature and Causes of the Wealth of Nations*, ed. by E. Cannan (New York: Modern Library, 1937), 284.

2. John Stuart Mill, *Considerations and Representative Government* (London: Routledge, 1905), 114; Jean Jacques Rousseau, The *Social Contract*, trans. by Maurice Cranston, book one, chaps.1–83 (New York: Penguin, 1968); Lindblom, *Politics and Markets* (New York: Basic Books, 1977), chap. 24.

3. John Stuart Mill, "Principles of Political Economy," in *Masterworks of Economics*, vol. 2, ed. by Leonard Abbott (New York: McGraw-Hill, 1973), 172.

4. Joseph Schumpeter, *Capitalism, Socialism and Democracy*, 3d ed. (New York: Harper Colophon Books, 1975), 205. For some review lessons in Europe, see J. Carby-Hall, *Worker Participation in Europe* (London: C. Helm, 1977), chap. 3; G. Garson, ed., *Worker Self-Management in Industry: The West European Experience* (New York: Praeger, 1977), chaps. 1–5.

5. Corey M. Rosen, Katherine J. Klein, and Karen M. Young, *Employee Ownership in America: The Equity Solution* (Lexington, Mass.: Lexington Books, 1986), chap. 2. Also Frederick Ungeheuer, "They Own the Place," *Time*, February 6, 1989, 50–51; and Joseph Blasi, *Employee Ownership: Revolution or Ripoff?* (New York: Ballinger, 1988), chaps. 1–3.

6. For such pioneering proposals, see Martin L. Weitzman, *The Share Economy: Conquering Stagflation* (Cambridge: Harvard University Press, 1984), 73–74; and his "The Simple Macroeconomics of Profit Sharing," *American Economic Review*, vol. 75, December 1985, 937–953.

7. Nicholas V. Gianaris, "Helping Eastern Europe Helps the West," *The New York Times*, February 8, 1990, A28.

8. Stephen Engelberg, "Lower House in Poland Approved Bill to Make Citizens Stockholders," *The New York Times*, July 14, 1990, A1, A4.

CHAPTER 5

1. More information in Morton Keller, *Regulating a New Economy: Public and Economic Change in America, 1900–1933* (Cambridge: Harvard University Press, 1990).

2. It is estimated that federal regulations in the United States are responsible for 12 to 21 percent of the slowdown in the growth of labor productivity in manufacturing. Gregory Christiansen and Robert Haveman, "Public Regulations and the Slowdown in Productivity Growth," *American Economic Review, Proceedings*, vol. 71, no. 2, May 1981, 320–325.

3. Further review on U.S. antitrust policy in John E. Kwoka and Lawrence J. White, eds., *The Antitrust Revolution* (Glenview, Ill.: Scott, Foresman, 1989); and William G. Shepherd, *The Economics of Industrial Organization*, 2d ed. (Englewood Cliffs, N.J.: Prentice Hall, 1985).

4. For pro and con arguments, see Robert Reich, "Leveraged Buyouts: America Pays the Price," *The New York Times Magazine*, January 29, 1989, 32, 36, 40; and Carl Icahn, "The Case for Takeovers," *ibid.*, 34.

5. John Kenneth Galbraith, *American Capitalism: The Concept of Countervailing Power* (White Plains, N.Y.: M. E. Sharpe, 1980).

6. U.S. Government, *Economic Report of the President* (Washington, D.C.: U.S. Government Printing Office), various issues; and Nicholas V. Gianaris, *Contemporary Public Finance* (New York: Praeger, 1989), 207.

7. U.S. Department of Commerce, Bureau of the Census, *Historical Statistics of the United States, Colonial Times to 1970, 1975*, 1117–1120.

8. For the effects of the dollar depreciation on the U.S. economy, see Nicholas V. Gianaris, *The European Community and the United States: Economic Relations* (New York: Praeger, 1991), chap. 7.

9. David L. McKee, ed., *Canadian–American Economic Relations: Conflict and Cooperation on a Continental Scale* (New York: Praeger, 1988); and Judith A. Teichman, *Policymaking in Mexico: From Boom To Crisis* (New York: Allen and Unwin, 1988).

10. Harold Crookell, *Canadian–American Trade and Investment Under the Free Market Agreement* (Westport, Conn.: Quorum, 1990), chap. 3.

CHAPTER 6

1. Nicholas V. Gianaris, *The European Community and the United States: Economic Relations* (New York: Praeger, 1991), chap. 2.

2. World Bank, *World Development Report* (New York: Oxford University Press for the World Bank), various issues; and M. W. Kirby, *The Decline of British Economic Power Since 1870* (London: Allen and Unwin, 1981).

3. H. Stephen Gardner, *Comparative Economic Systems* (Chicago, Ill.: Dryden Press, 1988), 167; and Shepard B. Clough, *France: A History of National Economics* (New York: Octagon, 1970), chaps. 1–3.

4. Charles P. Kindlerberger, "French Planning," in Max F. Millikan, ed., *National Economic Planning* (New York: National Bureau of Economic Research, 1967), 290–297.

5. For the use of public policy in the process of growth, see William J. Adams, *Restructuring the French Economy* (Washington, D.C.: The Brookings Institution, 1989).

6. More details in Otto Nathan, *The Nazi Economic System: Germany's Mobilization For War* (Durham, N.C.: Duke University Press, 1944); and Helmut Bohme, *An Introduction to the Social and Economic History of Germany* (New York: St. Martin's Press, 1978). Also William Ebenstein, *Today's Isms: Communism, Fascism, Capitalism, Socialism* (Englewood Cliffs, N.J.: Prentice Hall, 1970), chap. two.

7. For the support of economic neoliberalism, see Ludwig Erhard and Alfred Muller-Armack, *Sociale Markt Wirtschaft* (Frankfurt am Main: Ullstein, 1972). For the performance of the economy, see Gerhard Brinkman, *Okonomik der Arbeit*, vol. I (Stuttgart: Ernst Klett Verlag, 1981). Also Jeremy Leaman, *The Political Economy of West Germany, 1945–1985: An Introduction* (New York: St. Martin's Press, 1988), chap. 3.

8. Heinz Kohler, *Comparative Economic Systems* (Glenview, Ill.: Scott, Foresman, 1989), 428. Also Hans-Joachim Braun, *The German Economy in the Twentieth Century* (London: Routledge, 1990).

9. Salvador de Madariaga, *Spain A Modern History* (New York: Praeger, 1958), part I, chaps. 1–4; and John A. Crow, *Spain: The Root and the Flower* (New York: Harper, 1963), chaps. 1–3.

CHAPTER 7

1. Koichi Shimokawa, "Japan's Keiretsu System: The Case of the Automobile In-dustry," *Japanese Economic Studies*, Summer 1985, 13, 3–31; and C. G. Allen, *A Short History of Modern Japan* (London: Macmillan, 1981).

2. More information in Tessa Morris-Sujuki, *A History of Japanese Economic Thought* (New York: Routledge, 1989); and "An Outsider Takes A Look Inside At Japan's Corporate Culture," *Japanese Economic Journal*, May 3, 1986, 40–41.

3. Masahiko Aoki, "Toward an Economic Model of the Japanese Firm," *Journal of Economic Literature*, vol. XXVIII, March 1990, 1–27; and his *Information, Incentives, and Bargaining in the Japanese Economy* (New York: Cambridge University Press, 1988).

4. For related statistics, see Organization for Economic Cooperation and Development (OECD), *Economic Surveys: Japan*, various issues.

5. In Japan, large business and bureaucrats have more power than politicians. See Karen van Wolferen, "The Japan Problem Revisited," *Foreign Affairs*, vol. 69, no. 4, Fall 1990, 42–55; and Chalmers Johnson, *MITI and the Japanese Miracle* (Stanford, Cal.: Stanford University Press, 1982).

6. Edward J. Lincoln, *Japan: Facing Economic Maturity* (Washington, D.C.: The Brookings Institution, 1988), chap. 2.

7. Further review in William R. Nester, *Japan's Growing Predominance Over East Asia and World Economy* (New York: St. Martin's Press, 1990); and Bela Belassa and Marcus Noland, *Japan in the World Economy* (Washington, D.C.: Institute for Inter-national Economics, 1988), chaps. 2–4.

8. More information in Susumu Takamiya and Keith Thurley, eds., *Japan's Emerging Multinationals* (Tokyo: University of Tokyo Press, 1985); and Carl Kester, *Japanese Takeovers* (Boston: Harvard Business School Press, 1991).

9. Paul C. Judge, "Nissan Plans New Factory For Engines in Tennessee," *The New York Times*, January 19, 1991, L37.

CHAPTER 8

1. A general review in Erik Lundberg, "The Rise and Fall of the Swedish Model," *Journal of Economic Literature*, vol. 23, March 1985, 1–36.

2. For more details, see Barry P. Bosworth and Alice M. Rivlin, eds., *The Swedish Economy* (Washington, D.C.: The Brookings Institution, 1987); and Kristine Bruland, *Scandinavian Industrialization: Technological Transfer and Economic Growth* (New York: St. Martin's Press, 1990).

3. Kristina Ahlen, "Sweden Introduces Employee Ownership," *The Political Quar-terly*, vol. 56, April–June 1985, 186–193; For further description, see Frederic Fleisher, The New Sweden: *The Challenge of a Disciplined Democracy* (New York: McKay, 1967).

4. More information in Martin Schnitger, *The Economy of Sweden* (New York: Praeger, 1970).

5. Comparative Statistics in Organization for Economic Cooperation and Development (OECD), *Economic Survey: Sweden*, various issues; and U.S. Department of Commerce, Bureau of the Census, *Statistical Abstract of the United States* (Washington, D.C.: U.S. Government Printing Office), various issues.

6. For the use of monetary and fiscal policies for economic growth, see John B. Taylor,

"The Swedish Investment Reserve Funds System as a Stabilization Policy Rule," *Brookings Papers on Economic Activity*, no. 1, 1982, 57–106; and Carolyn Webber and Aaron Wildavsky, *A History of Taxation and Expenditures in the Western World* (New York: Simon and Schuster, 1986).

7. "Sweden Will Seek to Join Europeans," *The New York Times*, December 13, 1990, A15.

CHAPTER 9

1. For a historical development, see Peter I. Lyosh-chenko, *History of the National Economy of Russia* (New York: Macmillan, 1969); and Michael Kort, *The Soviet Colossus: A History of the USSR* (New York: Scribner's, 1985).

2. Paul R. Gregory and Robert C. Stuart, *Soviet Economic Structure and Performance* (New York: Harper, 1990), chap. 3.

3. Raymond Hutchings, *Soviet Economic Development* (New York: New York University Press, 1971), chaps. 4–6; and Alexander Erlich, *The Soviet Industrialization Debate, 1924–28* (Cambridge: Harvard University Press, 1960).

4. Gur Ofer, "Soviet Economic Growth: 1928–1985," *Journal of Economic Literature*, vol. XXV, no. 4, December 1987, 1767–1833. Also Paul R. Gregory, *Restructuring the Soviet Economic Bureaucracy* (New York: Cambridge University Press, 1990).

5. Heinz Kohler, *Comparative Economic Systems* (Glenview, Ill.: Scott, Foresman, 1989), 185–86.

6. More information in A. Hewett, *Reforming the Soviet Economy* (Washington, D.C.: The Brookings Institution, 1988); and U.S. Congress, Joint Economic Committee, *Gorbachev's Economic Plans*, vols. I and II (Washington, D.C.: U.S. Government Printing Office, 1987). Also, Maurice Friedberg and Heyward Isham, eds., *Soviet Society Under Gorbachev* (New York: M. E. Sharpe, 1987), 101–130; and Gail Sheehy, *The Man Who Changed the World* (New York: HarperCollins, 1990), chaps. 1–4.

7. Chris C. Carvounis and Brinda Z. Carvounis, *U.S. Commercial Opportunities in the Soviet Union* (Westport, Conn.: Quorum, 1989), chaps. 1–3.

8. For the western support needed for economic stability, see Richard Pipes, "The Soviet Union Adrift," *Foreign Affairs*, vol. 70, no. 1, 1990/1991, 70–87.

9. The U.S. voting power in 1990 was 19.10 percent for the IMF, 6 for Japan and Germany, and 5.5 for Britain and France. See *IMF Annual Report*, 1990, app. VI (Executive Directors and Voting Power on April 30, 1990); and William N. Gianaris, "Weighted Voting in the International Monetary Fund and the World Bank," *Fordham International Law Journal*, vol. 14, no. 4, 1990–1991, 910–945.

CHAPTER 10

1. For economic performance and comparisons, see Abram Bergson, *Planning and Performance in Socialist Economies: The USSR and Eastern Europe* (Winchester, Mass.: Unwin Hyman, 1988); David Turnock, *Eastern Europe: An Economic and Political Geography* (London: Routledge, 1989); and U.S. Congress, Joint Economic Committee, *East European Economies: Slow Growth in the 1980's* (Washington, D.C.: U.S. Government Printing Office, 1986).

2. Nicholas V. Gianaris, "Helping Eastern Europe Helps the West," *The New York Times*, February 8, 1990, A28.

3. Stephen Engelberg, "Polish Workers Wield New Power," *The New York Times*, December 28, 1990, D1; and "Poland, Pioneer of Capitalism," *The New York Times*, January 30, 1991, A22.

4. For problems and changes up to recent years, see Norman Stone and Edward Strouhal, eds., *Czechoslovakia: Crossroads and Crises, 1918–88* (New York: St. Martin's Press, 1989).

5. More information in Alexander Dubcek, *Czechoslovakia's Blueprint for "Freedom"* (Washington, D.C.: Acropolis, 1968).

6. Janos Kornai, *The Road to a Free Economy, Shifting from a Socialist System: The Examples of Hungary* (New York: Norton, 1990), chaps. 1–3.

7. A historical review of the Balkan countries in Nicholas V. Gianaris, *The Economies of the Balkan Countries: Albania, Bulgaria, Greece, Romania, Turkey, and Yugoslavia* (New York: Praeger, 1982), chaps. 1–3; and *Greece and Turkey: Economic and Geo-political Perspectives* (New York: Praeger, 1988), chap. 2.

8. Nicholas V. Gianaris, *Greece and Yugoslavia: An Economic Comparison* (New York: Praeger, 1984), 35–42. Also Jaroslav Vanek, *Participatory Economy* (Ithaca, N.Y.: Cornell University Press, 1971), 21–38.

CHAPTER 11

1. By 1923, in some cities, as many as 90 percent of men and 60 percent of women were addicts. L. Carrington Goodrich, *A Short History of the Chinese People*, 3d ed. (New York: Harper, 1959), 223. Further historical analysis in Mark Elvin, *The Pattern of the Chinese Past* (Stanford, Cal.: Stanford University Press, 1973).

2. For agricultural inefficiency and low wages in prewar times, see Thomas G. Rawski, *Economic Growth in Prewar China* (Berkeley, Cal.: University of California Press, 1989).

3. For economic changes under Mao, see Alexander Eckstein, *China's Economic Revolution* (Cambridge: Harvard University Press, 1977).

4. E. L. Wheelwright and Bruce McFarlane, *The Chinese Road to Socialism: Economics of the Cultural Revolution* (New York: Monthly Review Press, 1970).

5. Thus, the annual average growth rate of agricultural output increased only 1.2 percent during 1957–65 and 3.4 in 1965–71. Thomas G. Rawski, "Recent Trends in the Chinese Economy," *China Quarterly*, 53, January/March 1973, 32. For an overall evaluation of the performance of the Chinese economy at that time, see Colin Clark, "Economic Development in Communist China," *Journal of Political Economy*, vol. 84, no. 2, April 1976, 239–264.

6. Peter Nolan, *The Political Economy of Collective Farms: An Analysis of China's Post-Mao Rural Reforms* (New York: Westview Press, 1988), 115–116.

7. More on reforms in William A. Byrd and Lin Qingsong, eds., *China's Rural Industry: Structure, Development and Reform* (New York: Oxford University Press, 1990); and Robert F. Dernberger "Reforms in China: Implications for U.S. Policy," *American Economic Review, Proceedings*, vol. 79, no. 2, May 1989, 21–25. Also Victor Nee and Frank Young, "Peasant Entrepreneurs in China's 'Second Economy': An Institutional Analysis," *Economic Development and Cultural Change*, vol. 39, no. 2, January 1991, 293–310.

8. Developmental trends in Carl Riskin, *China's Political Economy: The Quest for*

Development Since 1949 (New York: Oxford University Press, 1987); and Mark Selden, *The Political Economy of Chinese Socialism* (New York: M. E. Sharpe, 1988).

9. World Bank, *China: Finance and Investment* (Washington, D.C.: World Bank Publications, 1984), chap. 10.

10. More statistics in U.S. Congress, Joint Economic Committee, *China's Economy Looks Toward the Year 2000* (Washington, D.C.: U.S. Government Printing Office, 1986); and World Bank, *World Development Report* (New York: Oxford University Press, for the World Bank, annual).

11. Nicholas D. Kristof, "China's Press Casts a Cold Eye on U.S. Vote," *The New York Times*, November, 1990, A8.

12. Harry Harding, *China's Second Revolution: Reform After Mao* (Washington, D.C.: The Brookings Institution, 1987), chap. 3; and Y. Y. Kueh, "The Maoist Legacy and China's New Industrialization Strategy," *The China Quarterly*, no. 119, September 1989, 420–447. Also Lucian W. Pye, "China: Erratic State Frustrated Society," *Foreign Affairs*, vol. 69, no. 4, Fall 1990, 56–74.

13. Self-employed shopkeepers increased from 140,000 in 1978 to more than 7.5 million in 1984, while wheat production more than doubled in seven years. Christopher Wren, "China Undergoing a New Revolution," *The New York Times*, April 24, 1984, A6. Also Richard Critchfield, "Aristotle, Deng, and China's Peasants," *The New York Times*, November 16, 1985, 27.

14. For legal and business issues, see Alfred K. Ho, *Joint Ventures in the People's Republic of China: Can Capitalism and Communism Coexist?* (New York: Praeger, 1990), chaps. 3–4. For Sino–American relations, see Michel Oksenberg, "The China Problem," *Foreign Affairs*, vol. 70, no. 3, Summer 1991, 1–16.

CHAPTER 12

1. Ragnar Nurkse, *Problems of Capital Formation in Underdeveloped Countries* (New York: Oxford University Press, 1953), 5. Other economists involved in this argument are Charles P. Kindleberger, P. N. Rosenstein-Rodan, and Hans Singer.

2. Nicholas V. Gianaris, "International Differences in Capital Output Ratios," *American Economic Review*, vol. 67, June 1970, 465–477; and "Projecting Capital Requirements in Development Planning," *Socio-Economic Planning Sciences*, vol. 8, April 1974, 65–76. Investment criteria in development planning in his *Economic Development: Thought and Problems* (North Quincy, Mass.: Christopher Publishing House, 1978), chap. 8.

3. World Bank, *World Development Report* (New York: Oxford University Press, for the World Bank, annual). For EC influence, see Marjorie Lister, *The European Community and the Development World* (Brookfield, Ver.: Avebury, 1988), chaps. 3–4.

4. John Kenneth Goldbraith, *The New Industrial State*, 2d ed., rev. (Boston: Houghton Mifflin, 1971), chap. 19; and, with Stanislav Menshikov, *Capitalism, Communism and Coexistence* (Boston: Houghton Mifflin, 1988), chaps. 9–10.

5. The limits of central authority were supported by the Stoics and Epicurian philosophers (fourth century B.C.), as well as by Thomas Hobbes (1588–1679), John Locke (1632–1704), and Jean Jacques Rousseau (1717–78), in addition to classical economists.

6. For privatization in some seventeen nations, see Dennis J. Gayle and Jonathan N. Goodrich, eds., *Privatization and Deregulation in Global Perspective* (Westport, Conn.:

Quorum, 1990). For cases of denationalization or privatization in China and other countries, see Emanuel S. Savas, *Privatization: The Key to Better Government* (New York: Chatham House, 1987).

7. Wlodzimierz Brus and Kazimierz Larki, *From Marx to the Market: Socialism in Search of an Economic System* (New York: Oxford University Press, 1989), part 2.

Bibliography

Adams, William J. *Restructuring the French Economy*. Washington, D.C.: The Brookings Institution, 1989.

Ahlen, Kristina. "Sweden Introduces Employee Ownership." *The Political Quarterly*, vol. 56 (April–June 1985): 186–93.

Allen, C. G. *A Short History of Modern Japan*. London: Macmillan, 1981.

Aoki, Masahiko. *Information, Incentives, and Bargaining in the Japanese Economy*. New York: Cambridge University Press, 1988.

———. "Toward an Economic Model of the Japanese Firm." *Journal of Economic Literature*, vol. XXVIII, March 1990, 1–27.

Baran, Paul. *The Political Economy of Backwardness*. New York: Monthly Review Press, 1957.

Barker, Earnest. *The Political Thought of Plato and Aristotle*. New York: Dover, 1959.

Belassa, Bela, and Marcus Noland. *Japan in the World Economy*. Washington, D.C.: Institute for International Economics, 1988.

Bergson, Abram. *Planning and Performance in Socialist Economies: The USSR and Eastern Europe*. Winchester, Mass.: Unwin Hyman, 1988.

Blasi, Joseph. *Employee Ownership: Revolution or Ripoff?* New York: Ballinger, 1988.

Bohme, Helmut. *An Introduction to the Social and Economic History of Germany*. New York: St. Martin's Press, 1978.

Borris, Moris. *Comparative Economic Systems: Models and Cases*, 6th ed. Homewood, Ill.: Irwin, 1989.

Bosworth, Barry P., and Alice M. Rivlin, eds. *The Swedish Economy*. Washington, D.C.: The Brookings Institution, 1987.

Braun, Hans-Joachim. *The German Economy in the Twentieth Century*. London: Routledge, 1990.

Brinkman, Gerhard. *Okonomik der Arbeit*, vol. I. Stuttgart: Ernst Klett Verlag, 1981.

Bruland, Kristine. *Scandinavian Industrialization: Technological Transfer and Economic Growth*. New York: St. Martin's Press, 1990.

Brus, Wlodzimierz, and Kazimierz Larki. *From Marx to the Market: Socialism in Search of an Economic System.* New York: Oxford University Press, 1989.

Byrd, William A., and Lin Qingsong, eds. *China's Rural Industry: Structure, Development and Reform.* New York: Oxford University Press, 1990.

Cairnes, John E. *Some Leading Principles of Political Economy Newly Expounded.* London, 1874.

Carby-Hall, J. *Worker Participation in Europe.* London: C. Helm, 1977.

Carvounis, Chris C., and Brinda Z. Carvounis. *U.S. Commercial Opportunities in the Soviet Union.* Westport, Conn.: Quorum, 1989.

Christiansen, Gregory, and Robert Haveman. "Public Regulations and the Slowdown in Productivity Growth." *American Economic Review, Proceedings,* vol. 71, no. 2 (May 1981): 320–25.

Clark, Colin. "Economic Development in Communist China." *Journal of Political Economy,* vol. 84, no. 2 (April 1976): 239–64.

Clough, Shepard B. *France: A History of National Economics.* New York: Octagon, 1970.

Commack, Paul, David Pool, and William Tordoff. *Third World Politics: A Comparative Introduction.* Baltimore: Johns Hopkins University Press, 1988.

Crane, George T. *The Political Economy of China's Special Economic Zones.* London: M. E. Sharpe, 1990.

Critchfield, Richard. "Aristotle, Deng, and China's Peasants." *The New York Times* (November 16, 1985): 27.

Crookell, Harold. *Canadian–American Trade and Investment Under the Free Market Agreement.* Westport, Conn.: Quorum, 1990.

Crow, John A. *Spain: The Root and the Flower.* New York: Harper, 1963.

de Madariaga, Salvador. *Spain A Modern History.* New York: Praeger, 1958.

Dernberger, Robert F. "Reforms in China: Implications for U.S. Policy." *American Economic Review Proceedings,* vol. 79, no. 2 (May 1989): 21–5.

Djilas, Milovan. *The New Class: An Analysis of the Communist System.* New York: Praeger, 1957.

Domar, Evsey D. *Capitalism, Socialism, and Serfdom: Essays.* New York: Cambridge University Press, 1989.

Dubcek, Alexander. *Czechoslovakia's Blueprint for "Freedom."* Washington, D.C.: Acropolis, 1968.

Duesenberry, James. *Income Saving and the Theory of Consumer Behavior.* Cambridge: Harvard University Press, 1949.

Ebenstein, William. *Today's Isms: Communism, Fascism, Capitalism, Socialism.* Englewood Cliffs, N.J.: Prentice Hall, 1970.

Eckstein, Alexander. *China's Economic Revolution.* Cambridge: Harvard University Press.

Ellman, Michael. *Collectivization, Convergence and Capitalsim: Political Economy in a Divided World.* Orlando, Fla.: Academic Press, 1984.

Elvin, Mark. *The Pattern of the Chinese Past.* Stanford, Cal.: Stanford University Press, 1973.

Engelberg, Stephen. "Lower House in Poland Approved Bill to Make Citizens Stockholders." *The New York Times* (July 14, 1990): A1, A4.

———. "Poland, Pioneer of Capitalism." *The New York Times* (January 30, 1991): A22.

————. "Polish Workers Wield New Power." *The New York Times* (December 28, 1990): D1.

Erhard, Ludwig, and Alfred Muller-Armack. *Sociale Markt Wirtschaft*. Frankfurt am Main: Ullstein, 1972.

Erlich, Alexander. *The Soviet Industrialization Debate, 1924–28*. Cambridge: Harvard University Press, 1960.

Fleisher, Frederic. *The New Sweden: The Challenge of a Disciplined Democracy*. New York: McKay, 1967.

Friedberg, Maurice, and Heyward Isham, eds. *Soviet Society Under Gorbachev*. New York: M. E. Sharpe, 1987.

Friedman, Milton. *Capitalism and Freedom*. Chicago: University of Chicago Press, 1962.

Galbraith, John K. *The Affluent Society*, 2d ed., rev. Boston: Houghton Mifflin, 1969.

————. *The New Industrial State*, 2d ed., rev. Boston: Houghton Mifflin, 1971.

————. *American Capitalism: The Concept of Countervailing Power*. White Plains, N.Y.: M. E. Sharpe, 1980.

Gardner, H. Stephen. *Comparative Economic Systems*. Chicago, Ill.: Dryden Press, 1988.

Garson, G., ed. *Worker Self-Management in Industry: The West European Experience*. New York: Praeger, 1977.

Gayle, Dennis J., and Jonathan N. Goodrich, eds. *Privatization and Deregulation in Global Perspective*. Westport, Conn.: Quorum, 1990.

Gianaris, Nicholas V. "International Differences in Capital Output Ratios." *American Economic Review*, vol. 67 (June 1970): 465–77.

————. "Projecting Capital Requirements in Development Planning." *Socio-Economic Planning Sciences*, vol. 8 (April 1974): 65–76.

————. *Economic Development: Thought and Problems*. North Quincy, Mass.: Christopher, 1978.

————. *The Economies of the Balkan Countries: Albania, Bulgaria, Greece, Romania, Turkey, and Yugoslavia*. New York: Praeger, 1982.

————. *Greece and Yugoslavia: An Economic Comparison*. New York: Praeger, 1984.

————. *Greece and Turkey: Economic and Geopolitical Perspectives*. New York: Praeger, 1988.

————. *Contemporary Public Finance*. New York: Praeger, 1989.

————. "Helping Eastern Europe Helps the West." *The New York Times* (February 8, 1990): 28A.

————. *The European Community and the United States: Economic Relations*. New York: Praeger, 1991.

Goodrich, L. Carrington. *A Short History of the Chinese People*, 3d ed. New York: Harper, 1959.

Gregory, Paul R. *Restructuring the Soviet Economic Bureaucracy*. New York: Cambridge University Press, 1990.

————, and Robert C. Stuart. *Soviet Economic Structure and Performance*. New York: Harper, 1990.

Hansen, Alvin. *Economic Issues of the 1960s*. New York: McGraw-Hill, 1960.

Harding, Harry. *China's Second Revolution: Reform After Mao*. Washington, D.C.: The Brookings Institution, 1987.

Hayek, Frederick. *The Road to Serfdom*. Chicago: University of Chicago Press, 1944.

Hewett, A. *Reforming the Soviet Economy*. Washington, D.C.: The Brookings Institution, 1988.

Hicks, John. *The Theory of Economic History*. New York: Oxford University Press, 1969.

Ho, Alfred K. *Joint Ventures in the People's Republic of China: Can Capitalism and Communism Coexist?* New York: Praeger, 1990.

Hutchings, Raymond. *Soviet Economic Development*. New York: New York University Press, 1971.

Icahn, Carl. "The Case for Takeovers." *The New York Times Magazine* (January 29, 1989): 34.

International Monetary Fund (IMF), *International Financial Statistics*, various issues.

Johnson, Chalmers. *MITI and the Japanese Miracle*. Stanford, Cal.: Stanford University Press, 1982.

Judge, Paul C. "Nissan Plans New Factory For Engines in Tennessee." *The New York Times* (January 19, 1991): L37.

Keller, Morton. *Regulating a New Economy: Public and Economic Change in America, 1900–1933*. Cambridge: Harvard University Press, 1990.

Kester, Carl. *Japanese Takeovers*. Boston: Harvard Business School Press, 1991.

Keynes, John M. *The General Theory of Employment, Interest and Money*. New York: Harcourt, 1936.

Kindlerberger, Charles P. "French Planning," in Max F. Millikan, ed., *National Economic Planning*. New York: National Bureau of Economic Research, 1967.

Kirby, M. W. *The Decline of British Economic Power Since 1870*. London: Allen and Unwin, 1981.

Kohler, Heinz. *Comparative Economic Systems*. Glenview, Ill.: Scott, Foresman, 1989.

Kornai, Janos. *The Road to a Free Economy, Shifting from a Socialist System: The Examples of Hungary*. New York: Norton, 1990.

Kort, Michael. *The Soviet Colossus: A History of the USSR*. New York: Scribner's, 1985.

Kristof, Nicholas D. "China's Press Casts a Cold Eye on U.S. Vote." The *New York Times* (November, 1990): A8.

Kueh, Y. Y. "The Maoist Legacy and China's New Industrialization Strategy." *The China Quarterly*, no. 119 (September 1989).

Kwoka, John E., and Lawrence J. White, eds. *The Antitrust Revolution*. Glenview, Ill.: Scott, Foresman, 1989.

Lange, Oskar. "On the Economic Theory of Socialism," in *On the Economic System of Socialism*. Minneapolis: University of Minnesota Press, 1938.

———, and Fred J. Taylor. *On the Economic Theory of Socialism*. New York: McGraw-Hill, 1964.

Leaman, Jeremy. *The Political Economy of West Germany, 1945–1985: An Introduction*. New York: St. Martin's Press, 1988.

Lenin, Vladimir I. "Imperialism, The Highest Stage of Capitalism," in *New Data for V. I. Lenin's Imperialism*, ed. by E. Varga and L. Mendelsohn. New York: International Publishers, 1940.

Lenski, Gerhard. *Power and Privilege: A Theory of Social Stratification*. New York: McGraw-Hill, 1966.

Leontief, Wassily. *Input–Output Economics*. New York: Oxford University Press, 1966.

Lincoln, Edward J. *Japan: Facing Economic Maturity*. Washington, D.C.: The Brookings Institution, 1988.

Lindblom, C. *Politics and Markets*. New York: Basic Books, 1977.

Lister, Marjorie. *The European Community and the Development World*. Brookfield, Ver.: Aveburg, 1988.

Lundberg, Erik. "The Rise and Fall of the Swedish Model." *Journal of Economic Literature*, vol. 23 (March 1985): 1–36.

Lyosh-chenko, Peter I. *History of the National Economy of Russia*. New York: Macmillan, 1969.

McKee, David L., ed. *Canadian–American Economic Relations: Conflict and Cooperation on a Continental Scale*. New York: Praeger, 1988.

Mandeville, Bernard. *Fable of the Bees*. Paris: J. Vrin, 1991.

Marx, Karl. *Capital*. New York: Modern Library, 1906.

Menshikov, Stanislav. *Capitalism, Communism and Coexistence*. Boston: Houghton Mifflin, 1988.

Mill, John Stuart. *Considerations and Representative Government*. London: Routledge, 1905.

———. "Principles of Political Economy," in *Masterworks of Economics*. vol. 2, ed. by Leonard Abbott. New York: McGraw-Hill, 1973.

Morris-Sujuki, Tessa. "An Outsider Takes A Look Inside At Japan's Corporate Culture." *Japanese Economic Journal* (May 3, 1986): 40–1.

———. *A History of Japanese Economic Thought*. New York: Routledge, 1989.

Nathan, Otto. *The Nazi Economic System: Germany's Mobilization For War*. Durham, N.C.: Duke University Press, 1944.

Nester, William R. *Japan's Growing Predominance Over East Asia and World Economy*. New York: St. Martin's Press, 1990.

Nolan, Peter. *The Political Economy of Collective Farms: An Analysis of China's Post-Mao Rural Reforms*. New York: Westview Press, 1988.

Nurkse, Ragnar. *Problems of Capital Formation in Underdeveloped Countries*. New York: Oxford University Press, 1953.

Ofer, Gur. "Soviet Economic Growth: 1928–1985." *Journal of Economic Literature*, vol. XXV, no. 4 (December 1987): 1767–1833.

Oksenberg, Michel. "The China Problem," *Foreign Affairs*, vol. 70, no. 3 (Summer 1991): 1–16.

Organization for Economic Cooperation and Development (OECD). *Economic Surveys: Japan*. Paris: OECD, annual.

———. *National Accounts*. Paris: OECD, annual.

Pareto, Vilfredo. *Cours d' Economie Politique*, vols. I and II. Lausanne, 1896–7.

Pipes, Richard. "The Soviet Union Adrift." *Foreign Affairs*, America and the World, vol. 70, no. 1 (1990/1991): 70–87.

Plato. *Laws*, in B. Jowett, trans., *The Dialogues of Plato*. New York, 1876.

"Poland, Pioneer of Capitalism." *The New York Times* (January 30, 1991): A22.

Putterman, Louis. *Division of Labor and Welfare: An Introduction to Economic Systems*. New York: Oxford University Press, 1990.

Pye, Lucian W. "China: Erratic State Frustrated Society." *Foreign Affairs*, vol. 69, no. 4 (Fall 1990): 56–74.

Rawski, Thomas G. "Recent Trends in the Chinese Economy." *China Quarterly*, vol. 53 (January/March 1973): 32.

———. *Economic Growth in Prewar China*. Berkeley, Cal.: University of California Press 1989.

Reich, Robert. "Leveraged Buyouts: America Pays the Price." *The New York Times Magazine* (January 29, 1989): 32, 36, 40.

———. "Secession of the Successful." *The New York Times Magazine* (January 20, 1991): 17, 42–5.

———. *The Work of Nations: Preparing Ourselves for 21st-Century Capitalism*. New York: Knopf, 1991.

Riskin, Carl. *China's Political Economy: The Quest for Development Since 1949*. New York: Oxford University Press, 1987.

Rosen, Corey M., Katherine J. Klein, and Karen M. Young. *Employee Ownership in America: The Equity Solution*. Lexington, Mass.: Lexington Books, 1986.

Rousseau, Jean Jacques. The *Social Contract*, transl. by Maurice Cranston, book one, chaps. 1–8. New York: Penguin, 1968.

Savas, Emanuel S. *Privatization: The Key to Better Government*. New York: Chatham House, 1987.

Schnitger, Martin. *The Economy of Sweden*. New York: Praeger, 1970.

Schumpeter, Joseph A. *Capitalism, Socialism and Democracy*, 2d ed. New York: Harper and Brothers, 1947.

Selden, Mark. *The Political Economy of Chinese Socialism*. New York: M. E. Sharpe, 1988.

Sheehy, Gail. *The Man Who Changed the World*. New York: HarperCollins, 1990.

Shepherd, William G. *The Economics of Industrial Organization*, 2d ed. Englewood Cliffs, N.J.: Prentice Hall, 1985.

Shimokawa, Koichi. "Japan's Keiretsu System: The Case of the Automobile Industry." *Japanese Economic Studies*, vol. 13 (Summer 1985): 3–31.

Smith, Adam. *An Inquiry Into the Nature and Causes of the Wealth of Nations*, ed. by E. Cannan. New York: Modern Library, 1937.

Stone, Norman, and Edward Strouhal, eds. *Czechoslovakia: Crossroads and Crises, 1918–88*. New York: St. Martin's Press, 1989.

"Sweden Will Seek to Join Europeans." *The New York Times* (December 13, 1990): A15.

"Ta Dekapente Kommatia tou Sovietikou Pazl" (The Fifteen Pieces of the Soviet Pazl), *To Vima*, Athens (September 1, 1991): A16.

Takamiya, Susumu, and Keith Thurley, eds. *Japan's Emerging Multinationals*. Tokyo: University of Tokyo Press, 1985.

Tawney, R. H. *Religion and the Rise of Capitalism*. New York: Harcourt, 1926.

Taylor, John B. "The Swedish Investment Funds System as a Stabilization Policy Rule." *Brookings Papers on Economic Activity*, no. 1 (1982): 57–106.

Teichman, Judith A. *Policymaking in Mexico: From Boom to Crisis*. New York: Allen and Unwin, 1988.

"The Soviet Union's Unequal Parts: Diverse and Restless." *The New York Times* (September 1, 1991): E2.

Turnock, David. *Eastern Europe: An Economic and Political Geography*. London: Routledge, 1989.

United Nations. *Yearbook of National Accounts Statistics: Analysis of Main Indicators*. New York: United Nations, 1987, Table 5.

———. *The World Economy at the End of 1991*. New York: United Nations, December 1991, Table 5.

————. *Yearbook of National Accounts Statistics*. New York: United Nations, various issues.

U.S. Congress, Joint Economic Committee. *China's Economy Looks Toward The Year 2000*. Washington, D.C.: U.S. Government Printing Office, 1986.

————. *East European Economies: Slow Growth in the 1980's*. Washington, D.C.: U.S. Government Printing Office, 1986.

————. *Gorbachev's Economic Plans*, vols. I and II. Washington, D.C.: U.S. Government Printing Office, 1987.

U.S. Department of Commerce, Bureau of the Census. *Historical Statistics of the United States, Colonial Times to 1970*. Washington, D.C.: U.S. Government Printing Office, 1975.

————. *Statistical Abstract of the United States*. Washington, D.C.: U.S. Government Printing Office, various issues.

U.S. Government, *Economic Report of the President*, Washington, D.C.: U.S. Government Printing Office, various issues.

Ungeheuer, Frederick. "They Own the Place." *Time* (February 6, 1989): 50–1.

Vanek, Jaroslav. *Participatory Economy*. Ithaca, N.Y.: Cornell University Press, 1971.

van Wolferen, Karen. "The Japan Problem Revisited." *Foreign Affairs*, vol. 69, no. 4 (Fall 1990): 42–55.

Von Mises, Ludwig. "Economic Calculation in the Socialist Commonwealth," in Friedrich A. von Hayek, ed., *Collective Economic Planning*. London: Routledge, 1935.

Webber, Carolyn, and Aaron Wildavsky. *A History of Taxation and Expenditures in the Western World*. New York: Simon and Schuster, 1986.

Weber, Max. *The Protestant Ethic and the Spirit of Capitalism*, transl. by Talcott Parsons. New York: Scribner's, 1958.

Weitzman, Martin L. *The Share Economy: Conquering Stagflation*. Cambridge: Harvard University Press, 1984.

————. "The Simple Macroeconomics of Profit Sharing." *American Economic Review*, vol. 75 (December 1985): 937–53.

Wheelwright, E. L., and Bruce McFarlane. *The Chinese Road to Socialism: Economics of the Cultural Revolution*. New York: Monthly Review Press, 1970.

World Bank. *China: Finance and Investment*. Washington, D.C.: World Bank Publications, 1984.

————. *World Debt Tables*. Washington, D.C.: World Bank Publications, annual.

————. *World Development Report*. New York: Oxford University Press, for the World Bank, annual.

Wren, Christopher. "China Undergoing a New Revolution." *The New York Times* (April 24, 1984): A6.

Index

About the Author

NICHOLAS V. GIANARIS is Professor and Program Coordinator of Economics at Fordham University, Lincoln Center, New York City. He is the author of six books, including most recently *The European Community and the United States: Economic Relations* (Praeger, 1991).

DATE DUE

~~APR 18 1994~~		JUN 2 9 2001	
~~AUG 31 1994~~			
			Printed in USA